To:

My parents, Alisa and Branko, who, against my strong opposition, somehow managed to instill in me a thirst for knowledge.

And my wife, Loli, who, despite enduring countless lonely nights and weekends, continued inspiring me to write, kept me sane, and took care of everything so that I could concentrate on the book.

Contents

About the Author

Ivo Raza is a branding consultant and founder of Brandhaus, a full-service marketing agency that specializes in integrated marketing solutions for hospitality, travel, and tourism clients. He has developed brand strategies, directed advertising campaigns, and managed marketing projects for a variety of companies and brands including Allegro Resorts, Viva Wyndham Resorts, Karisma Hotels, El Dorado Resorts, Jack Tar Village Resorts, Occidental Hotels, Royal Hideaway, Schick, Blue Diamond, Kraft Foods, Boston Beer, and others. For seven years, Ivo was in charge of marketing at Allegro, which he helped grow into the largest chain of all-inclusive resorts. His professional mantra is: "Don't out-spend. Out-brand." He lives in Miami, Florida, and may be reached at ivo@brandhaus.net.

Prelude

The purpose of marketing is to build brands, generate sales, and increase profits. This is my personal belief and the mantra of *Heads in Beds*. Whether you are a hospitality student, innkeeper, general manager, corporate director of marketing, director of tourism for a destination, the company's chief marketing officer, or someone who is simply interested in the marketing of hospitality, the principles and practices covered in this book should be relevant. Its premise is based on the following eight beliefs:

1. **Branding: The best way of generating strong sales is by building strong brands.** The beauty of branding is that when it is done properly, it works. Actually, it works so well that it is regrettable that so few companies do it right. Instead of employing a knowledge-based approach based on empirical data, creativity, and guts, companies unfortunately often dabble in dilettantish pseudoprofessional activities based on personal tastes, opinions, and company politics. Pair this with a lack of return-on-investment accountability, the ambiguity surrounding branding, and the corporate fear of dealing with brands' emotional properties, and you'll end up with the current garden variety of me-too brands.

   Nevertheless, in our world of parity products, marketing in general and branding in particular have become the main determining factors in the success of companies. This does not only apply to huge marketers such as Toyota, which through intelligent branding introduced Lexus (a new brand—not an extension!). It also applies to many giants of today that have not been around for very long and have succeeded in a short period of time due to well-planned, well-executed branding strategies; Nike, Starbucks, Swatch, Amazon, Expedia, Travelocity, and Yahoo come to mind. But branding is not limited to large companies. The principles of branding apply to the smallest operators just as much as to the mega brands. Study good branding, use it to your advantage, and your sales will grow. Strong brands have strong relationships with their consumers and generate strong profits.

2. **Knowledge: The more you know, the more you'll grow.** The best marketing is based on knowledge, and the only way to acquire knowledge is by doing your homework. The best creative ideas are not possible otherwise. You may occasionally stumble over a brilliant thought, but you will not be able to create good ideas and deliver results continuously unless you make a conscious effort to educate yourself as well as your organization.

   Don't mistake experience for knowledge, however. It is fairly easy to gain experience; stay at the same job for 20 years and you'll have it. But that won't automatically make you a guru. Practice alone doesn't make perfect. If you commit yourself to becoming an expert in your area, you'll produce better results faster. Thus, you'll do smarter marketing, which will help you grow personally, grow stronger brands, and grow your profits.

3. **Results: The right long-term strategy solves short-term needs.** In a world of instant gratification and quarterly results, it is painfully difficult to embrace a long-term approach, yet no great achievements have been accomplished without it. In reality, your entire professional life is a long-term project. And your biggest challenge is to make everything you do part of that long-term campaign instead of jumping from one short-term project to another (also know as "putting out fires").

   The long-term marketing approach is by its nature proactive; you will be recognizing patterns of behavior, thus gaining knowledge and insight. Then you'll develop long-term (and mid-term) strategies, which will be executed through actions that will deliver continuous (and immediate, i.e., short-term) results over extended periods of time, subject to continuous learning, monitoring, and tweaking.

   The short-term approach, on the other hand, focuses totally on immediate issues or situations that need rapid tactical solutions. Approaching marketing only with short-term, immediate actions is like trying to lose weight without a long-term commitment. You may have days when you do not eat anything and exercise for 10 hours, but the result will be major fatigue and no visible effect. If, however, you commit to eating well every day and exercising regularly, the results will come. And, as a bonus, by being (and staying) in shape for the long term, you'll easily be able to overcome short periods of inactivity or consumption of fatty foods.

   I know that it is especially difficult to champion a long-term strategy in an industry in which the entire inventory expires every 24 hours. At some point in his or her career, everyone will be faced with the short-term need to increase occupancy for next month by 22%. However, when you start with a strong long-term strategy, short-term problems will be easy to handle and will be solved successfully. You will have mechanisms in place that will allow you to achieve short-term goals, and you will have an ongoing positive momentum in the market, along with a strong brand, which will help you bridge difficult periods, deliver immediate results, and increase your sales over the long run.

4. **Big picture: It's not about style versus substance, it's about substance armed with style.** For some strange reason, the marketing community is missing the bigger picture by belonging to one of two schools of thought or conviction: style versus substance, form versus function, suits versus creatives, visual versus verbal. How about seeing the bigger picture, folks? How about creating a lethally powerful campaign by arming substance with style, by using a timeless visual and immortalizing it with outstanding copy? I'm talking about enlightened strategic creativity here. We all have a left as well as a right side of the brain; we have to use them both. In today's competitive environment, I don't know how I could survive without employing both sides. As a matter of fact, there are no "both sides." All sides must be on my side. The only one allowed on the other side is my competition. Let them debate whether form follows function and whether to focus on the sizzle or the steak. You've got to see the bigger picture. Your form must strengthen your function. You've got to sell the sizzle *and* the steak.

5. **Creative budgeting: Outthink versus outspend.** When it comes to marketing budgets, my belief is: outthink versus outspend. Creative marketing doesn't have to be wasteful. Vast budgets and lack of accountability have resulted in the perception of marketing as an expense rather than an investment. This is the main reason why marketing is often deemed dispensable when budget cuts are necessary. Don't get me wrong. Good money must be invested in marketing; otherwise, your company will never achieve the necessary critical mass. But there's a huge difference between smart allocation and splurging. Call me a budgetary Spartan if you will, but I feel very comfortable knowing that I have squeezed the most marketing action out of every single marketing dollar. If you create systems that enable you to truly maximize your available budget, not only will you look good to your board of directors, but your sales will grow. A caveat here: Beware of the bean-counter syndrome. If your company is run by accountants who consider a reduction in the marketing budget as another source of revenue, you may need to remind them of Thornton Wilder, who said: "Money is like manure. If you let it pile up, it just smells. But if you spread it around wisely, you can encourage things to grow." (Things such as brands.)

6. **Happiness: Enjoy what you do while you're alive, for you'll be dead a long time.** Indirectly, this book is about personal happiness. Finding the right job and career is a blessing and will bring happiness and fulfillment. Confucius said it better: "Choose a job you love and you will never have to work another day in your life." To me,

marketing is the only business discipline that provides an opportunity to be involved in all the aspects of any business—from creative work such as directing photo shoots and developing advertising to creating new products to more somber activities such as controlling budgets; all in all, it is enjoyable and truly rewarding work. Just make sure it is right for you.

7. **Dare to: Be different, explore, be silly, break rules, be funny, be crazy, be smart, make mistakes.** A famous bumper sticker reads: "WHY BE NORMAL?" Indeed, why? Not in the mental-institution sense, but rather in the breaking-away-from-the-usual sense. At the risk of sounding esoteric, the truth is that nothing in this world is exactly as we think it is. We just happen to believe it is so because of a variety of elements that surround us and that we have grown to accept. Often our mental boundaries are conditioned by society. But fresh thinking, entrepreneurship, and innovation have always been disruptive, not conformist. And disruption is good, provided that it is constructive. Disruption creates new views, frontiers, opportunities, and products. Making mistakes teaches us as much as studying. Unfortunately, society teaches us to conform, to play by the rules, to obey structure and keep our collective noses to the grindstone. Playing it safe, however, is not the way you build outstanding brands or have fun doing it.

8. **Success: Succeed by competing with yourself for your own excellence.** "Whether you think you can or you think you can't, you are right," said Henry Ford. Your success lies within you. This is not a shabby maxim to live by. All the brand-building principles apply to you as well. Think of yourself as a brand and follow the same steps you would follow with any other brand. What does the brand called YOU stand for? What are its strengths, positioning, strategy? What makes YOU different from any other brand? Why should someone pay more for brand YOU than any other? Then, once you have developed your strategy, don't waste too much time measuring yourself against others. The only way to truly succeed is by competing with yourself for your own excellence. The Austrian psychologist Viktor Frankl said it brilliantly in the preface to his book *Man's Search for Meaning*: "Don't aim at success—the more you aim at it and make it a target, the more you are going to miss it. For success, like happiness, cannot be pursued; it must ensue . . . as the unintended side effect of one's personal dedication to a course greater than oneself."

WHO WILL BENEFIT FROM *HEADS IN BEDS?*

This book was not written for a specific type of hospitality marketer, but rather for anyone responsible for (or interested in) marketing hospitality, tourism, and travel products. However, a basic familiarity with the terminology and concepts is required. So, if you are completely new to the topic, you should read it along with an introductory textbook on hospitality sales, marketing, and operations.

Heads in Beds is a book written for practitioners by a practitioner. So, whether you are a hospitality student, just starting a new job, a general manager, a sales and marketing director, or a seasoned veteran looking for methods to increase your yield, the material in this book will help you manage the marketing function and generate better results.

Miguel de Cervantes wrote: "There is no book so bad but something good may be found in it." I hope that "something good" from this one results in stronger brands, better sales, and bigger profits.

HOW THIS BOOK CAME TO BE

You have noticed by now that I am a strong believer in marketing and branding. I actually believe that branding is the key differentiating factor in any industry, and especially in hospitality, travel, and tourism. This is why I felt compelled to write *Heads in Beds*.

The initial idea for this book was conceived in 1996, when I joined Allegro Resorts Corporation and realized that I had no clue about what it would take to market a hospitality product. I had good experience in consumer products marketing, advertising, and branding, but knew nothing about hotels or hospitality distribution. I had never worked in a hotel or any type of hospitality company, and ADR meant no more than F & B.

A futile search for good hands-on literature about hospitality marketing turned up only Philip Kotler, John Bowen, and James Makens' excellent textbook *Marketing for Hospitality and Tourism*. But I needed something more than a textbook; I needed a book that would provide practical advice and insider information on most aspects of the hospitality marketing job. I needed a book that would help me shorten my learning curve. When I finally gave up the search, I vowed that some day I would write a hospitality marketing book for people in similar situations.

Fast forward to late 1999: I started writing *Heads in Beds*. After a few months I had written several chapters, which made me realize that some day I might actually finish it. And what's the purpose of finishing a book if it doesn't get published? So I started looking for a publishing agent, which was a major undertaking in itself. But I got lucky. My book idea seemed intriguing to Dianne Littwin, and we made an agreement. A few weeks later, she had several interested publishers and I signed on with Prentice Hall.

IN CONCLUSION

This book contains nothing about franchising, time-sharing, and other hospitality topics that are either covered extensively in other books or unfamiliar to me. It is not a book of rules. It is a book of concepts, principles, practices, and guidelines.

Nietzsche said that a good book is made better by good readers and clearer by good opponents. For either, my e-mail address is ivo@brandhaus.net.

ACKNOWLEDGMENTS

I am grateful to many "heads" without whose involvement this book would have never seen the light of day.

Let me start by thanking Dianne Littwin, my agent, for being a great counselor and finding a great publisher, and Vernon Anthony, executive editor at Prentice Hall, for believing in this project and providing valuable input and guidance. I thank the reviewers Nora Berkey-Campbell, Northern Virginia Community College; and Robert J. Sobieraj, Johnson County Community College for their invaluable assistance. A big thank you also goes to my copyeditor, Helen Greenberg, for seriously improving the flow without changing the meaning.

I am particularly grateful to three dear friends, Brad Tolkin, Lubo Krstajic, and Pamela Johnston, who have spent extensive time with me reviewing the work and providing exceptional input. They are superb professionals and have helped improve this book significantly.

Special thanks also go to all the people who have provided me with great information, materials, and insight along the way, including Gilda Noboa and Laurel Herman, as well as Bill Vervaeke, Miguel Poplawsky, and Lisa Ross, for their support long before this project was a reality.

Many thanks to two great friends, Gerhard Koenderink and Bill Sumner, as well as all the wonderful folks with whom I have worked on various projects and from whom I have learned plenty.

I would also like to thank all the people who, by replying to my informal survey, have provided important information; they are Alex Mager, Rafael Feliz, Steve Gorga, Rafael Blanco, Richard Doumeng, Benny Guevara, Paola Rainieri, Richard Kahn, Paul Rishell, Bob Gilbert, Michael Winfield, and Bill Vervaeke.

Great thanks to Maria Armenteros, a fellow author, whose success and encouragement were a great inspiration, and to my sister Dina, a remarkable designer and architect, whose sense of style and functionality has helped me develop an eye for purposeful aesthetics.

Finally, I am more than grateful to my family and friends, who relentlessly encouraged me with this project.

Ivo Raza

CHAPTER ONE

Hospitality and Marketing

"He was on one of my flights when a passenger reported that a toilet was broken. When I made it up there, I found Richard lying on his back, soaking wet, fixing the toilet."
—A flight attendant, interviewed by *Airways* magazine about her boss, Richard Branson, chairman of Virgin Atlantic

THE IMPORTANCE OF MARKETING IN HOSPITALITY AND TOURISM

Hospitality and tourism together comprise the world's largest industry. According to the World Travel and Tourism Council, this will translate into an estimated $9.3 trillion in economic activity by 2011—certainly a competitive environment.

And in such a competitive environment, no company can survive without a sophisticated marketing approach. While at traditional companies marketing is a business function performed by the marketing department, today's hospitality superstars have embraced marketing as a way of thinking and running the entire business. The role of marketing, once limited to pushing a company's products or services, has evolved into an overall business strategy. Today, no hospitality business, from the smallest restaurant to the largest hotel chain, can afford to leave marketing to the marketing people and run the rest of the business separately. Why? Because marketing communications comprise only a portion of the customer interaction, and the customer's product/brand experience and nonmarketing communication will have more impact than the company's traditional marketing activities. A flier, brochure, or advertisement may attract guests to a particular hotel, but once they enter the premises they will be exposed to the product/service/brand experience for an extended period of time; thus, their interaction will have more impact than the marketing itself. If all those points of contact are not driven by an appropriate marketing strategy—that is, if the staff is not equipped to handle customers correctly, the menu items are inappropriate, or the premises don't deliver what the brochure promised—no amount of brilliant marketing will replace or diminish that negative experience.

Companies may be product driven, process driven, finance driven, or technology driven, but none of that matters if they don't attract enough customers. Marketing-driven companies, on the other hand, will be guided primarily by their customers' needs, wants, and expectations. These will be reflected in the companies' products, processes, financing, and technology, all of which will ultimately result in high levels of patronage.

WHAT MARKETING IS

Marketing was once described as the four Ps: product, place, promotion, and price. This is no longer true. The marketing paradigm in today's environment is: customer, brand, distribution, price, and promotion. Today, the customer must be an integral part of the marketing process, because none of the remaining elements of the marketing mix matter much if the strategy is not focused on the needs and wants of the customer. The product has grown from an article of utility into an element of a larger concept called the "brand." And the place has evolved into distribution, also primarily driven by the focus on the customer. Marketing authors Philip Kotler, John Bowen, and Janes Makens define marketing as a "social and managerial process by which individuals and groups obtain what they need and want through creating and exchanging products and value with others." This is the way I define it: "Marketing is an ongoing process comprising various coordinated activities a company must perform to develop a needed and/or wanted product, bring it to the market, maintain it there, and maximize the customers' benefit as well as the company's yield from it over extended periods of time."

Thus, while for a coffee shop the entire marketing effort may consists of serving 44 unique types of coffee and distributing a black-and-white flier throughout the neighborhood, for a multinational cruise line marketing consists of strategic planning, product development, branding, franchising, advertising, public relations, Internet marketing, training, and a variety of related activities such as creating added value, developing new markets, entering different market segments, and up-marketing. So for a larger company, marketing is a variety of coordinated activities that are executed in one or many markets to deliver goods and services to customers and thereby achieve a desired revenue and profit objective in the marketplace.

WHAT MARKETING IS NOT

Marketing has many misconceptions. Let's eliminate the most common ones. Marketing is not magic. Marketing is not a miracle cure. Nor is it a substitute for bad products, a compensation for insufficient budgets, or a replacement for sales. Marketing is not advertising. Marketing is not a brochure. Marketing is not a website. Marketing is not something you do. It is something you do to achieve something else (sales, profits, brand equity).

CHARACTERISTICS OF SERVICE MARKETING

While pure services are completely devoid of physical properties, hospitality, even though often referred to as a service industry, actually combines services with elements of a physical product. For the purposes of marketing, however, hospitality should be considered primarily a service due to the following characteristics:

1. **Intangibility.** The first and foremost service characteristic refers to the period prior to consumption, when a potential guest may have nothing but a reservation number before arriving at a hotel. One of the key functions of hospitality marketing must be to create a perception of tangibility for the product in the mind of the consumer by communicating the benefits through branding and all points of customer contact.

2. **Inseparability.** Consumption of the hospitality product is not separable from the physical location. This makes it vital to synchronize marketing activities with product delivery.

3. **Perishability.** Unlike physical products, which may be sold today, tomorrow, or next month, the hospitality product expires every 24 hours. And while inventory control and yield management are therefore crucial for maximizing revenues, they are equally important for planning and ensuring operational quality at optimal (not necessarily maximum) capacity levels.

4. **Inconsistency.** Hospitality is a product that consists of many, often varying, elements. For this reason, it often suffers from inconsistent delivery. If is the job of operations as well as marketing to minimize product delivery fluctuation for maximum consistency and an optimal guest experience.

EMBRACING INCONSISTENCY

From the previous paragraph on product delivery to the chapters on branding, advertising, and brochure design, many parts of this book stress the importance of consistency. A high level of consistency in those areas will contribute to—if not define—the overall selling effort. However, one area of hospitality must maintain and embrace inconsistency: guest interaction. Just as no two guests are exactly alike, no two employees are exactly alike, and a business must use that reality to achieve maximum mutual benefit.

In an effort to create corporate consistency, hospitality companies have set out to create operating manuals that define every single aspect of their employees' interaction with the customer. Yet in doing so, they have stifled

Highlight: Southwest Airlines

To the question "Are customers always right?" Southwest Airlines' CEO, Herb Kelleher, answers, "No, they are not. The customer is frequently wrong. We don't carry those sorts of customers. We tell them, fly somebody else. Don't abuse our people."

Southwest Airlines is the perfect example of a service company that succeeds by embracing inconsistency through a unique brand culture. Operationally, they remain leaner than other airlines by operating mostly short-haul flights, using secondary airports, flying only one type of aircraft (Boeing 737s), not handling baggage transfers, and not assigning seats. Their frequent flier program, called Rapid Rewards, revolves around credits, not miles, and requires only eight round-trip flights to earn a free round-trip ticket.

But the key characteristic of Southwest, and its true reason for success, lies in the profound commitment of the entire organization. Their mission statement reveals that Southwest Airlines is dedicated to the highest quality of customer service delivered with a sense of warmth, friendliness, individual pride, and company spirit. And they really mean it.

They hire people for their attitude rather than their education or experience. They look for a sense of humor and warmth because they don't just want to provide the service of transportation; they also want to entertain and surprise their customers. That's why, on Southwest's flights, it is not uncommon for flight attendants to entertain the passengers with jokes. And even though they are highly unionized, their employees work significantly more hours than the competition, which makes them significantly more productive. This attitude starts at the top and permeates the entire company. Herb Kelleher interacts with customers whenever he flies. Southwest's stock symbol is LUV, and their safety announcement starts with the sentence "There are fifty ways to leave your lover but only six exits from this airplane."

All of this has paid off handsomely. Customers love them. Employees work harder. And the bottom line is that in an industry plagued by many problems, Southwest operates profitably year after year.

---

their employees' freedom to provide genuine service. The best customer service is based on allowing employees latitude in handling different (and often unexpected) customer issues (not just complaints) with personalized responses. In the end, a guest is a person who wants a response from another person, not a "customer service automaton." Hospitality providers who embrace the fact that they cannot control every aspect of the guest interaction and instead focus on hiring people with the right attitudes and instilling in them a service culture will reap remarkable benefits.

COULD THE REAL MARKETING DIRECTOR PLEASE STAND UP?

If there were an official guide called "How to Run a Company" that CEOs got when they started their jobs, I doubt that it would include a large section devoted to marketing. Chief officers are usually concerned more with earnings than with marketing. This is unfortunate because the most successful companies (in all industries) have a profound involvement in marketing, from the top officer (CEO or GM, regardless of company size) down. This makes sense: if marketing is directed from the top, it will permeate every department in the organization, resulting in a solid entity in which every strategy and every action is singlemindedly market driven. This market obsession will result in exceptionally high performance, which will impact the bottom line, financing, shareholder value, profits, and many other smaller and larger issues with which CEOs and GMs are traditionally faced.

Great hospitality marketers—on both the property and corporate levels— do not relinquish the role of marketing to the marketing staff. On the contrary, they are waist deep in it, because they know that they cannot control the destiny of their hotel or company without controlling its marketing.

Richard Branson's toilet repair is a perfect example of involvement from the top. And it started long before he ever got on his back. First, he was on the flight to interact with his customers, as he often does to stay in touch with his actual market. Second, by performing such a menial task, he communicated to his employees that no job is too dirty and that customer satisfaction is everyone's responsibility. Third, by performing this task himself, he communicated to the passengers that Virgin airlines truly cares about its customers. Coming from Branson, it wouldn't be surprising if the entire bathroom episode was a carefully orchestrated public relations stunt designed to reinforce the core values of the brand. Either way, it works.

Commitment starts at the top: Southwest Airlines' CEO Herb Kelleher.
Source: David Woo. Used with permission.

FACE-TO-FACE VALUE

Another key element of great hospitality marketers is that they do not confine themselves to their offices. On the contrary, they mingle with their guests as often as they can. This provides them with the opportunity to take the pulse of actual customers, collect plenty of feedback, and even uncover potential product problems. Marketers who are close to their customers are usually passionate about their products and can identify with those customers. By contrast, a hospitality company that relies solely on market research and focus groups can never reach the same level of customer understanding. How could it? The company in which management maintains close client contact and cross-references that information with market research is more likely to gain true insight into customers' needs than a group of marketing professionals reading a research study in a remote office.

DAVID VERSUS GOLIATH

With tremendous subsegmentation of markets and products, hospitality and tourism are served by a huge range of suppliers, from mom-and-pop establishments to corporate giants. Nevertheless, while large corporations have used marketing sophistication to dominate the industry for decades, today new and equally marketing-savvy smaller suppliers are carving out lucrative niches and stealing business from the monotonous chains and franchises. The industry has come full circle. Increased consumer knowledge, combined with an abundance of travel offers and readily available information, has created a playing field in which virtually everyone is competing in the same market. And rightly so. While large players have the advantage of large budgets, large size, and multiple locations, small players have the advantage of personalized services, unique products, and a high degree of flexibility and nimbleness. So, who is more likely to win, David or Goliath? Both (but only the best in both categories). The market is mature and segmented to such a degree that it supports the demand for large and small suppliers, as well as a whole range in between. The key success factor will not be size but market insight, quality of product, service, and marketing.

FOUR "MARKETING" FUNCTIONS

Besides the various marketing activities that are extensively covered in the chapters of this book, following are four functions that are paramount to the success of any business. Even though in many companies they may not be considered marketing functions, they should be, because the marketing department is likely to have the best perspective regarding competitive environments, products, and customer insight, as well as internal procedures. These functions are:

1. **Corporate identity.** A strong company image is one of its most valuable assets. It will help facilitate growth and entry into new markets,

attract better employees, and find investors. A weak company image is a liability. Control your company's image or it will control you. Thomas Garbett, a corporate communications expert, defines six key factors that control a company's image: (a) the reality of the company itself, such as its size, structure, industry, and products; (b) the newsworthiness of the company and its activities; (c) the diversity of the company (i.e., the more diverse the company, the less cohesive its image); (d) the company's communications effort; (e) time; and (f) memory decay.

The creation of a corporate identity starts at home, with the formal definition of what the company stands for; for example, is the company modern or traditional, aggressive or laid back, young or old-fashioned, conservative or liberal, serious or fun, relaxed or formal? This must be determined by the top management and the CEO. Once it has been defined, this corporate personality needs to permeate the entire organization. It needs to be communicated and integrated into every pore of the company. It needs to be reflected in the company's operation and translated into its communication vehicles. At the same time, it needs to be presented to the external environment—repeatedly, consistently, and cohesively. The CEO is the company's premier spokesperson, so he or she needs to devote enough time to reinforcing the company's identity and realize that his or her personality will represent the image of the company just as much as the corporate communications. Consider Richard Branson, the founder of Virgin, a company that is perceived as irreverent, offbeat, and fun, offering good-quality products and services. Much of Virgin's identity is due to the personality of its founder.

Mergers and acquisitions, new companies, old companies with new market realities, and other reasons may require you to create or change your company's name. There's a lot of good advice out there and many good naming consultants. I shall confine my comment to the following: avoid initials. They are confusing and meaningless unless you have millions of dollars and years to invest.

If your employer is large enough, it may decide to run a corporate campaign. If tend to believe that corporate campaigns are good strategies—but only if they have a specific communications objective such as wooing investors, creating perceptions, or changing public opinion. Unfortunately, many corporate campaigns have no clear objective. They are full of platitudes and self-indulgent chest thumping. They are meaningless outside the boardroom. If you are directing it, make it relevant for the audience, not the board.

Instead of spending money on corporate advertising, you may choose to spend it on philanthropy. There are plenty of worthy causes to support. And if your company is big enough, it may start its own cause. Keep in mind, though, that it's not enough to give money to charity from the ivory tower. A corporation must get seriously involved in a cause to show true support. Otherwise, the effort—regardless of the dollar amount—will be perceived as a covert promotional attempt. In other words, if you're going to advertise, advertise openly, intelligently, and responsibly. Don't hide the fact that you are advertising. But if you're going to contribute to a charity, contribute wholeheartedly and without ulterior motives. Let the goodwill ensue as a by-product of your actions and outstanding corporate citizenship.

2. **Pricing.** "The market defines our pricing." "The wholesalers define our pricing." "The competition defines our pricing." Do these statements sound familiar? Studies show that approximately 80–90% of companies conduct no in-depth pricing research and analysis. Yet price is one of the key factors that drive profitability.

By definition, profit equals price × sales − costs. So each of these three elements should get the same attention. Traditionally, however, everyone is accustomed to focusing on sales, or unit sales, or sales volume, or occupancy levels. Sales are considered the controllable result of sales and marketing activity; so, the thinking goes, if occupancy is high, the company must be doing well. Perhaps it is, perhaps it isn't. The question is, at what price? Cost is another element that is under close observation by most companies. Cost reduction, downsizing, and reengineering are all to some extent cost optimization programs. Cut your costs and profitability will increase. Seemingly so, but at what price? Price is the final element and most often the overlooked stepchild of management. Why invest time, money, and resources in something (presumably) beyond your control? As much research as you conduct, the market will define the price levels. Right? Wrong. Pricing is the final bastion of profitability and should be considered the reflection of your value proposition in the marketplace. Thus it should be considered a key element of your brand strategy.

For any product there is a price range with upper and lower limits. If you surpass these limits, you will price yourself out of the market. Yes, price fluctuations may be seasonal, regional, and subject to consumer behavior. But if you know your playing field and structure your pricing around maximizing value, you should strive and be able to remain within the upper limit of your allowable price range. And that will maximize profitability. Knowing the proper pricing range in which you can safely operate will help you not only generate volume but also avoid leaving money on the table. The Optimal Tariff Theory, developed by economist Charles Bickerdike, states that it is possible to improve your terms of trade by increasing the price and thus reducing the number of unit sales, allowing you to conduct a smaller amount of trade on more favorable terms. Following the principles of this theory is what pricing and yield management are all about: reaching an optimal balance of price level and unit sales.

The bottom line—especially in hospitality and tourism—is that anyone can increase unit sales by dropping rates. It takes no wizard or marketing guru to slash prices. Most companies are also quite good at reducing operational costs. If you serve only one olive instead of three with every meal, you will save 66.67% on olives, and if you reduce the operational hours of the front desk, and wash the towels only once a week, and stop serving bread, and charge for salt . . . You see what's happening. You are seemingly cutting the fat, but what you are in fact doing is severing the bone. This cost-cutting strategy will send any company on a downward spiral that will ultimately result in loss. Yes, it is crucial to operate at optimal cost levels, but quality costs money and you should not compromise your products. Nobody will accept compromised quality even at the lowest rates. People don't want to buy cheap products. They want to buy good products cheap. They are willing to pay good money for good products and good brands as long as they know what they are getting in return. They want genuine value. And the creation of value is your job as the marketing pro of your company. The right pricing level will merely be the reflection of that value. Value creation and perception will allow you to price according to your needs, thus setting your price for maximum return and profit by optimizing unit sales.

Pricing strategies should also be evaluated against the product and brand life cycles. Mature products may need less promotion at a lower price. New products may need high levels of promotions combined with an initially lower price for quick market penetration.

Finally, pricing is a marketing tool. Whether you like it or not, the price says as much (or more) about your brand as the smart copy in your advertisement. So, don't leave pricing to the sales or corporate finance departments, or your prices may end up being designed to increase sales quotas or to meet some unrealistic corporate debt repayment objective. Study pricing. Become an expert. Pricing should be the job of marketing, and you must be involved.

3. **Customer focus.** Research shows that customers cease using a product or frequenting an establishment for the following reasons:

   1. 70% because a company (i.e., a brand) doesn't seem to care about their needs
   2. 15% because their problems remain unresolved
   3. 10% because they find a better price
   4. 3% because they move away
   5. 2% because they die

Hence, excluding price adjustments, relocation, and death, the average business has the opportunity to adjust 85% of the reasons that could make them lose their customers. Nevertheless, at most hospitality companies, customer service is spotty, often dependent on the mood of a disgruntled employee or on his or her corporately defined limitations that prevent them from truly solving customers' problems. At many hospitality companies, customer service is considered an operational issue, as consumption occurs within the product operation. This is a mistake. While most customer service issues may be resolved within operations, the driving force behind the effort should be marketing. Tomes have been written about customer service and how to improve it, maintain it, and turn it into a secret weapon. Study all of them and make exceptional customer service your stealth branding tool. Or as Guy Kawasaki, the author of *How to Drive Your Competition Crazy*, states, "Pigs will floss before this maxim changes: The best way to drive your competition crazy is to make your customers happy. To make your customers happy, you have to focus on them."

And if you feel bad about your company's not being totally customer oriented yet, consider this statement by General Motors' former president, Charles Kettering: "It isn't that we build such bad cars; it's that they are such lousy customers." It takes time to shift an entire organization to truly commit to great service, and the impetus has to come from the top.

4. **Sales.** Although often used interchangeably, the terms "sales" and "marketing" are very different. The role of marketing is to divide the different markets into segments, create products that meet the needs of the identified segments, and generate demand and a call to action. The role of sales is to answer that call and convert it into a sale. Traditionally, the sales department focused mainly on pushing existing products or services through large-volume sales. In some hotels and hospitality companies, sales and marketing operate as separate business functions, sometimes almost as independent units. Results, however, are much stronger when sales operates as an element of the marketing process.

Businesses that view sales as the function of marketing will achieve three major advantages: First, the business will develop and fine-tune its product/service to meet the needs of its target market. Second, all of the marketing activities will be focused on achieving sales results and will be measured by the results they achieve. Third, the selling function will be supported by all marketing activities, and a marketing-driven sales approach will focus not just on reaching quotas, but also on building long-term relationships and achieving customer satisfaction.

MARKETING RESPONSIBLY

As a hospitality marketer, you are not just a proprietor or an employee, but also a member of your environment and society. And while marketing may represent the last competitive advantage, it should also be a covenant for creating value beyond the bottom line. Playing to win does not mean playing irresponsibly or unethically. Playing to win should be seen as a means of competing at the highest level of thinking and creativity, which should generate benefits for your company (more revenues), your employees (a better work environment, greater job satisfaction and personal growth), your customers (better products and services), your society (goodwill, contributions, jobs), and even your competition (fomenting improvement through innovation).

USEFUL LINKS

- ahla.com
  American Hotel & Lodging Association (AH & LA)
- arccorp.com
  Airlines Reporting Corporation (ARC)
- cruising.org
  Cruise Lines International Association (CLIA)
- ei-ahla.org
  AH & LA's Educational Institute
- fmi.org
  Food Marketing Institute (FMI)
- franchise.org
  International Franchise Association (IFA)
- hotel-online.com
  Online hospitality news
- hsmai.org
  Hospitality Sales and Marketing Association International (HSMAI)
- iaapa.org
  International Association of Amusement Parks and Attractions (IAAPA)
- iacvb.org
  International Association of Convention and Visitor Bureaus (IACVB)
- otid.com
  Travel Agent Magazine Travel Industry Directory
- str-online.com
  Smith Travel Research
- tia.org
  Travel Industry Association of America (TIA)
- ttra.com
  Travel and Tourism Research Association (TTRA)
- world-tourism.org
  World Tourism Organization (WTO)
- wttc.org
  World Travel and Tourism Council (WTTC)

CHAPTER TWO

The Market

"All animals are equal, but some animals are more equal than others."
—George Orwell, *Animal Farm*

Unlike most other industries, the hospitality, travel, and tourism industry is unique because it includes direct as well as single- or multilevel intermediary commerce.

Direct buyers are individuals or groups who book directly. They include walk-ins, repeat customers, members of a loyalty program, buyers who book through a reservation center via phone or the Internet, corporate meeting planners, and corporate travel buyers.

Indirect buyers are individuals or groups who buy through intermediaries such as travel agents, incentive companies, meeting and convention planners, Internet travel companies, junket representatives, travel clubs, associations, and transportation companies. All of these intermediaries may book either directly or through other intermediaries such as wholesalers or tour operators.

This reality has both pros and cons. On the one hand, a complex distribution system allows for a better variety of business sources. It reduces dependency on a single channel of distribution and creates opportunities for selective pricing. On the other hand, more distribution channels make marketing and selling more complex, more labor-intensive, and potentially more costly.

The key is to study the market mix and create a plan that balances the various market segments and channels by volume and profitability. This will provide the best foundation for developing focused product and marketing strategies.

DEFINING THE MARKET MIX

You cannot have a strong marketing strategy without defining your market mix first. Not to be confused with the original marketing mix (the four Ps), the

A targeted resort ad. The headline reads: "Naked is how our open-air showers are best enjoyed on a honeymoon."
Source: Brandhaus and Karisma Hotels & Resorts. Used with permission.

market mix is a composite of all the market segments that comprise your total source of business.

The hospitality, travel, and tourism market consists of two large entities—individual and group customers—so the market mix may contain any of the following segments: individual business guests, corporate group guests (meetings, group events, seminars, incentives), convention guests, and other group guests (social, military, educational, fraternal, religious, governmental, association), as well as individual nonbusiness guests such as tourists or special interest guests.

For vacation resorts, most business will consist of leisure travelers, while city hotels will focus on business travelers. Other locations may have a mix of both. Some destinations, such as New York City, will have a strong mix from a variety of markets—business travelers, conventioneers, tourists, educational groups, cultural groups, and so on.

The first step is to review and summarize historical data, which will tell you the percentage of business that you receive from each of the segments. A market mix for a city hotel may consist of 80% business customers and 20% leisure customers. The business segment would be further divided into individual business travelers (70%) and meetings and groups customers (30%). The leisure segment may be subdivided into tourists (60%) and local events such as educational group meetings, weddings, and meetings of fraternal organizations (40%).

Analyzing this information will initiate the process of further defining the various market segments as well as identifying potential new segments.

MARKET SEGMENTATION

The benefit of market segmentation is fourfold. First, it allows you, regardless of your company's size, to maximize your available budgets by specializing in and targeting smaller market clusters. Second, by going after specific targets, you will be in a better position to spot market opportunities. Third, you can tailor your product and service to the specific needs of your market segments and therefore create a stronger positioning and competitive advantage. And, fourth, your marketing program will be much more focused.

Many marketers fall into the trap of targeting "heavy users," "big-volume customers," "nonusers," and "new customers." This is unfortunate, because some (or all) of these segments may be quite unprofitable. Heavy users and big-volume customers may have highly negotiated rates, thus yielding lower margins. Nonusers may have no interest in your product category, so money spent on attracting them will be wasted. And constantly going after new customers is much costlier than maximizing returns from profitable existing customers.

Before you embark on a segmentation spree, make sure that the potential segments meet the following criteria: (1) the segment should be substantial enough to warrant a separate marketing effort, (2) the segment must be measurable in terms of purchasing power and size, and (3) the segment must be accessible, that is, you must be able to market to and serve it effectively.

Nevertheless, the key factors in determining target markets should be profitability and affinity, not merely number of transactions or size. The purpose of market segmentation is to identify specific profitable market clusters, develop products and services for them, and market to them with relevant communications and branding. The steps for defining potential market segments are:

- Identifying denominators common to individual market segments
- Defining the market profile for each segment
- Choosing segments based on size, level of profitability, and feasibility
- Defining product features and appeals for the chosen segments
- Developing the product and marketing strategy for the chosen segments

SEGMENTATION PARAMETERS

The different segments that constitute your customer mix (current or planned) may be based on the following parameters:

- **Transaction history and buying behavior**—which tracks and analyzes the purchase behavior of customers including shopping flows (information search, offer comparison, price evaluation, purchase), where and when (seasonality) they buy, how often (loyalty), how much they spend, how purchases are made (travel agent, phone, Internet, walk-in), what products or services they buy (features, benefits), who makes the buying decision, and who makes the purchase and determines its type/motivation (leisure or business).
- **Geography**—which groups clusters of customers by geographic areas. Location analysis reveals that people residing in certain areas and zip codes share common purchasing behavior characteristics.
- **Demographics**—which is based on age, gender, income, education level, occupation, religion, race, nationality, family life cycle (single, married, etc.), and family size. It is used to group consumers and evaluate patterns of behavior based on these parameters.
- **Psychographic or lifestyle analysis**—which groups people based on their special interest and common lifestyle traits.
- **Profitability**—which combines information from all of the above-mentioned parameters to segment target markets based on their value as clients. This is the optimal targeting measurement, as it is based on actual or potential value instead of size.

Plenty of good data is often available in house, yet companies often fail to use it for more than accounting purposes. This information may include registration files, fulfillment requests, payment records, customer service surveys, and so on. For example, guest registration cards contain crucial information such as the date and length of stay, rate paid, number of guests in the party, and type of party (adults, children), and may even provide zip code and contact information. This information, combined and overlaid with information from periodic surveys, can be transformed into outstanding marketing information.

The challenge, especially for companies with multiple locations, is centralizing this internal data for marketing purposes and integrating it into the daily operations process.

CONSUMER BEHAVIOR AND DECISION-MAKING FACTORS

Since marketing is the creation and management of demand and demand is a form of behavior, it is important to study behavioral patterns to better understand how and why consumers react to different stimuli such as pricing, product features, services, incentives, packages, and advertising appeals. And while the study of consumer behavior is an evolving field with no absolute rules, knowing the principles, and the different factors that influence buying decisions, will assist marketers in understanding what makes consumers tick and therefore in better managing demand. The key factors influencing the buying behavior of consumers are culture (the accepted values, views, and behavior systems in a society), social status or class, personal values, demographics (age, gender, income, occupation, family life cycle, geographic location), lifestyle, reference groups (private, social, and professional), personality, attitudes, motives (needs, wants, desires), perceptions (organization and interpretation of information), and learning (behavioral changes resulting from acquiring knowledge and experience).

Furthermore, to focus marketing communications on the appropriate target, it is important to understand the exact involvement of consumers in purchase decision making, as there may be one or several people involved in the process. First, there is the person who initiates the purchasing process (e.g., a business traveler, his or her supervisor, or a client). Then there is the user, the person who actually uses the purchased product (e.g., a business traveler). There is also the influencer, a person whose opinion may count (e.g., the spouse of the business traveler). There is the decider, the person who makes the ultimate decision (who may or may not be the user). Finally, there is the buyer, the person who makes the actual purchase (e.g., the business traveler's assistant).

Purchasing is a multistage process that starts when the consumer identifies a need, want, or demand for a certain product or service (e.g., overseas accommodations for the business traveler). Then the consumer (or someone on his or her behalf) is likely to gather information (e.g., searches the Web, calls for information, talks to a travel agent) on a variety of options to evaluate and compare the alternatives and choose the most appealing supplier (e.g., the hotel with the best mix of cost, benefits, appeals, and attributes). Finally, the chosen product is purchased, which usually ends the process for the user. For the marketer, however, the process shouldn't end here. The smartest hospitality marketers continue communicating after the purchase and consumption are completed.

Studying and understanding the nature of each market segment—its needs, wants, and desires—as well as knowing the factors and constituents that

The design sets the tone for the entire hotel: Hotel Unique in São Paolo, Brazil.
Source: Hotel Unique. Used with permission.

influence the consumption decision-making process will lay the foundation for developing products and marketing plans targeted for specific market segments and aimed at the appropriate audience members with the appropriate set of appeals.

Traditionally, the study of consumer behavior focuses on the individual end consumer. However, for many hospitality marketers, it may be imperative (and often more beneficial) to analyze the intermediaries (travel agents, meeting planners, corporate travel buyers, etc.) and the factors that influence their organizational buying behavior.

CONSUMER TRENDS

"When you're safe at home, you wish you were having an adventure. When you're having an adventure, you wish you were safe at home," said Thornton Wilder. This statement describes quite accurately the fickleness of consumers' wants and needs. Some of these grow into consumption patterns of certain population groups and eventually become trends.

Futurist and author Faith Popcorn researches the ever-changing population for patterns and trends. Because of the accuracy of her predictions, *Fortune* magazine nicknamed her the "Nostradamus of Marketing." Throughout the past two decades she has recognized a variety of trends that have assisted marketers in developing products and appeals. Several of these trends have strong implications for the hospitality, travel, and tourism marketer:

Down-aging—The age barriers of yesteryear are no more. Forty is the new 30, and the tendency of grownups is to act and feel young. This provides a great opportunity for adventure vacations and specialized camps.

Egonomics—Following the motto that mass equals no class, consumers are more in touch with their individuality and personal tastes. This provides a great opportunity for products that reflect the individuality of their target (unique locations, product features, food, etc.).

Fantasy adventure—Consumers need to escape the boredom of their daily routine. This is a fine opportunity for innovative vacation products such as theme parks and resorts.

Ninety-nine lives—Consumers are strapped for time, They have to juggle too many things at the same time, and convenience is a great benefit. This is an excellent opportunity for business travel products that help handle all the tasks from one location.

Small indulgences—Consumers are highly stressed. There is a great need for small indulgences that provide pleasure and brief escapes from the daily pressures. This is reflected in consumers taking more weekend trips rather than the annual 2-week vacation and provides a great opportunity to offer creative getaway packages.

Being alive—People realize that being healthy means living longer and better lives. Organic foods, supplements, and exercise are becoming consumption staples. Helping consumers to maintain a healthy lifestyle even when they travel has strong appeal for a growing number of travelers (especially business travelers).

Pleasure revenge—After decades of self-restraint, consumers are consciously enjoying so-called forbidden fruits such as red meat, tobacco, and alcohol. Being healthy means being happy, and that includes sometimes indulging in things that are not necessarily good for them. In contrast (or in addition) to the previous trend, offering guests an opportunity to indulge in pleasurable items may be an attraction.

Eveolution—Women are becoming the predominant influencers and purchase decision makers. They control 80% of household spending. Marketers will do well to create products and services that meet women's needs.

These are my interpretations of several of Popcorn's trends. For more information on her books and work, visit the website faithpopcorn.com.

MARKET RESEARCH

Market research sometimes seems a daunting task, yet its basic purpose is simply to answer a few questions to make marketing easier: Who are the existing or target customers (demographics)? What are their wants and needs (features, attributes, benefits)? What appeals and attributes attract them (preferences, tastes, lifestyle)? How do they become attracted (marketing, recommendations)? How do they purchase (channel, distribution, consumption patterns)? What competitive products do they buy (competition)?

Researching the market may take many forms, from gathering industry data and studying available statistics (secondary research) to conducting guest surveys, one-on-one interviews, phone surveys, mail surveys, focus groups, and others. You can research any aspect of the marketing mix:

- Customers (trends, preferences, demographics, competitive usage)
- Brands (product features, attributes, new product ideas, competitive analysis)
- Distribution (location, distribution patterns, channel members, costs, sales methods, competitive strategy)
- Price (competition, discount appeals, price variance and demand)
- Promotion (all aspects of the promotional mix: advertising recall, appeals, messages, awareness, brand names, competition, response rates)

A good research firm will be able to gather the information and provide the insight sought.

THE BENEFIT OF SURVEYING EXISTING CUSTOMERS

While some research techniques have more validity than others, many are partly flawed in that they do not measure actual behavior, but rather opinion or intent. And opinion and intent are very different from action. Focus groups can certainly provide valuable information, but especially for hospitality companies, there is one very effective way of conducting market research: surveying your actual patrons. They represent your market perfectly because they are actual customers, not a market sample. Disney World, for example, asks for every visitor's zip code. They use this information to profile their consumers based on available zip code demographic and consumer behavior data. It is amazing that destination organizations do not use more of this type of visitor profiling to optimize their marketing efforts. All it takes is the collection of zip codes. Embarkation forms filled out by the travelers collect all the necessary data to create extensive visitor profile reports.

While this form is very convenient for the patron, as it contains only one question, most guests will not object to answering a short survey with several questions. Optimally, you should obtain the following information:

- Zip code
- Age, marital status, family size
- Education level, profession, household income

- Household type: rent or own
- Commute: preferred mode of transportation
- Buying habits: what supermarket they frequent, what car they drive, and so on
- Preferred TV program(s), network, cable
- Preferred radio program(s), network
- Preferred newspaper(s)
- Preferred magazine(s), professional publications
- How learned about your brand: TV, newspaper, magazine, Internet, and so on
- Internet provider, connection type
- Primary purpose of the trip (leisure, business, etc.)
- Traveling: alone, with partner or spouse, children (how many, what ages and gender)
- Travel information: preferred airline, what loyalty programs they belong to

It may be a bit unrealistic to expect to obtain all of the above information, but you will get some of it. Regardless of how much you get, combining it with your available purchase statistics (length of stay, way of booking, rate paid, type of purchase, etc.) will soon allow you to build a powerful knowledge base that will help guide you in the decision-making process.

For example, if you market without this information, you may know the following: about 60% of your bookings are from the New York tristate area, as your three largest wholesale accounts are located there.

If, on the other hand, you consistently conduct this type of research, you may learn that of the 60% of the customers in the origin market, 50% live in urban areas and 50% in suburban areas, and that in the urban market, 40% live in Manhattan and in the suburban market, 60% live on Long Island. Furthermore, you may learn what magazines and newspapers they read, which TV shows they watch, and where they buy their groceries. You may learn that they commute to work on foot, or by car, train, bus, or subway, or you may learn that they have heard about your offer on the radio, which they listen to at work. You may also learn that they visited your website to find out more about your product. You may learn how many are married, how many have children, and how many are in a serious relationship or single. You'd be surprised how much market intelligence is available for the asking—not speculative data, but hard facts from your actual guests. The more information you collect, the less money you'll be wasting on "blind" marketing and the more precisely you'll be able to define your audiences. After a while you will start seeing patterns among your guests, and by combining this information with transaction data, you will be able to segment target markets based on their profitability. This will allow you to create clone profiles and target new customers with much greater accuracy.

If possible, structure your survey in the form of a multiple-choice questionnaire; these are easier and quicker to complete. If you think that your guests will not be willing to spend a few minutes providing this sort of information, bribe them. Offer them a small reward or turn the survey into a promotion. You could enter each completed survey in a weekly drawing for a free stay. Or ask them to complete the survey online, after which they will receive an added-value coupon for a return stay.

If much of your business is derived from intermediaries such as travel agents or meeting planners, survey them as well. Find out what attributes, appeals, and benefits they take into account when recommending a particular product or brand. Find out what motivates them to choose one location or

Controversial or insensitive? A Nike shoe with an insignia resembling the word "Allah" in Arabic.

Source: Aurora & Quanta Productions, Inc. Used with permission.

brand over another. Measure the importance of the various stimuli in their decision-making process.

Continuous study of your customers will make you a superb marketer.

THE MASS MARKET

The mass market has not disappeared; it has evolved. What has actually disappeared is the traditional way of reaching the mass market, not the need for mass market products. True, with the drastically changing tastes, preferences, and knowledge of consumers, products, brands, appeals, and media choices will continue evolving and transforming as well. But mass market products have not disappeared. What is Disney World if not a product for the mass market, or the scores of mega cruise ships and resorts, or destinations such as Las Vegas, Cancun, or Miami Beach, or restaurants such as Subway? These hardly qualify as niche market products. Yet, they continue thriving in a highly fragmented marketplace by changing their product offerings as well as marketing to meet the needs of the evolving population. The key to marketing a mass market product in today's environment is to approach it with specialized strategies (targeting) for the various subsegments, that is, to create appropriate appeals for the varying audiences. As consumers become savvier, marketers have to understand that the way to reach the new mass market is through a cluster of smaller and larger target markets.

SPECIAL INTEREST AND NICHE MARKETS

Niche marketing is not a new concept. Special interest segments have always existed. Have there not been ski resorts for many years, or family resorts, honeymoon resorts, and golf resorts? True, there are some new ones, such as the spa market, and some of the old special interest markets, such as the golf market, have exploded and have been further divided into subsegments (e.g., senior, female, and junior golfers). However, besides special interest segments, which are largely defined by special products, niche markets may be segmented by demographic groups including women, children, Hispanics, Asian-Americans, African-Americans, gays and lesbians, single parents, and seniors, as well as groups based on attitudes and lifestyles such as consumers of premium products or consumers who seek leisure time over money. The key lies in understanding that these niches are not watertight, may overlap, and have subsegments. For example, the guest at a luxury spa may be an administrative assistant or a top-level executive, both of whom are seeking pampering and relaxation after a stressful week. Or consider the affluent consumer who shops at Target and Saks. It is important to understand the motivation behind the differing purchase decisions across the niches to offer the appropriate blend of special product features and universal appeals that will help target varying customers more precisely.

The advantage of niche markets over general markets is that they are smaller, better defined, and more manageable. It is easier to reach them through specialty publications, programs, websites, clubs, and events. In many instances, products can be specialized for the particular needs or wants of certain market segments. Focusing on special interest markets instead of the general market can be very lucrative, as the tendency of these markets to look for discounts and price-off deals is less pronounced. For smaller competitors, a great reason for specializing in niche markets is to avoid direct competition with market leaders.

Success with niche markets lies in the knowledge and specialization of products, market segments, demographics, lifestyle, service area, region, and even price. Prior to developing a niche market strategy, each niche should be evaluated for:

- **Feasibility**—can you effectively serve the niche with your product offering, expertise, budget, and so on?
- **Profitability**—is the niche large enough, and do its constituents have spending potential?
- **Barriers to entry**—what barriers will you have to overcome before entering this niche market?

Are you sure you are targeting the right market?
Source: Getty Images Inc.—Hulton Archive Photos. Used with permission.

- **Exclusivity**—is someone else already serving this particular niche?
- **Opportunity**—can you establish yourself as the uncontestable leader in this segment, that is, dominate the niche?
- **Longevity**—is this a true niche market or just a passing fad?

EXTERNAL MARKET DATA

If you are serious about analyzing actual and potential user data, you should complement your internal research information with external consumer data to achieve greater accuracy and expand your potential markets. Good sources of hospitality and tourism information include visitors' bureaus, chambers of commerce, governmental agencies, industry associations and organizations, companies, suppliers and vendors, channel members (travel agents, wholesalers, tour operators), industry consultants, general publications (newspapers, business magazines), trade publications, research institutions, and colleges and universities.

The following organizations provide a variety of consumer information (category usage data, geographic data, purchase behavior, demographic and psychographic data), and some offer extensive databases:

- acnielsen.com   AC Nielsen
- americandemographics.com   American Demographics magazine
- arbitron.com   Arbitron
- cohorts.com   Cohorts
- claritas.com   Claritas
- esribis.com   ESRI Business Information Solutions
- equifax.com   Equifax
- experian.com   Experian
- mediamark.com   Mediamark Research
- smrb.com   Simmons Market Research Bureau
- symmetrical.com   Symmetrical
- sric-bi.com   SRI Consulting Business Intelligence
- census.com   U.S. Census Bureau

CHAPTER THREE

Products

Nothing can be created out of nothing.
—Lucretius

In the past, the purpose of marketing was to push existing products. Today, hospitality products are part of the marketing function, and it is absolutely crucial to develop products that are relevant for the intended target markets.

I was fortunate to be part of the team that developed and launched an innovative hospitality product called Royal Hideaway Resort & Spa. I experienced firsthand how a well-conceived product marketed to the appropriate market segments can achieve tremendous success.

All-inclusive resorts in general, and especially in the Cancun and Riviera Maya areas, suffered from the perception of being cheap, loud, and crowded mass market resorts with buffet-style restaurants serving food of average taste. The concept of Royal Hideaway was an answer to that perception: a five-star luxury all-inclusive resort that offered first-class accommodations, food, amenities, and services combined with the convenience of an all-inclusive program. The positioning of the property was "pampering," which was defined by the product. The unique all-inclusive features of the Royal Hideaway included five gourmet à-la-carte restaurants, a theater-style dining room with live shows and entertainment, premium beverages, beverage and fruit service on the beach and around the pools, 24-hour room service, large guest rooms with custom-made furniture, premium bedding, and amenities, personalized concierge service for every guest villa, a CD, video, and book library, and a variety of sports and activities with equipment and instructors. It also offered a full-service spa, which was not part of the all-inclusive program.

We knew that it would take too long to try to build a reputation based on the product alone, so we "acquired" initial credibility by making Royal Hideaway the only all-inclusive hotel member of the renowned Preferred

Hotels & Resorts organization. This helped us support the luxury claim we
were making and justified the high rates we charged from the very beginning.

Royal Hideaway was launched with premium materials and a dedicated
sales staff, and with no preopening specials or discounts (the rates were double the highest rates in the Riviera Maya). The success of this property was
due to a finely targeted market segmentation. In terms of distribution, instead
of trying to market the product through the traditional leisure channels
(wholesalers and tour operators), we aimed at the small groups and incentives market as well as high-end travel agencies. But, most important, the consumer target strategy was to aim at Caribbean vacationers, not travelers

With today's level of market clutter your product must stand out:
old Route 66 on a sunny day.
Source: Stock Boston. Used with permission.

interested in Mexico. This was done because Mexico is perceived as a more affordable destination than the Caribbean, so going after the Caribbean traveler allowed us to command higher rates. This was done in the geographic markets with the largest number of scheduled air flights into the Cancun airport and was promoted directly to consumers and travel agents, which created a significant stream of reservations at the rack rate. Another key success factor was that we didn't lower the rate or sacrifice quality during the first few months, when the property had low occupancy levels. This ensured exceptional product quality from day one and helped create extremely enthusiastic word of mouth.

Without the right product for the right people, no marketing—no matter how smart or creative—will produce significant results.

SPECIAL PRODUCTS FOR SPECIAL PEOPLE

While hospitality product segmentation used to be easy, with hotels, motels, bed and breakfast places, cruise ships for travel, upscale restaurants, diners, and street stands, today it is quite complex. There are luxury hotels, near-luxury hotels, ultra-luxury hotels, mid-market hotels, convention hotels, boutique hotels, business hotels, economy hotels, motels, family resorts, all-inclusive resorts, golf resorts, ski resorts, spa resorts, and sports camps. There are luxury cruises, family cruises, active cruises, singles cruises, barefoot cruises, and yacht charters. Then we have fast-food restaurants, family restaurants, ethnic-food restaurants, seafood restaurants, franchised upscale restaurants, home delivery, take-out restaurants, and all-you-can-eat restaurants. Specialization is what happens when an industry matures and the population's income grows.

Nowadays, key product differentiation doesn't lie in the core product (lodging), but rather in differentiation of the supporting products (services, facilities, and amenities), which should be developed according to the intended target market's needs, motivations, and appeals. The travel motivators are:

Business travel
- Meetings
- Events
- Group travel
- Trade shows
- Conventions
- Incentive travel
- Projects
- Research
- Seminars

Interior design is a crucial element of the hospitality product:
the Jean-Georges restaurant, New York City.
Source: Peter Paige. Used with permission.

Leisure travel

- Vacationing
- Entertainment and fun
- Escape
- Relaxation and stress relief
- Bonding (family, partner, children)
- Socializing
- Pampering and indulging
- Personal growth
- Exploration
- Sports and activities

- Affinity groups
- Events
- Group travel
- Seminars
- Events
- Education
- Weddings and honeymoons
- Sex

Except for sex tourism, all of these represent good market segments, and your product and marketing strategy should be focused on those that fit your operational capabilities.

A common mistake is to try to develop a product with such broad appeal that it becomes generic, that is, it doesn't appeal to anyone in particular. The key to success in any product category lies in specialization. Let's examine two cruise companies. Both operate identical 100-cabin ships. Cruise A is a generalist cruise and tries to project a broad enough appeal to attract a general market. Cruise B specializes in romance and targets weddings, honeymoons, and couples. Cruise A has nice but generic decor. Cruise B has decor that supports its romantic positioning. Which one do you think will have stronger positioning, lower marketing costs, higher rates, and more repeat business? Most likely Cruise B, since this company will be perceived as a specialist, which will give it a stronger presence in a smaller, yet profitable, market segment and allow it to command premium pricing.

THE PRODUCT AS A MARKETING TOOL

"If you build it, they will come"—the favorite statement of many hoteliers with empty hotels. Nowhere is this statement more untrue than in hospitality. Certainly, there are exceptions for "hot" properties in "hot" locations, but as for the rest, without proper marketing most hotels will remain empty. Unfortunately, many operators learn the importance of marketing the hard way. If they just looked hard enough, they would realize that marketing must start before the property is conceived, because the first element of marketing is the product itself.

Beyond the obvious purpose of its existence, the product has huge importance during all phases of the marketing process. This is called the "product role sequence." The first phase is the planning phase, during which the product must be conceived with a marketing strategy in mind. The second phase is the prelaunch period, during which no one can actually see or experience the product (usually 6–12 months prior to the opening). All information is based on imagination, computer renderings, and claims. During this phase the product is nonexistent and thus irrelevant, but the idea of the product is crucial. The third phase is the inaugural period, during which the primary driver is the initial product experience (usually the first 6–12 months). In the third phase, the product operation must shine, which is quite difficult because most hospitality products do not shine during the first few months. Yet, this is the period when initial media reviews, travel agent familiarization trips, and industry visits will happen, so it is absolutely essential to perform small miracles to deliver superb service, even though this may be difficult. (And forget about selling rooms during soft openings; this is the biggest disservice a hotel can do to itself. It's like selling a car with some parts still missing.) The fourth phase is the full operational phase, when all the initial kinks have been ironed out and the operation has reached a certain level of confidence. During this phase the product must become the key driver behind word-of-mouth marketing. Word of mouth is the *best* marketing tool, with the highest credibility and

The hip atmosphere of the Habita Hotel in Mexico City
differentiates the product experience.
Source: Habita and Deseo Hotels. Used with permission.

the lowest cost. And all it takes is to delight the guests. Hospitality companies, unlike most other product companies, have the opportunity to delight their customers on a daily basis. A bottle of badly flavored juice will remain badly flavored forever, but the hospitality product, even with an average physical property, can delight guests with fabulous service. It is that simple.

THE PRODUCT AS A BRAND ELEMENT

Make no mistake about it; the time when a product existed merely to fulfill its expected physical purpose is over. The product today is *the* key brand ingredient and should be conceived as such. It is impossible to sustain success and build a strong brand with a feeble and undifferentiated product. This is discussed in more detail in Chapter 4.

PRODUCT QUALITY

Product perfection has been touted as the killer strategy in a variety of industries, but in reality, it is virtually impossible to satisfy all customers all of the time. Especially in the hospitality industry, variables beyond our control

A great location will help define the product experience: a view from the Westin Stamford Hotel restaurant in Singapore.
Source: Getty Images Inc.—Stone Allstock. Used with permission.

will occasionally affect the product experience. Furthermore, operating for perfect quality means increasing training, staffing, and operational costs to such high levels that quality improvements (real and perceived) become marginal. It is wiser to seek optimal quality at optimal cost and be prepared for the occasional dissatisfied customer with exceptional customer service.

PRODUCT DEVELOPMENT

New products are the drivers of growth for any company. They deliver new revenue streams, open new markets, and create new opportunities. In the hospitality industry, new product development encompasses:

1. Improvement of old products by adding new features (e.g., new menus and menu items; product upgrades; improvement of common areas and rooms; expansion of services; new facilities)
2. Repositioning of old products by narrowing the focus (e.g., a regular hotel refocusing only on couples and honeymooners)
3. Developing new products with differentiating new features (e.g., specialized and improved new products within existing categories that offer better, more convenient, or attractive customer features and services)
4. Expansions of related existing products (e.g., Disney's new Animal Kingdom)
5. Entering new segments (e.g., a hotel company opening resorts or a budget operator entering the mid-market segment)
6. Entering new categories (e.g., a cruise company opening hotels or vice versa)
7. Developing new categories (e.g., all-inclusive resorts or boutique hotels)
8. Developing new "real estate" (e.g., new locations or ships within an existing category)
9. Developing new products or features for promotional purposes

Regardless of the type of development project, following are some vital questions that need to be answered for a successful product development project:

- What is the reason for the new product?
- What is different about the new product?
- How complete is the research on which the new product plan is based?
- What are the product's competitive advantages?
- What is the objective of the new product?

- What market segment(s) does it target?
- Is the segment sufficiently large and profitable?
- What consumer needs or wants does it address?
- What consumer appeals does it have (rational, emotional)?
- What competitive products exist in the category? How loyal are its users?
- How populated is the category?
- What market risks are associated with this product category?
- What are the barriers to entry in this category?
- How does it fit into the existing product portfolio?
- How does it fit into the existing brand portfolio?

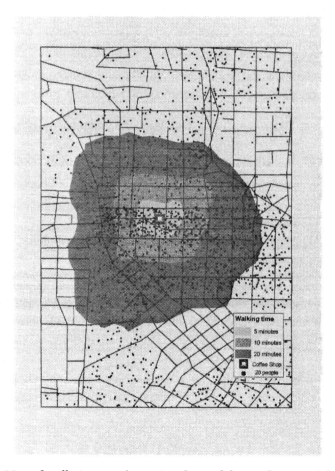

Map of walk times to determine the usefulness of a potential
site for a Starbucks coffee shop.
Source: Compass Rose Consulting, Inc. Used with permission.

- How will the new product affect the core brand value?
- How does it fit into the core operational and promotional skills of the company?
- How does it fit into the existing distribution channels? In addition to those channels, how else will the new product be distributed?
- How quickly can the product be brought to market?
- Who is on the development team?
- Does the project have full buy-in from top management?
- What is the development cost?
- What is the marketing budget?
- What are the financial risks?
- How long will it take to achieve critical mass?

Answer these questions and you'll have a good head start. Product development plans must be based on facts and realistic expectations. Otherwise, they will fail.

Highlight: Allegro Essentials—A New Product

In 1998, as corporate director of product development for Allegro Resorts, one of my projects was to develop and implement a brand new idea: Allegro Essentials, a concept of total, all-inclusive hospitality that would allow virtually luggage-free travel. Basically, it was an addendum to the company's all-inclusive program, but packaged as a unique product. It was to be developed at Allegro's Jack Tar Village Resort in Puerto Plata, Dominican Republic, a four-star all-inclusive resort for adults. The objectives of the project were to generate awareness and differentiate the property, as well as position Allegro as an innovative hospitality company.

The Allegro all-inclusive package was already quite complete. It included accommodations, unlimited food and beverages at a variety of on-property restaurants, snack stands and bars, access to all hotel facilities, a daily sports, water sports, and activities program (including instructors and equipment), a nightly entertainment program with shows and a discoteque, and an activities and entertainment staff, as well as tips and taxes. In addition to these standard features, the Essentials program included:

- A set of resort wear for her (shorts, polo shirts, T-shirts, canvas shoes, sandals, underwear, bathing suits, wraps, blouses, linen dresses, skirts, a sun visor, and sunglasses)
- A set of resort wear for him (shorts, polo shirts, T-shirts, canvas shoes, beach sandals, a belt, a cap, swim trunks, long linen pants, long-sleeved linen shirts, underwear, and sunglasses)
- A set of toiletries for both (sun protection lotion, toothpaste and toothbrush, mouthwash, hair brush, talcum powder, deodorant, shaving cream and razors, skin lotion)

- An Essentials boutique where guests could choose, try, and exchange their items
- Alterations
- Laundry and dry cleaning during the guests' stay
- A duffle bag so that guests could take the items home with them (I guess it was only 50% luggage free)

The objective of Essentials was more promotional than operational, yet the development was quite an undertaking. It included complete design and manufacturing of the product line, from shoes to caps. Izod manufactured part of the clothing, and the remaining part was an Allegro private label line of clothing manufactured by Manutex, a Dominican clothing manufacturer and retail store chain. As there was no way to predict future customers' sizes and tastes, all clothing needed to be ordered in a range of sizes and designs to provide variety and prevent guests on the property from looking uniformed. All the remaining merchandise, such as sunglasses, caps, visors, and toiletries, needed to be procured as well. Further, we had to design, construct, and staff a complete retail complex to serve as a welcome lounge, boutique, and alterations facility. It needed to be large enough to handle significant traffic, as arriving charter flights would bring up to 100 guests at a time. Also, since this was a prepaid package (i.e., there were no per item transactions), a smart inventory system was necessary to handle arriving customers. This problem was solved by using a voucher system.

Essentials was launched only in one test market, Germany, and only with one tour operator, TUI, with a retail price for the supplement of $295 per person. The first guests were scheduled to arrive on the afternoon of May 3, 1998, the final merchandise arrived May 1 and the boutique was finished on the morning of May 3, following many tribulations. Whomever we had mentioned the project to during development called us crazy. We, however, knew that if we pulled it off, the payback would be worth the effort.

And it was. The project was a major promotional success. We received tremendous publicity in the German media, and many writers traveled to the property to see for themselves that there were people daring enough to travel halfway across the globe with only their passports and wallets. Our original objectives of creating awareness by differentiating the property, as well as helping us position the company as innovative, were more than achieved. Moreover, this project spawned an interest in our other properties and helped us grow business in that market.

WHY PRODUCTS FAIL?

Unfortunately, many new products fail for a variety reasons. The most common ones are the following:

Insufficient planning. Companies sometimes approach new product development projects haphazardly, without paying sufficient attention to whether the new product fits the company's growth strategy, can be easily distributed through existing distribution channels, fits operational standards, is in a profitable category, has real appeal for consumers, can be developed and marketed at a reasonable cost, and so on.

Proper planning and feasibility assessment is a crucial investment for any new product launch.

Lack of consumer focus. Products conceived in the boardroom may have little appeal to actual consumers. Sufficient customer feedback is imperative.

Incomplete or misinterpreted market research. Market research is valuable only if it is complete and the results are correctly interpreted. Results can be presented in many different ways to project wanted messages. Consider this funny example from Guy Kawasaki's excellent book *How to Drive Your Competition Crazy:*

Does this describe how your research is transformed in your organization?

Customer	It is a crock of shit, and it stinks.
Researcher	It is a container of feces, and most unpleasant in smell.
Manager	It is an earthenware vessel of excrement, and it is very strong.
Director	It is a vase of fertilizer, and no one can resist its strength.
Vice President	It contains substances that aid plant growth, and it is very potent.
Chief Operating Officer	It promotes growth, and it is robust.
President	Let's implement this terrific idea because it will promote growth.

You get the idea.

Poor direction. Often development projects are not assigned to a single person or group. As a result, they get passed around and end up as orphans without a parent. On the other hand, projects developed by large committees have an equally low chance for success; remember the old adage about too many chefs in a kitchen. New products must have a champion who will lead the project and give it clear direction.

Weak concept. New products must offer unique benefits. If they do not offer real differentiation or innovation they are merely new, which isn't enough for success. Products based on strong concepts deliver strong and unique benefits to potential costumers. However, new products can also have too many benefits, confusing the market or becoming prohibitively expensive.

Poor execution. Even with a good concept based on solid planning and research, a product can fail if its execution falls below market expectations.

Insufficient funding. This may result in project abandonment or feeble products. Often projects start with lofty goals and then are whittled down in order to fit the budget. Products should be developed well or not at all; starting strong only to cut corners along the way will result in weak products.

Other reasons. Other products fail because they are merely corporate ego projects, conceived for the purpose of corporate or management aggrandizement instead of meeting market needs.

DESTINATION FASHION

Destinations are products and brands. As such, just like shoes, clothes, and cars, they are subject to fashion. One year a destination may be in vogue, while next season it's a different island. This is quite different from the gradual decline in popularity of a destination, such as Acapulco, which was all the rage in the 1950s and 1960s but, by the end of the twentieth century, had become a secondary destination (this is very unfortunate, as it is one of the most exciting places in the world). What can a destination do to combat this boom-bust cycle? Quite simply, keep its product up-to-date.

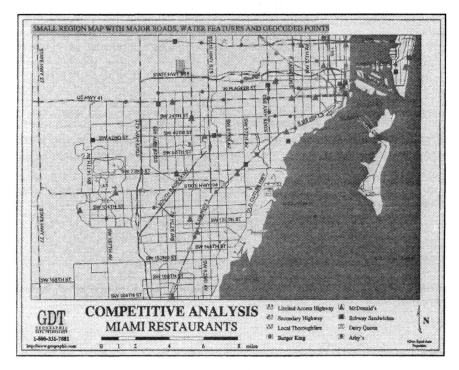

Competitive analysis: a street map of Miami, Florida, showing the locations of various fast food restaurants relative to highways and thoroughfares along the shoreline.

Source: Geographic Data Technology, Inc. (GDT). Used with permission.

One example of doing an excellent job of continuously keeping the destination fresh and relevant is the island of Aruba. I've always been intrigued with Aruba's popularity, as there are many prettier islands that are closer to the U.S. mainland and have lusher vegetation. But that's partial product reality. Aruba's success lies in creating the right brand perception: the island is extremely clean, everyone speaks English, the roads are good, overall safety is higher than in an average U.S. city, and the tap water is drinkable. Aruba has curbed hotel development, so rooms are plentiful but the island is not overbuilt; this keeps overall rates high and attracts a more affluent clientele. There are a variety of restaurants, casinos, excursions, and shops. Overall, Aruba is a complete and safe vacation choice. Make no mistake; Aruba is not an adventurous destination. Serious thrill seekers will not choose it, but thrill seekers are not its target. The target is the main U.S. market, for which the island offers the perfect product. It attracts this market with the positioning slogan "Where Happiness Lives." In addition, to ensure a steady market interest and flow of traffic, its tourism office invests significant dollars in the promotion of the island (promotion consists of consumer and trade advertising, as well as marketing through the distribution channels by educating travel agents and cooperating with airlines and wholesalers). You should see their marketing plan!

PRODUCT ANALYSIS

Periodic analysis of the company's as well as the competitors' products is about the only way to remain up-to-date and honest. Example after example shows that when management confines itself to the boardroom and stops personally experiencing the product, they often lose touch with the core product values. Managers, on the other hand, who continuously experience the product, not only have a chance to see and feel it for themselves but also to collect immediate feedback from actual customers. And that may often be more valuable for uncovering product weaknesses than multiple consultants' reports. Following is a checklist of the main categories that a detailed product and competitive analysis should cover:

Reservation experience (speed, friendliness, accuracy, efficiency, billing convenience)

Reception (speed, friendliness, accuracy, efficiency)
- The check-in and check out experience
- Valet service
- Front desk
- Bell service

Public spaces and property grounds
- Appearance and architecture
- Decor

- Overall cleanliness
- Aesthetic appeal
- Landscaping
- Functionality

Accommodations

- Guest rooms (number, sizes, decor)
- Room type (suite, standard room, categories, views)
- Bathrooms (shower, tub, both, hydro-massage tub, hair drier, scale)
- Amenities (standard, deluxe, premium)
- Room service (hours, menu, options)
- Television (basic, cable, prepaid, closed-circuit information program, games)
- VCR and CD players
- Phone (lines, units, Internet connection, dialing information and options)
- Iron and board
- Minibar
- Convenience (bathrobes, slippers, guides, product information)
- Safety deposit box
- In-room fax machine

Restaurants, bars, and lounges

- Number of restaurants and bars
- Types of restaurants (formal, grill, specialty, casual, healthy food, coffee shop, snack bar)
- Types of bars (lobby bar, lounge, sports bar, bar with live entertainment, pool bar, beach bar, disco, cigar bar, wine cellar)

Guest services

- Concierge
- Information
- Tour desk
- Car rental
- Shops and boutiques (snacks, gift shop, shops for clothing, flowers, logo items, jewelry, sports equipment)
- Guest transfers
- Hair salon
- Laundry and dry cleaning
- Shoe shine

Business center

- Opening hours
- Services (faxing, printing, Internet access, computers, cell phones, pagers, paper and writing supplies)

Meeting services

- Meeting spaces (variety, sizes, setups)
- Prefunction space
- Meeting services (audiovisual equipment, food and beverage services, business services)

How about a 7-Star property? The unique Burj Al Arab Hotel in Dubai.
Source: Peter Arnold, Inc. Used with permission.

Recreation and sports

- Property facilities (fitness center, pool, spa, massages)
- Sports (tennis, golf, bicycles, water sports, archery, volleyball, etc.)
- Beach (quality, public/private, size, services)
- Off-property facilities (nearby, transfer to and from)
- Activities (activities staff, children's activities, playground, game room, theater, etc.)
- Services (classes, equipment rental, club cleaning and storage, pro shop)
- Library (books, videos, CDs, games)

If you are working for a large hospitality corporation, you probably have a quality control department. If you are working for a smaller hospitality company, everyone is probably so busy doing their job that quality control is an afterthought. Neither of these situations is sufficient. Once a year, the marketing department should perform a competitive product analysis, which for your product should be completed by a total unknown in the company—a virtual customer—to get unbiased customer-quality feedback. Then and only then will you have true information about your product's quality and how it compares to those of your competitors. If the competitors' products are better, you will know where to improve. If your product is better, you can use that information to command higher rates.

PRODUCT TRENDS VERSUS PRODUCT TRENDINESS

Like all products, hospitality and travel products are subject to trends. Yet it is very important to distinguish between real trends—things that guests and travelers grow to expect—and trendy fads that may be costly to implement and don't add to the guest's experience. Based on comments from the participants in an unofficial survey I conducted, as well as my own observations and research, following are several trends that are likely to remain:

Leisure: Quality

Even the mass market is going up-market. Quality leisure time is not seen as a luxury but as a necessity, and the attitude of the customer seems to be "If I'm going to spend (and I am going to spend!), let me spend on something I'll truly enjoy." Just as it is not uncommon to see clerks toting Gucci bags, the demand for better leisure hospitality products is growing strongly across the different market segments. For the mass market, the opportunity lies in offering a near-luxury product (and brand) and delivering it at upper-mid-market pricing.

Business: Convenience, Lifestyle, and Leisure Combinations

The key trend in business travel remains convenience. Business travelers want to take their lifestyle on the road, which means maintaining specific eating, exercising, working, and relaxing habits. And that means convenience of location, services, features, timesaving amenities, and, quite important, the convenience of booking leisure add-ons for business travelers. Another trend that is likely to grow is extended-stay accommodations.

Indulgence

A large segment of the population is stressed and strapped for time. They look for opportunities to have quality time for themselves or with their loved ones through indulgences such as massages or spa treatments, gourmet food, premium beverages, learning and exploration opportunities, and many other pampering, growth, and bonding experiences. Hospitality companies have an opportunity to develop products that cater to this need for pampering (and not just at luxury product levels).

Mass Customization

The wave of mass customization that has engulfed many other product categories will have a huge impact on the hospitality industry. With merchandisers such as Nike, which allows sneakers to be customized online, personalized makeup available at reflect.com, and custom-fitted jeans that can be ordered at the Lands' End's website, it is only a matter of time when hotels and other hospitality providers will harness the Internet to deliver preordered services. There is huge potential for prearrival customization of anything from food to bathroom toiletries, to sheets and mattress firmness. Why not? It is something customers will both grow to expect and expect to pay for.

CHAPTER FOUR

Branding

A good name is better than riches.
—Miguel de Cervantes

❖ BRANDING BASICS ❖

Miguel may well have been a branding consultant. But while a good name is indeed better than riches, a brand is more than just a name. And the process of branding is much more than just coming up with a name for a product and slapping it on an advertisement or brochure. Branding itself is more than a marketing concept; it is a business concept and, if executed properly, the most profitable one. Just how profitable? Consider one of the most successful brands of all times: Marlboro. What comes to mind? Cowboys, horses, masculinity? Would you, then, believe that Marlboro was originally a rather obscure cigarette for women? All white, with an ivory tip and the tag line "Marlboro—mild as May, ivory tips protect the lips." That's how it was marketed for 30 years since its inception in 1924, until it was repositioned in the 1950s to what it is today: one of the best-known brands and the best-selling cigarette in the world.

This is the power of a properly (re)positioned brand: not just imagery but superb sales and profits over the long run. Why? Because—don't be shocked—of the way the brand makes the user feel. Sure, the (perceived) tangible benefit (flavor) is part of the experience, but the way the brand makes us feel is the key driver.

Branding consists essentially of creating positive associations for products and charging extra for them. It works for large and small hospitality companies, individual hotels as well as destinations. The challenge is to quantify and organize the creation of those associations and package them successfully for the marketplace, a process formally known as "building brand equity." This

The world is a branded place: Ken and Barbie strolling down
a street full of brand names.
Source: Aarow Goodman. Used with permission.

chapter explores a variety of brand-building issues that should assist in the
process.

IS BRANDING REALLY THAT IMPORTANT?

Shouldn't it be enough to have a good product at a good price? Well, yes, basically that's all it takes, but by doing just that, you have already started the
branding process. Because if you don't actively manage your branding yourself, the marketplace will do it for you. And then you will not be in control of
your destiny. How? Let's say that you buy a ship and start offering cruises.

Since you just want to focus on the product and you don't want to deal with branding, you decided not to have a name for your cruise. You just branded yourself as the no-name cruise. The market did it for you. By entering any market segment you are automatically entering a branded environment, and you must be prepared to embark on the ongoing journey called branding.

Why is branding important? For the consumer, brands are crucially important because they identify the product or service, associate it with the operating company, and reduce the cost and time necessary to search for it in the vast marketplace. Furthermore, brands reduce various risks involved with the purchasing decision (financial, social, functional, emotional), they serve as covenants of product or service quality, and they establish a sense of familiarity and comfort, a virtual bond. For you, the hospitality provider, brands are important because they are a way of providing legal asset protection. They serve as a platform and a device for communication and market education, creating differentiation and maintaining loyalty. Brands also deliver financial benefits (premium pricing, attracting investors). They represent one of your key competitive advantages.

But the true importance of brands lies in the fact that they are the only way left to effectively differentiate products. Why? Because the marketplace has changed. Even the most innovative product features are likely to be copied (and often improved) by the competition. Even the lowest prices can be beat by a larger or cheaper competitor. But brands provide an opportunity to create intangible and ownable associations, which are not only difficult to copy but may even be legally protected. Consider a commodity that is free: water. Yet, Evian sells hundreds of thousands of bottles at premium prices due to a strong brand. In today's marketplace, not just marketing but everything a hospitality company does must be managed as an element of its brands, including service, reservation systems, distribution, and the products themselves. When consumers are faced with the choice of spending their money on commodities or branded goods, which are they more likely to buy? My bet is on branded goods.

WHAT MAKES SUCCESSFUL BRANDS SUCCESSFUL?

It's evident that branding pays off. Especially in recent years, branding has become the new corporate mantra. But what makes successful brands successful?

The first key element of any successful brand is a good product. Unlike what some brand consultants would have you believe, and especially in the hospitality industry, products are not mere commodities differentiated only by perception. Truly great hospitality brands are largely defined by their products. Products are crucial brand elements, and no amount of intelligent branding will ever turn a feeble product into a successful brand. The consumer has a keen sense of product quality. Four Seasons could never be Four Seasons without a Four Seasons product. A good product will serve as the foundation for brand differentiation, strategy, and communication. This becomes increasingly true as you move up the pricing ladder. The more exclusive the brand, the more it is driven by the product itself; that is, product usage becomes the brand experience. But even at budget and mid-market levels, there are successful and very well differentiated brands that are supported (if not defined) by the product's delivery. Southwest Airlines is one example. Their promise: a comfortable flight with a low price and a sense of fun. Their delivery: a comfortable flight with a low price and a sense of fun. Southwest truly took the maxim "less is more" and built a brand around it. And this philosophy is ingrained in the entire organization. Southwest's flight attendants, mechanics, and pilots are among the hardest working in the industry; they all understand this commitment and are motivated (personally and financially) to help achieve it. The product is an element of the brand, not the other way around.

If a product largely defines the brand, what is the difference between a brand and a product? The difference between a brand and a product is the difference between a banana and a Chiquita, a motorcycle and a Harley, an amusement park and Disney World, a hotel and a Four Seasons. A product is an item in a category (a hotel, a resort, a cruise, etc.) designed to satisfy a consumer's need, which makes it one of the brand's key elements. A brand, on the other hand, is a set of various real and perceived character qualities, benefits, experiences, and feelings. It is also the element that, in addition to satisfying tangible needs, satisfies desires, wants, aspirations, and emotional needs. The differentiating factor in branding is the level of ownership of these differentiating brand attributes and perceptions in the mind of the consumer. The purpose of the physical product, service, or both is to fulfill those brand expectations. Thus, you could say that, on an emotional level, a product could be described as an acquaintance (you are aware of its existence and you have rational expectations), while a brand is a friend (you feel you know it, and you have both rational and emotional expectations; there is a sense of mutual commitment; plus, a friend makes you feel good).

What if you're competing in a commoditized segment such as rental cars or air travel? In any industry and segment, there are many unique attributes you can use to set your brand apart, and having the right attributes is the second key element to success. These may be inherent in your product or you may develop them consciously to make them part of your brand's character. Avis has been trying harder for decades. Hertz has the most convenient locations. Enterprise picks you up at home. American Airlines has the most routes to the Caribbean and Latin America. The differentiation doesn't have to be a tangible benefit; it can be a service, an added value, or a perceived benefit. It can be a character trait or a product-implied attitude (e.g., Club Med's antidote to civilization). It can be the lack of something (e.g., Southwest's lack of frills). It can be a company claim (e.g., Avis is number two). However, truly great brands don't just brand their product offering; they brand a "higher ground." Do you think Disney World brands their theme parks? Of course not. They brand the higher ground of Disney magic and then use that higher-ground branding to reflect positively on the theme parks (and everything else they promote). That's powerful stuff. Of course, Disney is a world in itself (pun intended), with the "magic" woven throughout the company, but this approach works in any category. You just have to search hard to find your brand's higher ground and then use it. Only creativity limits the attribute and differentiation factor you can use and own for your brand. Just make sure that it is relevant to your market, that your product and/or service can deliver it, and that it is not easily copied by your competition. Easy enough, right?

The third element of success is consistency, both of the product and of the brand. Especially in hospitality, where third-party management contracts and franchise systems abound, control is difficult and consistency is often hard to achieve. Who has not had the experience of staying in a hotel with a big, franchised brand name, only to have a terrible experience due to miserable conditions and service? Of course the corporate office established quality standards,

Those ears are a powerful branding element.
Source: Getty Images, Inc.—Liaison. Used with permission.

but if a hotel is operated by a sloppy general manager, this will reflect negatively on the brand.

The fourth element is perceived value. Whatever your brand offers, it must hold value in the mind of the user. Perceived value is the factor that tips the pricing scale. The more of it is loaded in your brand proposition, the more you can expect in return.

The fifth element is the communication of your brand to the world. If you don't let people know you exist, they won't know the unique benefits of your brand. And if that communication is not in sync with your brand's character—and actually pushes its limit—they may hear about you but perceive you incorrectly.

The sixth and final element is the feelings a brand commands from its users. These feelings are created through the usage of the first five elements and should not be neglected or seen as fluff. If feelings were not the ultimate driver behind successful brands, how would you explain someone paying $700 per night at the Peninsula when she could have had just as good a night's sleep at the Best Western? The best brands maximize this emotional bond to achieve ridiculous competitive advantages. What's the best way to measure the feelings of your customers or guests? Never confine yourself to your ivory tower; keep talking to customers and keep being a guest yourself. A few incognito conversations in the lobby or restaurant may provide more insight than various research studies.

So, what makes a successful brand successful? The physical qualities of the product (i.e., product and brand experience delivery), along with the relevance and uniqueness of one or more brand-owned attributes and perceived value, combined with an overall brand personality, delivered consistently over time, held together with outstanding brand communications, and maximized by positive brand feelings are what make successful brands successful.

WHAT IS BRAND EQUITY?

"Brand equity" is the buzzword of businesses around the world. Everyone talks about it. But what is it?

The author of *Managing Brand Equity*, David Aaker, defines it as "a set of brand assets and liabilities linked to a brand, its name and symbol that add to or subtract from the value provided by a product or service to a firm and/or to that firm's customers." He further states that "The five categories of assets that underlie brand equity are 1) brand loyalty, 2) brand awareness, 3) perceived quality, 4) brand associations (reason-to-buy, differentiation, attitudes, etc.), and 5) other proprietary brand assets (patents, trademarks, channel relationships, etc.)."

Young & Rubicam, one of the largest global advertising agencies, has developed a brand equity measurement system called BrandAsset Valuator. This tool evaluates brand equity on the following four levels: (1) differentiation, which measures the brand's perceived uniqueness; (2) relevance, which measures how relevant a brand is to its user base; (3) esteem, which measures the regard, liking, and reputation of a brand; and (4) knowledge, the ultimate measure of brand equity, which measures the market's understanding of the brand, its benefits, its associations, and what it stands for.

I define brand equity as the difference between the value of a branded product and the value of that same product without the brand. This represents more than the difference in pricing that branded products command over generic products. It also represents the total value, comprised of all brand elements, that a brand brings to a product: financial, perceived, social, emotional, even irrational.

Thus the benefits of a brand with strong equity include larger margins, less susceptibility to economic fluctuations, higher pricing flexibility, greater marketing effectiveness, a greater share of the market and customer, more consumer loyalty, and easier marketing through the distribution channels. The active building of brand equity means employing the full arsenal of brand-building tools and actively managing all the elements that comprise a brand.

The key challenge of brand equity is measuring it, as it is quite difficult to quantify things such as reputation, feelings, and goodwill. Nevertheless, it is possible. European companies do it. And it seems that plans are in the works to include intangible assets on the balance sheets of American companies as well. Following, in its entirety, is an excellent commentary on the subject written by *Business Week's* senior editor, Neil Gross, that appeared in the August 6, 2001, issue.

Valuing "Intangibles" Is a Tough Job, but It Has to Be Done

As any business-school prof can tell you, the value of companies has been shifting from tangible assets—the bricks and mortar—to intangible assets, such as patents, customer lists, and brands. These are the keys to shareholder value in a knowledge economy, but our accounting system does little to acknowledge the shift. You won't find balance-sheet entries for those assets except in rare cases, even though at some companies they may account for the bulk of overall value. For example, at Apple Computer (AAPL), No. 49 in our rankings, brand value equals a huge 80% of market capitalization.

Ignoring those intangible assets may have been fine 30 years ago; not anymore. Investors need a sense of the assets' value and whether expenses to support them—such as advertising—are really productive. If accounting can't take stock of that, boards can't allocate capital intelligently, analysts can't evaluate the companies they cover, and investors can't get a fix on the market. "You end up with the blind leading the blind and being evaluated by the blind," says Jonathan D. Low, senior fellow at Cap Gemini Ernst & Young.

NEW RULES

Now, after years of dithering, architects of accounting rules are finally taking the first steps on the issue. It's a start, but more needs to be done. In June, the Financial Accounting Standards Board issued rules for how companies record assets in a merger. The rules, effective for most companies next Jan. 1, mean that when businesses acquire others using standard accounting, they will no longer have to amortize goodwill. That makes sense because most of those assets don't really depreciate. You don't wear out research or run out of brand power—at least most of the time.

Sometimes, however, those assets can be damaged, and the new rules require companies to recognize that. If your assets become impaired—say, your biggest brand suffers a massive safety recall—then you must account for the damage. To do so, companies will have to assign a value to the intangibles. Crusaders for accounting reform who care about knowledge assets applaud this outcome. "The idea that you will identify acquired intangibles and periodically measure what they are worth—this is definitely a move in the right direction," says Baruch Lev, accounting professor at the Stern School of Business and author of *Intangibles: Management, Measurement and Reporting.*

So why not go a step further and require companies to account for intangibles on the balance sheet all the time, regardless of whether or not there's a purchase? After all, in places such as Britain and Australia, companies already must, at times, report brand valuations on the balance sheet.

VOODOO ACCOUNTING?

First of all, get real. It took the conservative FASB 30 years to make the latest set of changes. A quick, radical overhaul simply isn't in the cards. And that may not be the solution, anyway. When it comes to brands and other intangibles, says FASB Research Director Timothy S. Lucas, "there are very significant measurement and definition problems." Even the reformers seem content to go slow. "To get into the financial statements, information should be reliable," says Paul B.W. Miller, a professor of accounting at the University of Colorado and a longtime FASB watcher and critic. The biggest problem? Valuing intangibles, even using the most rigorous methodology, calls for subjective judgments—something accountants abhor.

There are, however, other ways to balance the need to track the value of intangible assets and the need for easily verifiable financial statements: Simply report the value of the intangible assets elsewhere in the financials—for example, in the footnotes. That way, investors would have at least some sense of whether their investment was gaining or losing value. Intentionally or not, FASB has put the need to value intangible assets front and center. BusinessWeek's new brand ranking will provide good grist for the whole debate.

Senior Editor Gross writes about research, patents, and other intangibles.

Source: Reprinted from August 6, 2001 issue of *Business Week* by special permission, copyright © 2001 by The McGraw-Hill Companies, Inc.

THE BRANDING STRUCTURE

Sooner or later, you will be faced with a branding decision that will affect the future of your company and potentially could mean millions of dollars: choosing the correct branding structure. There are five basic branding structures:

1. The company name is also the brand name. Example: Carnival Cruises.

2. The company name is just a corporate brand and operates different market brands. Example: Starwood (Westin, Sheraton, W, Four Points, St. Regis, Luxury Collection).

3. The company name is also the brand name and operates in different categories. Example: Disney (cruises, parks, resorts, movies, cartoons, television, toys).

4. The company name is also the brand name and operates different brands as well as sub-brands. Example: Marriott (Marriott Hotels, Courtyard by Marriott, Renaissance, Ritz Carlton, Residence Inn, Fairfiled Inn, TownPlace Suites, Springfield Suites, Marriott Conference Centers).

5. The brand is a market brand with several sub-brands. Example: Holiday Inn (Holiday Inn Hotels and Resorts, Holiday Inn Select, Holiday Inn SunSpree, Holiday Inn Family Suites, Staybridge Suites by Holiday Inn).

These are not watertight structures and each of them may have subdivisions, but for the purpose of our discussions, this is how the basic structures are primarily used. Each of the five structures has its advantages and disadvantages; there are no right or wrong answers, as this decision depends on many past, current, and future variables. The key in choosing the correct structure is to approach the process wisely and evaluate the following issues:

Critical mass. Do you have enough products in the portfolio to allow for a multibrand system? Will each of the brands have enough critical mass or would it be best to unify the product under an umbrella brand?

Corporate contribution. Will the corporate brand contribute to the consumer brand and vice versa?

Long-term strategy. Is the proposed branding structure in sync with the growth plans? If expansions into unrelated divisions are on the horizon, perhaps the corporate brand should remain separated from the market brands.

Clarity. Will the branding structure be clear and transparent to the consumer and the distribution channel? While it may be understood by management, it may remain very confusing to the marketplace.

Brand budgets. What are the available brand budgets? A multibrand system requires multiple budgets. A unified branding approach maximizes available budgets.

THE CHALLENGES OF BRANDING

The main challenge of branding is that a brand (or brand equity) is an intangible asset. The true value of a brand lies in the perception of it in the marketplace, not in any physical property. Even though the physical product of a hospitality brand has significant value, such as real estate for hotel companies and restaurants or ships for cruise lines, the true value lies in what the brand's associations bestow on those products. Carnival could replace its entire fleet tomorrow, but it would have a difficult time replacing the value of its brand. And while this intangible brand value affords the owners a significant competitive advantage, it makes it difficult to quantify the value of brand equity and determine the return on brand investment. Valuing brands has been one of the most mulled-over issues in recent business history.

The second key challenge of branding is that corporations are not organized to nurture brands. If they were, they would put customers, employees, and long-term brand value before short-term financial gains. Instead, most companies pay lip service to branding but operate as they have for decades. This point is very well illustrated by David D'Alessandro, author of *Brand Warfare:*

> The truth is that even the best American corporations tend to be full of people who actually think they are doing their job by keeping branding down. There are the lawyers who slow down a company's response in a crisis because they believe that short-term liability concerns ought to trump long-term brand considerations. There are the clerks who allow scandals to brew because they feel they have little to gain by reporting the dicey things they uncover. There are the financial types who allow good brands to atrophy because they resent the dollars it takes to build a brand. And there are the advertising managers who spend millions on campaigns that mean nothing to consumers because they fail to understand that the brand ought to drive the advertising and not the other way around.

Sad, but true.

Furthermore, brands in general, and hospitality brands in particular, are burdened by emotional challenges, misunderstanding, discounting, product parity, lack of positioning, competition, insufficient marketing, underfunding, inconsistency, weak strategies, and lack of consumer focus, as well as market clutter and fragmentation:

Emotional challenge   Branding is about the creation of feelings, yet it is a business discipline. The feeling a customer has for a brand is not quantifiable, nor can it be explained with numbers, which makes branding a tangible activity for creating intangible assets. The solution is to overcome the fear of dealing with feelings and take advantage of the opportunity while most companies are still emotionally challenged. I believe that the branding superstars of tomorrow will be women, as they are more emotionally intelligent than men.

Misunderstanding   Branding is much discussed but often misunderstood. You may often hear "Just put the two logos together in the ad and you've solved your branding problem." Branding is not about creating an ad or placing a logo. True branding is at the heart of marketing and the overall business strategy. If it is not the driver behind your company's market approach, it is your job to change that situation. Educate yourself first and then your organization.

Discounting   This is a tough one. If you don't have a strong brand value perception, it's hard to command or even maintain profitable price levels. If you don't maintain prices, it's hard to build brand value perception. Convince your company to invest in brands.

Product parity challenge Copycats are everywhere. They steal your brand strategy, advertising techniques, and product ideas. Make sure that you keep ahead of the curve with innovative product features, great service, and customer happiness so that the competition can merely play catchup. It just might position you as a market leader.

Lack of positioning There is *no* reason for this. Positioning is your responsibility, and you just have to do it.

Lack of responsibility The responsibility for managing and protecting a brand is often not very well defined, and lack of responsibility ownership will have an adverse affect on the brand. This responsibility needs to rest with someone who has enough experience, knowledge, vision, and clout to make the right decisions and implement them throughout the entire organization.

Competition Hospitality has one of the fiercest competitive environments of any industry. How can you gain a competitive advantage? By building a strong brand and delivering an excellent product.

Insufficient marketing Some hospitality brands just don't market enough. They may have a steady flow of customers and forget that this situation may not last forever. When you don't need to market is the best time to market. Don't wait until it is too late.

Underfunding See Chapter 14.

Inconsistency This is one of the greatest evils, but also one of the easiest to fix. Get buy-in from the top executive and make brand identity a priority. The big problems start when you have a chain of managed properties or a franchise organization. Often the general manager or property sales and marketing staffs want to operate independently, which creates headaches for the corporate marketing office and vice versa. You can control this problem by putting in place an identity system, material templates, and support infrastructure so that individual properties have no option but to follow the branding.

Weak strategy Some companies just don't know how to develop a strong strategy. Their products are bland, and therefore their strategies are bland. Get unbiased help from the outside. Dare to make tough decisions. Dare to leap, not walk.

Lack of consumer focus It is very easy to get entangled in the inner workings of a company. Corporate growth plans, financial burdens, bureaucracy, lack of leadership, and many other issues cause companies to lose their focus on the consumer. Get back to basics. Your brand exists because of your customers, not the other way around.

Market clutter and fragmentation The market is fragmented and cluttered. It is helpful to constrict your brand positioning to narrow the playing field. You cannot be all things to all people. Instead, try to mean something to one group of people. Turn a negative into a positive. Take advantage of the fragmented market and become a specialist for a few market segments instead of competing with everyone for everyone.

Immediate gratification challenge   Wall Street's quarterly earnings approach has created immense pressure on companies (and not just publicly traded ones) throughout the nation to forego midterm brand-building strategies in favor of short-term sales results. Until brand equity becomes a quantifiable item on the books, this situation will remain.

Corporate greed   Hand in hand with instant gratification goes corporate greed. Strong brands today are sacrificed, extended, and neglected for lack of corporate focus and the search for new profit opportunities. Often the best profit opportunity lies right under your nose. Perhaps the biggest asset is the one you already have.

PROTECTING BRAND VALUE

Protecting the value of your brand must be a conscious effort. The brand value is what differentiates your product from a commodity and allows you to charge a higher price. Probably the best lesson comes from premium brands. These do not have factory outlets, and they do not sell scratch-and-dent inventory. They leave these to their inferior competitors. Quality is an investment, and the only way to keep delivering quality is by protecting the value associated with your brand.

❖ BRANDING TOOLS ❖

BRANDING ELEMENTS

A brand consists of a set of different elements, all of which must be managed for maximum brand value. These are:

- The product (location, architecture, features, facilities, amenities, services, decoration, size, condition, attributes, uniqueness)
- The service (friendliness, accuracy, speed, efficiency, variety, consistency)
- Primary communication elements (name, logo, symbol, signage, guest materials, advertising, brochures, displays, public relations materials, photography, sales kits, presentations, displays, web site)
- Secondary communication elements (support materials, tickets, ticket jackets, stationary, invoices, forms, contracts, memos, internal communications)
- Character elements (country of origin, heritage, user profiles, usage situations, personality, corporate association, customer relationships, size)

- Strategic elements (positioning, differentiation, user benefits, perceptions, associations, strengths, reputation, perceived quality, aspirational quality, attitude)
- Price

ONLY ADVERTISING BUILDS BRANDS, RIGHT?

Wrong. One of the biggest myths is that brands are built by advertising alone. Thus, if you have no advertising dollars, the fallacy goes, you might as well compete on the commodities exchange. New brands are actually built mostly with publicity, not advertising. Advertising, albeit a key ingredient, is just one of the brand-building tools you have at your disposal. The product itself, public relations, customer service, guest experience, signage, pricing, marketing, promotions, and the Internet are all key weapons in you branding arsenal. You can build a powerful brand with those alone, before you have even started allocating money for advertising. Smart companies recognized this long ago, and use advertising to drive and integrate what all the other activities have helped create.

POSITIONING

What is positioning? It is what your brand stands for in the marketplace. Simply put, a brand's positioning defines what the brand does, how it is preemptively different, and for whom it is intended. Answering the question of what a brand does simply by stating what need the brand's product fulfills is wrong. The answer lies in what benefits (physical, emotional, rational, and aspirational) the brand delivers to its users and how these are perceived as distinctive from others.

There are few limitations to how you may choose to position your brand. Some hospitality brands are starting to establish a strongly differentiated positioning in the minds of consumers. Examples include Carnival Cruises, which positions its products as fun ships at a great price. Royal Caribbean has recently started positioning itself as the cruise line for active people. Sandals has positioned itself as a brand for couples and honeymooners. Club Med used to have a strong position as "the antidote to civilization." British Airways has been positioning itself as the world's favorite airline. Ritz Carlton, Four Seasons, and Mandarin Oriental have positioned themselves as über-luxury brands, but not with any particularly well-differentiated positioning.

To have a strong position in the prospect's mind, you must be singleminded. You cannot be cheap, luxurious, romantic, and corporate all at the same time. Your positioning must reflect the relevant function (what your brand does) and differentiation (what it stands for and how it is preemptively different from the competition) and thus defines the audience (for whom it is intended). This doesn't mean that your narrow positioning excludes other attributes. On the contrary, your positioning claim will imply and legitimize the remaining attributes.

An example of exceptional positioning is Heinz ketchup: "thick and slow-pouring." That in itself doesn't mean much, but it *conjures up images* of a slow-pouring, rich, high-quality ketchup, which, in turn, *implies* great taste. So, the positioning is: relevant function (what your brand does): it's ketchup; differentiation (what it stands for and how it is preemptively different from the competition): it claims to be thick and thus slow-pouring. This defines the intended audience: anyone who uses ketchup on food and refuses to use the "thin" stuff (implication: cheap, lower quality). Moreover, "thick" lends itself to stunning advertising execution.

As you can see, being preemptively different means choosing a claim for your brand that has not yet been claimed (pun not intended) by another brand. Using the previously mentioned examples, any cruise line could have claimed to provide fun ships. No major physical differentiation was necessary to make that claim. But Carnival did so first; they preempted the claim. Other ketchup brands could have claimed to be thick, but Heinz preempted the competition and now they own that claim.

Positioning is a branded product claim, which may be a product attribute, an attitude, or a specialization for a market segment that helps a brand embody a specific quality in the consumer's mind. But whatever claim it is, all the product adjustments necessary to support that positioning must be part of the branding strategy. So, what is positioning? When perception becomes reality, that's positioning.

POSITIONING TOOLS

There are a few tools that come in very handy when crafting a positioning strategy.

First, analyze your product. Many products contain some unique feature that can be used as the differentiating factor.

Second, if you do not have a unique product feature, analyze the usage problems within a product category to determine if there is an opportunity to deliver solutions and thus provide unique positioning. For example, a problem in many business hotels may be noise from the outside environment and the neighboring rooms. A company that detected this problem may have soundproofed its rooms, positioned itself as the "boring" hotels (as in "we're boring because we're quiet"), and created a hilarious campaign around it.

Third, analyze the higher ground of the category. Every product in the category must comply to a degree with this higher ground, as this is the reason for its existence. What you need to look for are any unclaimed pockets of this higher ground. For example, for restaurants, the higher ground is food and taste, so when Burger King proclaimed "Have It Your Way," they had uncovered the unclaimed pocket of customizing orders in the fast food category.

Fourth, analyze any potential gaps between consumers' needs and products' delivery. This is different from the first point, as it is based on consumers' stated needs or wants, whereas the first point lies in uncovering pockets that have not been recognized by customers. For example, one such gap may have been customers' need for vacations that don't require taking a wallet to the beach—to which the all-inclusive vacation would have been the solution (and, earlier, positioning). Today the all-inclusive vacation is a category, so operators need to look for gaps within the category.

Fifth, analyze the behavioral patterns, trends, and attitudes of current users, potential users, and nonusers to uncover any aspirational or differentiating claims.

Sixth, analyze the attitudes and positioning of competitive brands in the category and industry, as well as what claims they are making. Chances are that most of them are quite bland, which may allow you to develop unique attitudes and positioning for your brand.

If you're lucky, your positioning will be so well differentiated that you'll create a whole new category of which your brand will become the leader.

POSITIONING CHALLENGES

Positioning is a key—perhaps *the* key—strategic branding decision, yet it is one of the most misunderstood branding concepts. The major challenges facing a strong positioning strategy are:

Weak positioning. The company thinks it has positioning, but it doesn't. Check the perceptions in the marketplace.

Fear. Companies often fear that singleminded positioning will exclude certain market segments, so they position their brands too widely. The key to positioning is to choose a claim that defines the brand, not one that excludes market segments.

Lack of relevance. You have positioning, but it's irrelevant. "The hotels with the biggest shower heads" may be a differentiation, but the market probably doesn't care. Test it in the marketplace.

Insufficient critical mass. You have strong positioning but no one knows about it. Make sure that your budget is large enough to deliver the message.

Size. You have grown so big that you have lost any real positioning; you are just big. But this, big brother, is a mistake. The bigger Nike grows, the more they just do it.

Frequent campaign changes. Good brand-building campaigns are built around a single brand idea that does not change. Frequent campaign changes will confuse the marketplace and erode brand equity.

THREE STRATEGIES TO AVOID

It would be impossible to list all the possible brand-positioning strategies, but these are three you should avoid.

Welcoming everyone   By its very nature, hospitality's core trait is to welcome everyone. Unfortunately, that is exactly what prevents most hospitality brands from having strong positioning strategies. "How can we exclude anyone? We are a hotel company," the comment goes. But, guess what? You already are excluding many people with your pricing, location, product features, appeals, service, and many other factors. Strong positioning will not exclude anyone; it will just fortify your perception and presence in the interested market segments. BMW's positioning around performance doesn't exclude other qualities such as luxury, quality, and prestige. On the contrary, it serves as the conduit for defining and communicating them in an ownable way.

Emphasizing low price Many brands focus on low price, which is a weak strategy. It is not preemptive, nor does it differentiate your brand. Keep in mind that there's a huge difference between being cheap and providing value. That difference is called "quality," and it must be the core of your brand strategy. Even price-conscious shoppers don't want to buy cheap products; they want to buy good products cheap. If you operate a budget motel, position it as the best budget motel in the area and then deliver on this promise. Anybody can lower the price, but not everyone will deliver superior quality. Daryl Travis, the author of *Emotional Branding*, said it well: "If you run a hotel and sell all your rooms at 75 percent off the regular price, you could keep a 100 percent occupancy rate and go broke. Selling on price is never as valuable as selling on the premise of quality and service that begets loyalty that begets repeat purchase that begets wonderful word of mouth, all of which begets higher profit—*much* higher profit."

Emphasizing value Finally, don't focus your positioning strategy on value alone; because value is a benefit, not a strategy. Look at Mercedes-Benz cars, for example. Despite their high price, they are an excellent value because they are reliable, and have great resale value and prestige. But the value is intrinsic; the strategy is based on superb quality engineering.

BEWARE OF MULTIPLE PERSONALITY DISORDER

Creating a brand personality means creating an image. Just as you have a personality, so does your brand. And just as your personality projects an image about you, so does your brand. The good news is that while it may be difficult for you to adjust your personality (genes, childhood experiences, and so on), you can do it for your brand. And if you don't, the market will. What your brand personality and image will be, you must decide. Elements that define your brand's personality include anything from its name, logo, advertising, pricing, and service to the product itself and the way your accounting department handles billing. The point here is that whatever you choose it to be, make sure it is the correct one and then stick to it in every possible contact with the marketplace.

BRAND IDENTITY VERSUS BRAND IMAGE

Everyone is talking about brand image, but image is the interpretation and perception of the brand's identity. In other words, before you can have a favorable brand image, you must develop (and project) a favorable brand identity. Consumers form an image of your brand based on a variety of identity elements such as the brand's name, logo, symbol, characters, advertising, promotions, publicity, the product, your brand's presentation in the distribution channels, and the usage experience, so the creation, maintenance, and control of the brand's identity must be a conscious effort. This effort must define how all these identity elements present the brand in the marketplace and how they make the recipients feel.

BRAND IMAGE VERSUS BRAND EXPERIENCE

In 1996 Norwegian Cruise Lines launched a new advertising campaign headlined "It's Different Out Here," created by Goodby, Silverstein and Partners. It used supermodels that swam with dolphins and projected seductive imagery that was quickly accepted by the marketplace and became the talk of the town (the campaign, not the brand). Eventually, it resulted in many taking a Norwegian cruise for the first time. But the campaign flopped. The brand experience did not support the brand imagery. Upwardly mobile clients who hoped to run into the likes of supermodels instead had belly-flopping contests with average Joes and felt taken for a ride. Someone should have known better.

We all have aspirational perceptions of our brands, and while a little upward mobility may actually be beneficial, the usage experience must jive with the image; otherwise, you are jeopardizing your brand's credibility. Remember that you are the keeper of your brand. No one knows (or should know!) your brand and product better than you, so make sure that you keep the creative strategy and product operation in equilibrium.

BRAND BODY LANGUAGE

It is amazing how feeble most travel branding is, considering the fact that hospitality, travel, and tourism brands offer one unique branding advantage: the consumption happens within the product, not of the product. This is what I call the brand's "body language," and it may very well be the key defining element for a brand. While small hospitality companies may not have the budgets or resources of the big players, they do have more flexibility and nimbleness. It would cost a large hotel chain millions to change their brand experience dramatically by adjusting the product. A small or medium-sized company, on the other hand, may turn ideas into reality quickly and at an acceptable cost.

One hotelier who uses the brand body language concept very well is Ian Schrager, whose hotels include the Delano in Miami Beach; the Morgans, Royalton, Paramount, and Hudson in New York; the Mondrian in Los Angeles; the Clift in San Francisco; and the San Martins Lane and Sanderson in London. I cannot remember ever seeing an advertisement or brochure for any of his hotels, yet everyone seems to know them and talk about them. How is this achieved? All of these hotels are unique products but have common brand traits. First, their overall design is fresh, clean, and understated. The bars are usually popular hangouts on their own, as are the restaurants. The rooms are minimalist, and the

The product is the most important branding element.
Hotel Deseo in Playa del Carmen, Mexico.
Source: Hotel Deseo. Used with permission.

facilities all fit the general look and feel. No detail is left out (fixtures, signage on property, furniture, etc.). And it doesn't hurt to have designer Philippe Starck's hands in the process. So, one could say that the product (a key branding element in itself) has become one of the key branding tools. It drives the hotel's brand body language, which makes the brand experience unique, memorable, and relevant and fulfills consumers' expectations and aspirations.

BRANDING ON THE PREMISES

The first time I flew on Virgin Atlantic from New York to London, everyone in coach class received a lovely amenity kit. It contained a sleeping mask, toiletry items, and a shoehorn with "Wakey-Wakey" written on it. It was cute

Cool design features define the "body language" of the Hotel Deseo in Playa del Carmen, Mexico.
Source: Hotel Deseo. Used with permission.

and silly but practical, and I still have it. It made me feel great. And even though Virgin doesn't fly my frequent routes, I will always remember that flight's special—branded—attention, and I'm sure that whenever an opportunity arises, I'll use them gladly again.

It is quite surprising to see how few hospitality companies use the tools they have on the premises for branding. Every company in the world seems to be searching madly for clients and going out of their way to reach them, and here you are with a captive audience *inside* your brand for at least a few minutes! Take advantage of this. Don't bore them with the generic pastel colors and Helvetica typeface on the room service menu. Why not make the menu exciting, different, unique—indeed, branded? This needs to be done anyway, so why not use it as a branded communications device? You can brand:

Public areas: property signage, general information, property maps, displays, posters, elevators, hallways, restrooms

Facilities: restaurant menus, bar menus, fitness center information, spa information, other facility information, displays in the bathrooms, billboards, posters, storage tickets, business center information

Front desk: parking stubs, card-key jacket, welcome card or letter, good-bye card or letter, creative guest kits (welcome kit, departure kit, family kit, kit for couples, etc.), a lending system (CDs, books, magazines, games, puzzles)

In the room or cabin: in-house television, services directory, menu, phone directory, general information, company publication, amenity kit, matches (if it's a smoking room), do-not-disturb signs, laundry bags, stationary

Restaurants and bars: decoration, signage, menus, displays in the bathrooms, billboards, posters, while-you-wait information

and much more. The possibilities are endless, and branding on the premises is simple: you can either have a boring, generic do-not-disturb sign or you can make it part of your brand strategy. Some airlines and restaurants have done a better job than hotel companies of maximizing the time during which they have a patron's undivided attention. And of course, who's the best one of them all? You guessed it: Disney World. The shower curtains have Disney characters, the soap packaging is branded, and on and on. They truly understand

You will always know that you are having coffee at a Starbucks.
Source: Andrew Garn. Used with permission.

this on-premise branding process and also manage to generate extra revenues through merchandising.

BRAND EXTENSIONS AND BRAND FLEXIBILITY

Are brand extensions the lazy marketer's solution for growth? Yes, but not entirely. There are legitimate reasons for extensions, and brands are usually flexible enough to support some of them. However, brand extensions should be approached with caution. The challenge of managing extensions is that the decision to extend is generally made in a vacuum, that is, in the boardroom. Here the financial projections of future line extension models have infinite corporate appeal. Here mega-brands and sub-brands are the solution to stagnant growth. The true question is: what about the appeal and consequences of extensions to the marketplace? The key factor when considering an extension is to look at it from the perspective of the consumer. Will an extension of my core brand be beneficial to the consumer? Is there a logical association with the core brand? Is there any core brand dilution? Brand extensions should be considered only if the extended brand will not only be a new business opportunity in itself, but will also strengthen the core brand; that is, the formula must be $2 + 2 = 5$.

How do you successfully extend a brand? By looking at its flexibility. Each brand is flexible vertically, horizontally, and spatially. The vertical flexibility is the brand's positioning on the price axis: budget, mid-market, luxury, and so on, as discussed at the beginning of this chapter. Horizontal flexibility denotes the market segment range, that is, from business to leisure. The third form is product category flexibility; thus, potential flexibility must be evaluated spatially, in any direction.

Vertically, flexibility is limited. You cannot move much up or down on the pricing scale or you'll end up pricing yourself out of your market. Ideally, you should always stay within your core brand's price positioning segment. However, if necessary, a safe strategy is to keep your extended brand within one-half of a category. Thus, if you operate in a four-star hotel segment, you should be able to venture safely into the three-and-a-half- or four-and-a-half-star market segment. A great example of the limitation of vertical flexibility is Crowne Plaza. Originally, it was introduced as Holiday Inn's up-market brand, Holiday Inn Crowne Plaza. But despite a good product, it didn't do well because potential guests at those price levels didn't want to stay at a "Holiday Inn." Finally, Crowne Plaza was separated from the Holiday Inn name and is now run successfully as a separate brand.

Horizontally, flexibility is a bit greater. You can use your brand to operate vacation products as well as business products. Unless you have strictly a leisure or business brand—say, a downtown conference center—you should be able to venture safely into both segments as long as you stick to the core values of your brand. An example of a brand that would not be appropriate for the business environment is Club Med. Their core value for 50 years has been leisure properties in exotic destinations combined with an inclusive product. It would be impossible to bridge the gap from that positioning to a downtown business environment. Nevertheless, this does not prevent them from going after groups and incentives, a business market segment.

While the pricing and segment axes are quite structured, spatial flexibility is very difficult to define. On what product or category of products can you safely place your name? Club Med recently licensed its name for a perfume called Club Med Ocean. Bulgari will operate a hotel in Milan. McDonalds operates the Golden Arch Hotel in Ruemlang, Switzerland. It remains to be seen how these extensions will reflect on their core brands; they are flexible with the product (spatially) but remain firm with pricing (vertically).

An otherwise remarkable hospitality company, Marriott, on the other hand, seems to be doing the reverse mistake of Crowne Plaza by putting the Marriott brand on real estate as different as a JW and a Fairfield Inn. Besides these two and the Marriott branded hotels and resorts, they have also placed their name on Courtyards, Residence Inns, TownPlace Suites, SpringHill Suites, Marriott Vacation Club, and Marriott Conference Centers—nine sub-brands in all. A smarter strategy would have been to stay with Marriott Hotels and Resorts, Marriott Vacation Club, Marriott Conference Centers, and perhaps Courtyard. Everything else should have been left without Marriott brand associations, as they did with the Ritz-Carlton and Renaissance Hotels, two other Marriott brands. Sure, the corporation's portfolio has increased. But

Outside view and logo of the Golden Arch Hotel, the world's first McDonald's hotel in Switzerland.
Source: CORBIS BETTMAN. Used with permission.

Woman in bed at McDonald's Golden Arch Hotel.
Source: AP/Wide World Photos. Used with permission.

what about the Marriott brand itself? How has it been affected by down-market associations? How have its rates and revenues been affected? Brand erosion doesn't happen overnight. It's a slow process. Yet, once you've realized what's going on, it is usually too late to make a quick recovery.

There are no federal branding laws that govern extensions. Who is to say what should or shouldn't be done with or to a brand? Granted, it is virtually impossible to survive with a one-product, one-brand business model, and some flexibility is necessary. But the *models* under an umbrella brand must be in sync. And that's what they are: models, not sub-brands, line brands, or flank brands, regardless of all the corporate convincing otherwise. To the consumer the Camry is a model of the Toyota brand, not a sub-brand of the Toyota super-brand. Consumers don't think in terms of superbrands. They think in terms of products, some of which have strong brand attributes and associations that make them enjoy, like, and therefore use those branded products more often. That's about it. The fact remains that while no one will slap your wrist for overextending your brand, example after example shows that the strongest and most profitable brands are the ones with the tightest focus.

FROM HOSPITALITY BRANDS TO CONSUMER BRANDS

Since we're on the topic of extensions, the lack of branded cross-merchandising from and to the hospitality industry is intriguing. Westin launched a unique catalog of accommodation-related products such as beds, linens, and bath products. They even offered a bridal registry. That is an excellent branding strategy. Not only do these products have the potential of generating extra revenue, but the company is selling items for which their product stands for (accommodations), thus positioning their brand as an expert in accommodations (2 + 2 = 5). The challenge in this sort of expansion is to limit the number and type of items in your catalog to prevent a brand proliferation effect. As mentioned before, Club Med recently launched the fragrance My Ocean by licensing their name to Coty, the fragrance manufacturer. They could have done this and much more decades ago. In the 1970s and 1980s, Club Med was a brand name with very strong brand associations; they had an opportunity to build a consumer brand around it. Today it will be much more difficult, as Club Med is just one of many vacation brands. TGI Friday's offers packaged snack foods. The Swiss Mövenpick hotels also operate restaurants and sell packaged food products such as coffee and ice cream.

Besides these, there are only a few examples of cross-branding, even though the potential for it is great, as many brands lend themselves to safe and strategically sound expansion into related consumer segments. Four Seasons could create a line of luxury travel gear. Hyatt could publish a series of "How to Do Business in 39 Countries" guides. Mandarin Oriental could develop a line of fine stationary. These are all products that would protect the core brand and reinforce the consumer perception of the brand's high level of expertise or commitment to quality.

With a few exceptions, consumer brands, on the other hand, have not made much foray into hospitality products. Why not create a branded floor at W hotels with Calvin Klein home collection products? Or Royal Caribbean ships with cabins by Nautica? The opportunities are there, but the waters are uncharted. It will take intelligent and visionary marketers to navigate correctly, profitably, and, most important, carefully to protect the core brand.

BRANDING WITHOUT MARKETING

Well, almost without marketing. Every product has a chance to differentiate itself as a brand, and every brand has a chance to become a superstar. Branding is not a marketing concept. It is a business concept, and to work properly it must be woven throughout the entire organization.

Following is a six-point list I've developed on the importance of branding for general managers and operations employees. It shows them that they are at the front line of branding and that any hospitality company can brand without doing significant "marketing."

1. Count your blessings for every new guest who sets foot in your establishment and twice for every guest who returns. Even the most sought-after products and destinations have their ups and downs. It is a mistake to believe that the steady traffic flow will continue indefinitely

or that a particular product will remind in vogue forever. Have this be understood and appreciated by every employee.

2A. Take the opportunity to enchant your guests. Unlike any other industry or category, hospitality, tourism, and travel products have an opportunity to do this. It goes without saying that guests should feel welcome, *but great brands will make them feel special, wonderful, appreciated.* Wow them. Knock them off their feet. This is your single most powerful branding tool.

2B. Take the opportunity to enchant your employees. Many companies proclaim that employees are their most important assets. In reality, employees in general, and especially line employees such as the front desk staff, housekeeping staff, and the waiters, are considered easily replaceable. But guess what? *It's those employees who define your guest's experience.* The official Ritz-Carlton motto is "We Are Ladies and Gentlemen Serving Ladies and Gentlemen." How true. You may have an average hotel building, an older ship, or a far-off restaurant, but if your staff is happy, appreciated, and empowered to serve your guests well, they will create and maintain an enchanting atmosphere. The six-figure-salary marketing vice president may be a terrific lady, but she's not the one who checks guests in, serves them their food, organizes their tours, or handles their complaints.

3. Brand the product experience. The product experience may be great but not branded. Make sure that you take every opportunity to brand it appropriately. A fabulous product experience is a key part of the process, but you have to brand any point of contact by avoiding cheap unbranded signage, old and dirty uniforms, sloppy in-room information, generic menus, and so on. If you have an international clientele, make sure that the translations are perfect. All these minor details will have a major cumulative branding impact.

4. Brand the brand experience. Okay, you have an enchanted staff. They help create (and maintain) an out-of-this-world guest experience. Your product branding is magnificent. It's time to brand the brand. This is the most intricate part of the process, since it requires going beyond merely delivering a branded product. Branding the brand means creating the higher ground, positioning your brand as the end-all and be-all of your product category. The single best example of this is Disney World; they brand the brand experience with cross-branding and maximize their brand differentiation by using the company's reputation for innovation, creativity, and creating special—magical—moments, whether in movies, on television, in print, or in the parks. Overall, Disney is the ultimate branding company. Of course, their war chest is formidable, but one can learn from their systematic approach.

5. Continue branding with follow-up. Your guests leave with enchantment in their collective hearts, promising they'll be back next week, month, or year. While those intentions are wonderful, why leave it to chance? Continue with the branding process. It doesn't matter if you don't have a huge budget. In fact, you may have no marketing budget at all. How much will it cost to produce postcards and send thank-you notes to your guests? You can list them under office expenses. Still too much? Then how about e-mail? It's free. The point is: there is no excuse for not following up, thanking your guests for their patronage, and letting them know that you have a new item on the menu or a new treatment at your spa. Just don't make your mailing too promotional or pushy (as in "Come back within 72 hours and you'll get an extra 50% off."). *Enchanted (and loyal) guests don't expect a discount; they want to pay full price* because they loved the experience. Rather, make it genuine; continue to use the same tone you set with your branding while they were guests.

6. Remember them and surprise them when they return. Some customers will return; many will not. That's reality. The ones who do return, however, deserve extra special attention. Wow them with a small surprise, a little added value. And then enchant them with the service they have come to expect.

The Art Deco buildings provide a unique and ownable look to Miami Beach.
Source: Corbis Digital Stock. Used with permission.

When you have an ownable look, maximize its usage: a stylized Art Deco lifeguard station on Miami Beach.
Source: Getty Images, Inc.—Taxi. Used with permission.

At the end of the day, the true difference between hospitality brands lies in how they treat their customers. And this is a branding approach that can be applied by any hospitality company, large or small. It does not require large marketing budgets, an advertising agency, or a marketing department. It just requires commitment from the top and continuous training and reinforcement throughout the entire organization. In essence, hospitality branding is the creation of positive feelings for fun and profit. But it takes dedication: while the decision to implement super branding may take only a moment, it takes every single day to maintain it.

BRANDING DESTINATIONS

Regions are brands. Countries are brands. States are brands. Cities are brands. Even some neighborhoods are brands. Actually, some of those are brands. The rest are just what they are. While branding other hospitality and tourism categories is commonplace, branding countries and destinations has been sporadic at best. Yet a strong branding strategy could constitute the difference between success and failure for many destinations. Just like product brands, countries can create strong perceptions in consumers' minds. France, for example, has a perception of pleasure; Italy, style; and Germany, precision. These perceptions, however, have not been the outcome of positioning strategies, but occurred over time as by-products of the respective countries' attributes.

But as for any other product, branding applies to the product destination. How can you brand a destination? Approach it as you would any other product category. Conduct a destination audit; evaluate its strengths and weaknesses. Analyze the existing and potential markets; evaluate opportunities. Develop a destination vision; what do you want the destination to become? Develop a branding strategy; define the destination's uniqueness and positioning and determine which markets you want to attract. Invest in its product (infrastructure, attractions, safety, etc.), extend the branding strategy to include all the constituents of the destination (transportation, local businesses, airports, information centers, employee training, environmental signage, etc.), and develop a differentiated communications program.

One of the best examples of destination branding is the "I Love NY" campaign. This positioning projected a slightly defiant attitude about the city during a period of less than positive perceptions. It provided a platform to explain why one should love New York with "product" facts, such as attractions, tours, theater, and so on. It also provided a platform for brilliant visual execution with the ubiquitous I "heart" NY symbol.

HELPFUL STEPS IN DEVELOPING A BRAND STRATEGY

Branding is like sculpting. Consider Michelangelo's recommendation:

> As when, O' lady mine!
> With chiseled touch
> The stone unhewn and cold
> Becomes a living mould
> The more the marble wastes
> The more the statue grows

The same with branding: the strategy lies within the product and the company. You have to extract it, and the more narrowly you can define it, the more your brand will grow. Following are a few basic steps that have proven to be very helpful in developing a brand strategy.

The physical product   All branding starts with the product, whether you already have one or not. Analyzing the product, itself a key brand element, and defining its features should be the first step in the branding process. In hospitality, whether for new products or existing ones, the capacity for adjusting, adding, or removing features and services will help support the branding strategy.

Defining the price level   Pricing has an intrinsic branding value, perhaps the most discerning one. By providing the other tip on the value proposition scale, it defines the category in which consumers will place your brand. Do not take pricing lightly.

You have basically three possible pricing strategies: (1) budget or economy, (2) mid-market, and (3) luxury. Anything else is a variation on one of these three (e.g., super-cheap, mid-economy, lower mid-market, upper mid-market, entry-level luxury, super high-end, and so on). The pricing level will help you determine in which category you will compete and help you establish the basic operational and promotional parameters.

Analyze your category You have determined your segment. What else is out there? What are those brands? What are their personalities? What are their price levels? What do they offer? How does their usage feel? What reputation do they have? What types of employees do they attract—and retain? What feeling do you get when you call their reservation line? What are their positioning strategies? What are their differentiating ideas? Do they have any? What are their strengths and weaknesses? What types of customers do they attract?

Analyze your brand Now that you have a market segment narrowed down and you know against whom you'll be competing, it's time for some introspection. If Brand X were a person, who would it be? A man, a woman, or both? Fun or serious? Young or old? Conservative or liberal? What job would it hold? What car would it drive? What restaurants would it frequent? How would it dress? What music would it like? What books would it read? Where would it shop? Would it be married? Would it have children? What would its name be— Joe or Donald or Agamemnon, or perhaps Daisy or Victoria or Gertrude? What, where, how . . . ? Ask as many questions as you can think of. Write the answers down. Organize them. You now have a decent brand personality framework.

Sounds silly? Don't kid yourself. As simple as it seems, this is an excellent tool. Of course, branding is more complex than this simple exercise; the idea is to establish a foundation for the personality of your brand. It will help you narrow your brand's strategy and positioning significantly.

This applies just as much to existing brands as it does to new brands. After you have done this exercise, ask yourself a final question: does your physical product support this brand personality? Don't choose a modern personality if your product says rustic unless you're prepared to invest a lot in refurbishing.

Value proposition Developing your brand's value proposition means defining the functional, emotional, and self-expressive benefits customers will derive from the brand. For example, for the Windjammer Barefoot Cruise, the functional benefit is a unique vacation product; the emotional benefits are the mystique of tall ship cruising and romance; and the self-expressive benefit is doing something different—barefoot cruising is not for everyone.

Brand, new "Nomen est omen," as the Latin saying goes, so you'd better choose wisely. If you are lucky enough (or unlucky, depending on your viewpoint) to have to develop a brand from scratch, you will have to choose a name. Hospitality, travel, and tourism brands are often named after their regional or aspirational origin, such as American Airlines, Southwest Airlines, Club Mediterranee, and Mandarin Oriental. Others use the names of their founders, such as Marriott or Disney, both of which do not mean anything per se. There is no formula, and naming a brand is not easy. Good names are fewer every day, and coming up with a good one will be a major effort. Strive to avoid the descriptive and too-obvious-to-be-unique name trap. The initial impulse is often to give the brand a descriptive name, such as ExtendedStay America. The truth is that brand names over time become verbal symbols in the marketplace, far beyond their initial meaning. Holiday Inn, for example, is not limited to leisure travel, even though its name on a literal level would indicate just that. ExtendedStay America would have done better even with a name such as Extay or Xtay, which, while not pretty, would at least be more memorable and ownable and would sound less generic. Chances are that for brevity, the company will start using the abbreviation ESA on its internal communications. And after it enters the company's vernacular, someone will say, "Hey, ESA Hotels is not a bad name; it's short and simple," and another company name will have fallen into the proverbial alphabet soup. Far more important than explaining the product or its regional origin is to choose a name that is unique and ownable. Even though I am not a fan of using initials, an example of unique naming is the W brand of hotels. It goes totally against the grain, thus achieving recognizable differentiation. A good name for a resort product is Sandals; it suggests images of vacation, beach, and warmth by being evocative, not literal. Another good name is Carnival Cruises, which implies fun and celebration; it relies on the intelligence of the consumer to make the connection.

Position the brand   Once you have defined the personality of your brand, you need to position it. What does the brand do? How is it different from the competition and thus for whom it is? How can it own a perception in the customer's mind? Part of the answer will come from the product. Every category has a high ground (e.g., for restaurants, it's food and taste; for business hotels, it's accommodations with convenience and comfort). Find a way to position your brand in connection with the pertinent high ground. Keep in mind that most brands are multidimensional, which makes positioning more difficult.

Chose the brand driver (an idea, attribute, or claim)   You now have a value proposition, a personality for your brand, a name, and a positioning. You have given it character traits. It is time to narrow down your strategy to one focal point that will be used as the foundation for all your future efforts, from product to marketing. Sandals chose love, Carnival has fun, and Royal Caribbean has action. (Remember, you are choosing only one focal positioning point to differentiate your brand and telegraph your positioning; this will not limit or exclude other brand and product benefits.) If you are branding a parity product, the positioning will be more difficult. Look for a distinct personality, an aspirational or unique self-expressive user trait to be the driver.

Make sure your product can support that claim   Aspirations can be tricky; we often want our brands to be something they are not. Choose a claim you can deliver, never promise something you cannot. Go back to the beginning and evaluate the product from this new perspective. It is better to make a simple claim, which you can deliver honestly and vigorously, than one your product cannot support.

Feelings   After you have completed all of the above steps, you must evaluate how this new brand gestalt will make its users feel. All of your other strategies may be well done, but if your brand doesn't strike the right emotional chord, it is highly unlikely that it will achieve greatness.

Develop a killer communications package   Even though your advertising agency should have been part of the process since the beginning, here's where they take center stage. Provide them with all the information you have. Lead them toward a strategy. Allow them to explore and help them achieve greatness for your brand. Refuse the average or good; request the unique and exceptional (more on this in the following two chapters).

Branding globally, thinking locally.
Source: Robert Brenner/Photo Edit. Used with permission.

A good brand strategy is preemptive (no one has claimed it before), unique, differentiating, ownable, narrow but not constricting, and it somehow stems from and defines the product.

2 + 2 = 5

"When you sell a man a book, you don't sell him 12 ounces of paper and ink and glue—you sell him a whole new life," said Christopher Morley. Gestalt psychology theory states that what counts is the overall, the bigger picture, not the components. The same is true for brands. You're not just selling the sum of all the elements that go into a brand, but rather a whole new (rational and emotional) relationship. This relationship is what will allow you to achieve unfair advantages over competing products and allow you to command a premium price. And getting top dollar is not just good for you, it is good for the consumer too. Companies with large profits invest in product development and growth, which provide jobs, and they contribute to good causes. If everyone operated at cost, few innovations would ever be developed, let alone reach the market. Investing in brands is truly the best investment any company can make. If you do your job properly—and there is no reason why you shouldn't—your brand will deliver in many more ways than are initially visible.

CHAPTER FIVE

Advertising

*People dream about visiting foreign countries. The job of
your advertising is to convert their dreams into action.*
—David Ogilvy

David was right. Sadly, there are few outstanding ad campaigns for hospitality, travel, and tourism brands out there. My personal belief is that due to the nature of the product, many advertisers are not able to focus their message. They are trying to be all things to all people, thus missing the boat with any audience. For example, a typical resort or destination needs to appeal to honeymooners, married couples, families with children, singles, young adults, seniors, and incentive meeting planners. Following a natural impulse, the creators of advertising try to jam everything into the campaign. The motivation behind trying to be all things to all people is compelling and understandable: potentially capturing as wide a market as you can and not leaving anyone out. At the end of the day it's the occupancy that counts, and you can't blame any business for wanting to maximize the bottom line.

But that's no excuse. Such a strategy will not build your brand. Maximization will not be achieved by doing feeble, nontargeted advertising, and ad agencies should prevent their clients from doing this. Instead of focusing on billings, they should focus on creating strong brand campaigns with a positioning that will allow your brand to appeal to a variety of audiences. So, if you have to sell to all those market segments, differentiate yourself based on personality or a unique product feature instead of a specific market segment appeal.

Much has been written about the creative processes of advertising, and you should read all of it. This chapter, however, is devoted to the process of managing advertising.

Inventive use of outdoor media in midtown New York City by Delta Airlines.
Source: Corbis/Stock Market. Used with permission.

THE JOB OF ADVERTISING

Let's start with a key point: in advertising, the end doesn't justify the means. Just generating sales is not enough. Your advertising must be more than a mere scream for sales. It has to contribute both to the brand and to the marketplace. Make no mistake about it, while your agency may create the ads, you will approve them. So the ultimate responsibility lies with you to make sure your ads don't reek. To quote Luke Sullivan (a U.S. ad man) quoting Norman Berry (a British ad man) in his excellent book *Hey Whipple, Squeeze This:*

> I'm appalled by those who judge advertising exclusively on the basis of sales. That isn't enough. Of course, advertising must sell. By any definition it is lousy advertising if it doesn't. But if sales are achieved with work which is in bad taste or is intellectual garbage, it shouldn't be applauded no matter how much it sells. Offensive, dull, abrasive, stupid advertising is bad for the entire industry and bad for business as a whole. It is why the public perception of advertising is going down in this country.

You may handle dozens of marketing activities, but you will be judged by your advertising.

ADVERTISING IS NOT A SCIENCE

Bill Bernbach, the legendary advertising man, made this statement over 30 years ago: "Marketing direction would be infinitely easier if advertising was a science, but it would also be infinitely duller." This is still true today.

HARD VERSUS SOFT SELLING

Imagine that you are a salesperson for a cruise line. Your job is to visit potential customers, explain the benefits of your product, and try to sell them cruise packages. Would you whack their doors with a baseball bat and when they opened, scream your offer at them, all the while flicking them on their foreheads, and then repeat the pricing information several times (screaming) while banging your fist on their kitchen tables? Probably not. You would not want to offend them, disgust them, or insult their intelligence. Well, that is the equivalent of hard-sell advertising: loud announcers, stupid messages, huge letters with exclamation points, bursting bubbles in all colors of the rainbow—all in all, primitive screams for attention. When inexperienced marketers approach advertising, they are often under the impression that their message has to be loud, intrusive, repetitive, and literal. Yet that is exactly what turns consumers off. If you approach your advertising just as you would a one-to-one conversation, it will be more effective. Showing and telling, but not yelling, will make advertising, like personal selling, much more convincing (rhyme purely coincidental).

BRANDVERTISING VERSUS BLANDVERTISING

What is the by-product of bland management? Bland advertising. It has to appeal to everyone and it must not displease anyone. Don't get me wrong; advertising should not be offensive or insulting, but people need to have a sense of humor. If I see an ad poking fun at Europeans, I will laugh, not get insulted. The fact that I'm depicting a certain group of individuals in a funny or silly way doesn't mean that I want to insult them; it means that I actually like them enough to depict them as users of my brand—just in a funny way. However, in an effort to create an omnibus appeal, creative work has become bland. "Never mind the right appeal, just don't exclude anyone" seems to be the modus operandi for most advertisers today.

Combined with the explosion of media options, as bland advertising creeps into consumers' homes, more of it is necessary to have even a chance of grabbing their attention. Who benefits from this? Media companies and a few bold brands that refuse to fall into the blandness trap, but certainly not the consumer.

The fact remains that you do have to appeal to different market segments. But even if you have to cover a lot of ground, segmentation doesn't have to be based strictly on demographics, age, or income. It can be based on attitude, personality, appeal, usage patterns, emotions, attributes, and benefits.

One such example is the campaign we developed for Viva Resorts. Their appeal is broad: families, couples, honeymooners, and divers. Thus we decided to position them based on attitude, which is fresh and young at heart, with a sense of humor, summarized under the brand strategy "Pure Viva" (which communicates pure life, enjoy life, and grab life by the horns). We wanted to avoid the stereotypical "plastic" vacation shots, so the ads featured shots with editorial quality. Instead of showing a typical wedding shot, we submerged the bride and groom and shot them underwater. Instead of showing kids playing in the sand, we showed two feet sticking out of the sand in the foreground and three children burying their father in the background and out of focus. Instead of putting a big logo on the cover of the corporate brochure, we spelled "Viva" with cloud formations; the support images were intended as snapshots—both of which combined create story appeal. Captured beautifully on film by Blake Fisher, they didn't show the entire scene, but rather left some of it to the imagination of the viewer. One ad, however, created controversy: it depicted a couple running down a beach, with the female chasing the male and trying to pull down his shorts, exposing part of his behind. The headline read: "supervised kids club = pure viva flirting." The body copy spoke about flirting and how Viva is an excellent choice for parents, since they will be able to leave their children

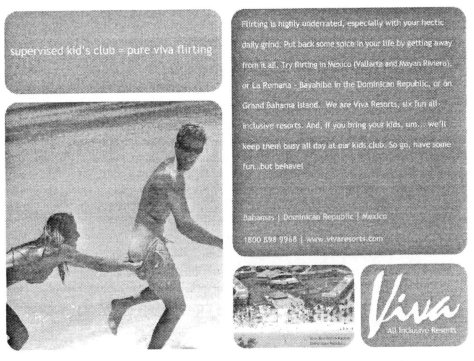

When you don't have a large media budget, a little controversy will help create momentum.
Source: Brandhaus and Viva resorts. Used with permission.

at Viva's supervised kids club, which will allow them some time for flirting and romance. Some travel agents were offended. What do you think?

❖ WORKING WITH AN ADVERTISING AGENCY ❖ (AND WHY IT PAYS TO BE A GOOD CLIENT)

A friend who used to be art director at a large agency once told me, "You would not believe the number of times we have taken existing or old presentations, slapped a new logo on them, and won the account." Unfortunately, this statement illustrates one of the biggest problems of advertising agencies: lack of credibility. It used to be that a company hired an ad agency to help it sell more products because the agency knew more about the market than anyone else. Nowadays, many agencies are so focused on pleasing clients that they will do almost anything to maintain billings. Fortunately, there are still great agencies. It is said that clients get the advertising they deserve. But agencies also get to work with clients they deserve. Both sides should choose carefully.

A NEW BREED OF AGENCY

Agencies create advertising because advertising builds brands. This is the paradigm as it has been for the past 50 years. However, the paradigm has shifted. Brands are not built by advertising alone anymore, and agencies need to adjust their knowledge base to develop insight into brand-building strategies and activities. And while many agencies are trying to position themselves as shops that understand marketing and offer integrated services, the bottom line remains that in the end they focus on advertising. I predict that in the next decade, advertising agencies as we have known them will start to disappear and a new breed of *branding agency* will emerge. This agency will not only know more about branding, it will also understand the client's complex marketing needs and will be able to formulate strategies and provide plans for solutions. Dare I claim that Brandhaus is one such agency?

BIG OR SMALL?

Whether to choose a large agency or a small one will largely depend on your company's size, but it is also a matter of preference and taste. Unless you need the status of a large agency name or are running a multinational campaign that requires offices in 30 countries, a mid-sized or even small agency may be the way to go. Large agencies are large companies, and large companies are by default less nimble and more bureaucratic. If your company is small or mid-sized, it will not get the same attention as a big one at a large agency. Large agencies offer certain in-house capabilities, such as research or promotions; smaller shops outsource those services to specialists. But size is irrelevant when you have the right team on your side. So, whether the agency is big or small, make sure it's the right one for you.

HOW TO FIND THE AGENCY THAT'S RIGHT FOR YOU

Choosing an ad agency is serious business and should not be taken lightly. Don't try to rush the process. You will spend a lot of time, energy, and money with your ad agency, so it is imperative to do your homework. It's somewhat like marriage—if you rush into it, you may regret it later.

The best place to start is by reviewing existing advertising. Flip through magazines, newspapers, and trade publications, surf the Web, study billboards, watch TV, and listen to the radio. Look for ads that you would have loved to have for your brand. Then choose the ads you feel are aligned with your company's needs and find out if they impacted the advertiser's sales. Then find out who created them. Since for hospitality and tourism marketers superb collateral is imperative, don't forget to get brochures and sales literature from companies you respect, and find out who created them. You may not have a budget to advertise, but I have not seen a single hospitality marketer that did not have a dire need for good collateral.

After you have a list of top 10 agency picks, check which ones are handling conflicting clients. If you are a direct competitor of their clients, look elsewhere. If, however, the conflicting client is merely another one in a related industry, sharing an agency should not be a problem. Unless it is a tiny agency, the folks working on your competitor's account will probably not be working on yours. Keep in mind that you don't even know if your bank or accounting firm is servicing your competitors, so why should sharing an ad agency be different?

Once you have a short list, set up meetings with the heads of the agencies, if possible, at their office. This will show you their microcosm, and you'll be able to get a feeling for the shop's energy level. Energy is important; you want an agency that is brimming with it.

Another good reason for meeting at the agency is that you'll be able to meet people who will be working on your account and get a better feeling for the chemistry between you and them. Chemistry is a crucial factor, so choose people with whom you share tastes, preferences, and viewpoints, because you'll be spending a lot of time with them. Another thing to look out for is agencies whose staff has had experience on the client's side. This will help them better understand your needs and communicate those needs internally. A staff with only agency experience may have limited or skewed views.

If the chemistry's right, study their portfolio. Thoroughly review all materials, from the smallest black-and-white newspaper ad to the collateral pieces and the large-production TV commercials. Don't forget, however, that most agencies today can present a portfolio of quality work, whether it is theirs or compiled from the agency's principals' or designers' previous work.

If you like what you have seen, discuss your industry, your brand, and your competitors. Get a feeling for the agency's knowledge, experience, and understanding of your market and other markets, and take a look at their client list.

Also, keep your ears open for recommendations. Ad agencies work almost entirely on referrals and recommendations, and the good ones will be recommended more often. Regardless of recommendations, don't forget to check an agency's references. Talk to former and existing clients, employees, and media representatives.

Don't forget that choosing an agency will depend largely on your budget. Many agencies will tell you that this is not important, but it is. Not that you can't get a New York City agency to accept your $500,000 account, but by simple order of size, your account will rank at the bottom. Instead, look for a petite hot shop with hunger for growth—whose survival will depend largely on your success—and you may end up with some superb work.

Finally, don't choose an agency based on the number of awards it has won; choose on the basis of results. Agencies are proud of their awards, and they should be. But don't forget that those awards are industry acknowledgments given to advertising people by advertising people. They are not awards for sales results.

What truly sets agencies apart are the knowledge, strategic creativity, and relevant experience they bring to the table, so make sure you pick the one best suited for your brand.

WHAT SHOULD YOU EXPECT FROM A GOOD AGENCY?

Starting to work with a new agency is exciting. You are getting a new partner and are expecting great results. Here is what you can and should expect from your new agency:

1. It does its homework. There is nothing more frustrating than working with agencies that do not learn enough about your product, market, consumers, distribution, competitors, and industry. Ask the agency to conduct an extensive audit and analysis before commencing any work.

2. It is branding driven. Strong branding is more important than ever. The only way to break through the market clutter is by having a clearly positioned brand. Your agency must be able to coordinate all marketing activities into brand-contributing communications.

3. It understands market fragmentation. The mass market is no more. Markets are fragmented, media exposure is spotty, and media opportunities are vast. Your agency must be able to target your audience in this cacophonous environment.

4. It is Internet savvy. Whether in-house or through a strategic partner, your agency must be able to deliver Internet solutions in sync with your offline marketing.

5. It is focused on results, not just activities. Too many agencies focus on what they do, not on why they do it and what results should be derived from those actions.

6. It knows how to use research data as market intelligence. True market insight is crucial for competing in today's marketplace.

7. It delivers on time and on budget. You have to move fast. Your market is changing, and the traditional way of doing business is becoming obsolete. Your agency must help you in this process by controlling costs, and a swift operation should be a standard modus operandi.

CAVEAT EMPTOR

A few words of caution before you sign a new agency:

- **Beware of the disappearing principal syndrome.** Most agencies are led by an outstanding individual who is largely responsible for bringing in new business. Nevertheless, once you sign on, the principal disappears in pursuit of new clients and you are left to deal with inexperienced junior staff. For daily routines this is fine, but you need to make sure that the top brass leads the strategic and creative work. Therefore, before you sign on, discuss this issue and get a commitment that the key senior people will be involved in all important projects and decisions.

- **Beware of creative work that's over 5 years old.** An agency's job is to continuously produce quality creative work. An agency that presents only old campaigns and has no good recent creative work to show may have lost all its creative and strategic talent.

- **Beware of hidden costs.** Some agencies lure clients with seemingly low monthly fees, only to add miscellaneous "other" charges when the billing starts. Before finalizing the contract, have the agency explain in detail and in writing all charges that will be included in the fee or commission payments, as well as all extra charges you will have to pay. This will avoid billing disputes and potential delays.

- **Beware of binding contracts.** Some agencies demand exclusivity, and some have a 6-month cancellation policy. Negotiate whatever is best for you. If you know you'll have freelancers working on smaller projects, make sure everyone understands this.

- **Beware of BS.** Some agency people have an incredible capacity for gab. Their eloquence, however meaningless, may fool you long enough to sign on.

BE A GOOD CLIENT

Some agency people think all clients are pigs, and some clients feel that all agencies are phonies. In reality, clients get the agency they deserve (and vice versa). Being a good client will substantially raise the level of commitment and enthusiasm from the people working on your account. Being a good client does not, however, mean being an easy client. You should never approve lousy work just to be nice. You can and should be as demanding as necessary. Setting high quality standards is good. And there is nothing wrong with demanding excellence, but you don't have to be uncivilized.

When you start working with a new agency, you should devote plenty of time to the brief agency about the product and the brand. Don't just hand them a corporate presentation and think that this is enough. Provide them with all materials and information you can. Give them copies of research, competitive studies, samples of work, and anything else that will help them better understand your product and brand. Some agencies are extremely diligent in conducting an audit and analysis before they commence work, while others are notorious for doing it the "quick and dirty" way. Make sure you pick the former.

WELCOME HONESTY

It is very important for honesty to be the foundation of your relationship from day one. Sometimes we all get blinded by the proximity of our daily work and fail to realize flaws in our system, product, or decision making (forest vs. trees). Or it may be difficult for us to hear negative comments about our product or brand. Nevertheless, demand brutal honesty and welcome constructive criticism from outside partners. You want to be the first one to hear about problems so that you have a head start on correcting them.

By the same token, be honest with your agency. Tell them when you don't like something and why. But be sensitive; criticizing somebody else's work is always hard. Remember that the advertised product may be yours, but the creative work is their baby. When you criticize, focus on the work or the idea, never on the person. True professionals will appreciate this and make an effort to improve.

There will come a day when you will feel compelled to say, "Well, I'm the client and I tell you to do it." You should carefully weigh the reason before saying those words. This is a sure way to turn agency people off. They already know this, and being dogmatic will intimidate them. If you feel that otherwise you will not get the job done, you should not be doing business with them in the first place. Shakespeare said it better:

> O, it is excellent
> To have a giant's strength
> But it is tyrannous
> To use it like a giant

HOW TO GET GREAT CREATIVE WORK FROM YOUR AGENCY

All of the above advice will assist you in getting good work from your agency. But what will truly make you stand apart as a client is allowing the agency plenty of space for discovery. Agencies thrive on freedom of thought,

How to get your ads read: combine the right appeal with the right media choice.
Source: Getty Images Inc. —Hulton Archive Photos. Used with permission.

and they will appreciate your willingness to explore unorthodox ideas. As a matter of fact, why not hold the brainstorming session together with the agency staff over a weekend on board your company's cruise ship or other enjoyable site? Let everyone bring their craziest ideas and have fun with them. Welcome outrageousness, inspire unconventional thinking. And remember that welcoming doesn't mean implementing. Demented suggestions that have nothing to do with your brand strategy will serve the great purpose of unleashing the creative juices. Keep in mind, though, that while exploration is good, you must also be prepared to take creative risks. Exploring cutting-edge creativity only to settle for the bland will just frustrate everyone.

CAMPAIGN APPROVALS

At some point in your marketing career, you will have the glorious and frustrating task of approving advertising. Glorious because you have achieved a high level of marketing expertise and market knowledge so that your company will entrust you with this important duty. Frustrating because you'll have to defend your ads and decisions against other people's likes and opinions. It seems that everyone has an opinion on decoration and advertising. There will be plenty of people who will tell you they didn't like it, why they didn't like it, and what you should have done to make the ad at least a little better. Advertising should be judged based on its strategy, not on personal preferences. More likely than not, your ad critic is not the target market.

Another (perhaps the largest) problem of campaign approvals is that too often too many people are involved in the approval process. Someone once said that a camel is a horse designed by a committee. The same thing could be said about advertising. Blend several opinions with a variety of objectives and a touch of personal tastes, and the campaign will undoubtedly stink. A committee of one gets things done (you may want to bargain for campaign approval responsibility during your job negotiation).

BEING A GOOD CLIENT IS NOT EASY

When I was director of marketing for Allegro Resorts, I once suggested to our agency that they should consider a typographic change,[1] only to be told that they didn't tell me how to fold towels, so I shouldn't meddle in their business. Later, after they presented a single idea as a creative solution, I said that I'd like to review a few more ideas—a creative exploration—only to be told that they knew what was best for us and that they did not intend to waste their time showing me pretty pictures. This didn't make me love them, and we parted soon afterward. Being a good client may not be easy, but as in any relationship, it's a two-way street.

AGENCY COMPENSATION

Agency compensation used to be quite simple. Agencies placed media ads and collected a 15% commission. Today, there are several ways you can compensate your agency. You can maintain the media commission approach, pay them a fixed fee for a fixed amount of work, or a combination of the two. Or, if your budget is large enough and you can track results accurately, you may compensate the agency based on the achievement of stated goals. Regardless of which form you choose, make sure to include all the necessary work that needs to be done. It is not very productive to have a fee that covers only print and radio ads if you know that a few months later you'll have to produce television commercials.

Don't forget that you will also have to pay for production charges. These charges are in addition to the fee or commission your agency is being paid, and they can add substantially to the cost of advertising. Production charges may include small items such as scanning, development of mechanical artwork,

---

[1] I suggested that changing a long all-caps headline to sentence case would increase readability.

color separations, and print supervision. Larger production charges include photography, video, music, commercial production, and billboard production. Even though, nowadays, a lot of the production work is handled digitally, it pays to know what may be involved, especially if you're dealing with technologically less advanced markets where traditional production methods are still being used. Evaluate your budget allocation to make sure that you're not spending half of it on production.

AGENCY COMPENSATION: HOW MUCH SHOULD YOU PAY?

Even though I'm running the risk of subliminal messaging, as I am myself the proud owner of an agency, I will make this claim: do not nickel and dime your agency. Agency services are not a commodity. The knowledge level, as well as the strategic and creative quality of agency employees, are directly related to the salaries agencies pay and therefore the fees they charge. Pay peanuts, the saying goes, and you get monkeys. I wouldn't want my branding and advertising to be developed by a group of monkeys. And neither should you.

PAY YOUR BILLS ON TIME

An old Croatian proverb says, "A settled bill means lasting love." In any business, there's nothing more frustrating than unpaid bills; equally so at agencies. Continuously inconsistent cash flow will disrupt the flow of information and smooth project execution, which will ultimately affect the timing and quality of your work. Just like you, agencies are in business to make money. Having work halted for weeks by your agency due to unpaid bills will cause you to miss media deadlines and affect sales. If nothing else, pay bills on time for selfish reasons: if you are a profitable account, your agency will assign the best people to work for you.

◈ ADVERTISING TOOLS ◈

THE BIG IDEA

What is a big idea? Marlboro country. The Absolut Vodka campaign. I Love NY. Avis' We Try Harder. American Express' Member Since. Nike's Just Do It. The Rolex performance campaign. Rolling Stone's Perception vs. Reality. The Got Milk? campaign. Although I'm trying to list more examples, I'm having a difficult time finding them. I am sure I've missed some good ones, but that's why these ideas are big; they are very, very rare.

The problem with big ideas is not so much coming up with one, it's recognizing one. While your ad agency will create them, it is up to you to recognize them. And that is not an easy task. How do you spot a big idea? Study good advertising to train your brain for clues. Open your mind and explore

Using humor to target prospects with a promotional offer. The headline reads: "Boy Toy is what your new hubby will become after you tell him the wedding was free."

Source: Brandhaus and Karisma Hotels & Resorts. Used with permission.

ideas from every different angle. Let your advertising agency go crazy. Ogilvy lists these five questions for help:

1. Did it make you gasp when you first saw it?
2. Do you wish you had thought of it yourself?
3. Is it unique?
4. Does it fit the strategy to perfection?
5. Could it be used for 30 years?

If you are lucky enough to find a big campaign idea, hold on to it and protect it. Don't let some eager marketing manager change it because he wants to make his mark. Don't let the CEO change it because she's bored with it.

It used to be a search for a big campaign idea. Today it is a search for a big branding idea that will also extend itself into advertising. Nike's Just Do It campaign is a big branding idea brilliantly extended into a campaign.

APPEALS

Again, you are not creating those ads; your ad agency is. But you'll have to approve them. So, here's a brief list of various appeals that they may use in your ads. There are dozens of choices.

- Humor (poke fun at yourself, your product category, your competitors, even your clients; e.g., a hilarious campaign for the European Club 18-30)
- Honesty (admit a flaw in your product and turn it into a strength; e.g., Avis is number two, that's why they have to try harder)
- Emotion (romance, family, friends, children, parents, patriotism, home; e.g., the American Airlines' Welcome Home commercials)
- Audience self-interest (stress relief, rest, fun, socializing, partying, learning, exploring; e.g. Royal Caribbean's active campaign)
- Sex (romance, partner fun, intimacy, sexiness)
- Status (price, brand name recognition, trendiness, celebrity usage, exclusivity)
- Self-expression (independence, ruggedness, adventure)
- Rational appeals (price, value, product benefits)
- Extol the benefit (don't promote the hotel room, promote a good night's sleep)
- Contrast (find a worthy competitor, X, and advertise as the anti-X; e.g. Club Med's "The Antidote to Civilization")
- Outrageousness (shock, provoke, push the envelope)

All of these appeals have their appropriate uses. Whatever appeal you are considering, choose it for the right reasons. If it's not relevant, it's just stupid. Don't

"I think the dosage needs adjusting. I'm not nearly as happy as the people in the ads."

Remember, underpromise and overdeliver, not the other way around.

use humor because you're a stand-up comedian at heart. Don't use sex appeals because you like big breasts. If the appeal is not relevant to the brand, product usage, or usage situation, it will be merely cheap and obtuse. The best campaigns appeal to both sides of the consumer's brain with a combination of emotional, rational, and self-expressive appeals.

Whichever appeal you use, don't insult the intelligence of the consumer by overstating or oversimplifying. They do get it. You don't have to tell the whole story. Ads with story appeal actually omit parts of the story purposely to induce a mental completion from the reader; that way, they invite the reader to participate. Determining how much to include or omit is the job of your ad agency. The better they are, the better they'll be able to gauge this. The best ads are mini stories initiated on paper or film but concluded in the mind of the consumer.

PRINT ADVERTISING: FACT VERSUS FICTION

Don't clutter up your print ads with unnecessary elements. One logo is enough, and you really don't have to list all of your 50 hotels in every ad. The best print ads are simple; they grab you with a stunning visual and a solid headline, and if you're intrigued enough by these two elements, you will be pulled into interesting and factual body copy. The headline and the visual should complement—not explain—each other. There is nothing more frustrating than seeing an ad with a wonderful visual and a headline that restates what the visual is showing. And the body copy? Don't worry too much if it's short or long. Worry about it providing the right information in the right way. As with all good writing, you have to refine it until you have presented the essence of the message in the absolutely best way.

Unfortunately, there seems to be a template for print ads these days: a large main visual, a short headline, and a modicum of meaningless body copy. What these ads are doing is following a fashionable look. What advertisers in many categories do not realize, however, is that while for a fashion brand a visual and a logo may be plenty, certain categories and certain brands require more information. The amount of necessary information also depends on the media weight and the life stage of a brand. Brand awareness is good, but brand knowledge is better.

I have found the following misconceptions about print advertising among agencies and advertisers alike:

1. For some strange reason (I think it may be laziness), everyone tries to avoid long copy as if it were the pest. Yet, well-written factual copy can actually increase sales. A consumer who is not interested in your type of product will probably not read your long-copy ad. A housewife and mother of three is not going to read an ad for a business hotel but may read an ad for a family resort or theme park. Write your ad for your target audience. The housewife will not ignore it because the long copy turned her off; she won't read it because she is not interested. On the other hand, with the availability of the Internet, your ads can have short copy and provide more information on the website. There is no rule that long copy is bad and short copy is good or vice versa. Use long or short copy as you please, but do it for the right reasons. Use it because it fits your strategy and fulfills your communication needs, not because it seems fashionable.

2. Advertising is omnipotent. Advertisers often wonder why their sales have not doubled after placing two ad insertions. Advertising and branding take time, frequency, and patience.

3. Including a price will somehow cheapen an ad. Including price information doesn't mean placing a big bursting bubble with 40-point letters and three exclamation points. The price is just as much a brand attribute as the location. Moreover, if you have to create advertising for a luxury brand, include the price as a differentiating tool.

4. Ads have to look like ads. Try different formats. Make them look like editorials. There is no rule that the logo must be in the lower-right-hand corner. Eliminate the visual clutter by being different. There is no rule that your ad must even contain a logo. Some "Avis is only No. 2 in rent

a cars" ads never featured a logo. Why should they? The headlines start with the brand name.

5. Too many headlines don't say anything specific. Generalities such as "It's About Time," "Experience the Magic," "A World Apart," and "A Different Destination" mean nothing, and they don't do anything to make your brand grab the reader and pull her into the copy. The problem is, the majority of readers (some research suggests as many as 90%) will never go past the headline, so if your headline doesn't work hard, most of your media dollars are wasted.

TYPOGRAPHY AND OTHER DESIGN ELEMENTS

Most marketing directors either don't pay enough attention to details or nit-pick every detail to death. Try to avoid being either of them. A critical eye for a balanced look is very important. Mixing three different typefaces because you can't decide between Trebuchet, Lucida Console, and Haettenschweiler is not.

One of the key issues in dealing with type is that it needs to facilitate reading. If it's too small, too large, too squiggly-wiggly, upside down, or too ghosted, it will be difficult to read and thus useless. Type effects can and should be used as design elements, but for accentuation and sparsely. Too many gimmicks look amateurish. Simplicity is elegant. If you have a large enough budget, it pays to invest in the development of proprietary typographic elements.

Other design elements may include a unique color, layout, shape, or picture. If you're lucky enough to own one of those rare birds, use it for maximum recognition. I am surprised that no hospitality company has commissioned a famous designer to create a uniquely patterned set of bed linens. The design would have to reflect the personality of the brand and be completely ownable (such as the famous Burberry pattern). Then it could be used in all communications efforts, making it a branding tool.

Typefaces and other design elements are subject to fashion. If you don't believe it, flip through the advertising and design annuals of past years and you'll notice similarities. The idea is to avoid being trendy. How? By staying simple. By letting your agency or graphic designer do their job well. If they are good, you should trust them. If they are not, you should fire them. And, more than anything, focus on achieving a balance of substance and style. What you say is still more important than how you say it.

COPY

My favorite headline was a billboard by Virgin Atlantic after they started giving massages on their flights: "BA don't give a shiatsu"—a brilliant example of "what you say" and "how you say it" in perfect harmony. Copywriting used to be the engine of advertising. Today it's art direction. I still feel that the art:copy value ratio is 50:50. "Just Do It" is first a word concept, then a visual concept. People think in words, not pictures. Even the most spectacular visual means nothing without at least the brand name (even if you only use the brand symbol without the name, as Nike does with the swoosh symbol, the reader will think the *word* Nike, not the *picture* Nike). Great campaigns use visuals to grab attention and differentiate but use words to fortify the message. The best ones incorporate words as part of the visual solution. How can you recognize great copy? When words conjure up palatable images. Here's an example: "Coffee should be black as hell, strong as death, and sweet as love" (an old Turkish saying).

How many times have you heard the adage "A picture is worth a thousand words"? But guess what? Confucius actually said, "A picture is worth a thousand pieces of gold."[2] Not words, gold. Talk about a long-lasting misinterpretation! A picture is indeed worth a thousand pieces of gold, but combined with words (at least in advertising) it is worth triple.

PHOTOGRAPHY

As we are on the subject of pictures, once the brand strategy and positioning are developed and a campaign concept has been approved, it is time to hire the best possible photographer to capture the essence of the brand.

Many companies complain about the cost of photography. So, let's make a quick calculation here. A 200-room hotel with year-round occupancy of 73% at an average rate of $120 per room makes around $6.4 million in revenues (excluding any nonroom revenue). A few day shoot with an excellent photographer, some models, and props will set you back somewhere between $35,000 and $50,000. This represents around 0.4–0.8% of your annual revenues. Add to that the fact that you are allowed to amortize the cost of photography over several years (because good photography will be usable for several years), and the percentage becomes laughably small.

Another absurdity is that hospitality companies do not dedicate sufficient resources during the photo shoot on the premises. Assign a dedicated team of operations people with a senior person in charge for these few short days. They will be crucial in making sure that everything runs smoothly. And, no, it is not enough to have a maintenance assistant come by twice a day. Be lax and you may waste a significant amount of money. Photography consists of long periods of preparation and waiting for the right moment, and if all available support resources are fully deployed, the photographer may concentrate on taking the perfect picture instead of organizing some trivial detail. Remember, it is your photography, and the photographer and crew are on the premises once and for a very short time. Doesn't it make sense to give them maximum support? You will end up with better results.

The photography you use in your advertising must imply the experience of your brand. It does not, however, have to tell the whole story. Too many hospitality advertising campaigns show the same imagery over and over again: a hotel

---

[2]Jack Trout, the positioning expert, had the saying translated from Chinese.

Don't just show the product, show it off: a luxury cruise in the Grenadines.
Source: Woodfin Camp & Associates. Used with permission.

building, a hotel room, a smiling concierge, and so on. Avoid these visual clichés by investing in the development of branded visuals. Does it matter if you have a commodity product? Your visuals can focus on anything, from architectural details to an attitude. Good photography is not cheap. But it is an investment that's worth its weight in gold. For more information on photography, see Chapter 6.

MAGAZINE ADVERTISING

Magazine advertising is *the* brand advertising medium for most hospitality and travel brands. It provides great quality reproduction in full color and is an exceptional medium to make the reader's mouth water. It's too bad, then, that most hospitality and travel magazine ads look alike. Yes, we've all seen pictures of the busy executive and the smiling chef. But there is more to travel advertising than these. And it is so easy to find good examples of travel photography. Just take a look at the editorial sections of travel magazines. Look at what they are depicting—dramatic shots of nature, fun, activity, architecture, people, experiences, and food. If you flip through travel magazines, you will find that many of the ads show a hotel room—not a wonderfully decorated room that would be worth showing, just a run-of-the-mill room. Do these advertisers think that this will entice anyone to stay with them? Look, we're a hotel and we have . . . a room. Hurray! Remember your positioning? What about the brand strategy and your differentiation? The photography that will be used in print ads must be based on these factors.

Suppose that you're a small advertiser with a budget barely enough to place quarter-page ads in two publications; it's understandable, that you want to show your product since nobody knows it. Go ahead, but don't just show your product; show it off. Dramatize it, make it spectacular, show a defining detail. You have to show something, so why not show something better? The smaller your company is, the harder your advertising needs to work, not vice versa. Or try a different strategy. Instead of using four quarter-page ads, buy one full-page ad and then maximize its media value by mailing out reprints of that ad.

Let's say, for example, that you operate a small cruise ship and position it as a romantic getaway for couples. Your ad could say "This is a romantic cruise for couples" and show the picture of a ship or it could say "Our chef personally hand-dips the strawberries in a proprietary blend of Swiss and Belgian chocolate" and show the picture of an empty tray with an out-of-focus couple relaxing in the background. Which one do you think will have a stronger appeal to a woman looking for a romantic getaway with her beau? The advertising doesn't have to be literal. Trigger readers' imagination and let them paint their own mental picture. This is just one approach; there are many more. Explore them and find what works best for your brand and market.

Media advertising to the travel trade consists of magazine advertising in the trade books. What works well? Relevance. There is an ongoing debate about how advertising to travel agents or meeting planners should look. The truth is, there is no rule. It all depends on the brand, product, and message. I believe that providing plenty of factual information in trade advertising is good. Think about it: you are educating travel agents with familiarization trips, educational seminars, and educational presentations; shouldn't your advertising educate them as well? This seems like a great opportunity to me. True, not every agent will read your factual copy, but the ones that do should get something out of it—some fact, news, or information that will be useful when they need to make a booking for their next client. The "Pure Viva" campaign was a very factual campaign presented in a different way. Instead of saying "Viva offers honeymoons," it said "Fun in the sun + fun in the room = pure Viva honeymoon"; instead of promoting "Viva Dive Packages," it said "6 to 60 feet under = pure Viva diving"; instead of saying "Viva offers a Kids Club," it said "Love 'em & leave 'em . . . at the Viva Kids Club." Viva is a friendly, fun, and active brand, so we reflected their attitude in the copy, which was humorous and lighthearted but loaded with facts.

Magazine advertising gives you the opportunity to try different approaches with special features such as poly-bagging, spectaculars, sampling, scratch and sniff, microchips with sound, pop-up ads, and brochure inserts. Explore some of these to further differentiate your brand or offer. If your cruise is famous (or you want it to become famous) for chocolate desserts, you may want to include a sample.

NEWSPAPER ADVERTISING

Sunday travel section advertising is one of the primary retail media for travel products. Readers have a travel-shopping mindset and are looking for offers. The job of your advertising is to entice them to look at your offer. Cynics will say that the key decision factor in newspaper advertising is price. I disagree. Price can be a marketing tool and a differentiating factor. If you have a well-known brand, a low price will only chip away at your brand quality perception and perhaps induce some price buyers. If you have an unknown brand, a price at or above that of well-known brands will indicate quality.

Creative for newspapers must be branded. Even though a newspaper is a short-lived and predominantly black-and-white medium, your ads do not have to look cheap or be unbranded.

If you're promoting a hospitality offer unique to a specific target market, consider placing your ad in other sections. Club Med sometimes places small ads in the employment section of newspapers, prompting people to take a break. An "island" in the stock market listings will always be prominent. Just make sure that the advertised product and message are relevant.

Things to avoid in newspaper advertising: First, large amounts of black ink. People consider newspapers a "dirty" medium already, so why turn them off further by making their fingers even dirtier? Also, avoid loud colors, huge pricing displays, and other blatant visual effects. They cheapen your brand.

TELEVISION

Television is the big brother of all media categories. Once you're doing TV commercials for your brand, you've made it. You're in the big league. Well, not entirely. There is spot television as well as cable, both of which do not require huge media budgets. I'm sure you've seen your share of local television commercials—the neighborhood furniture superstore or car dealer. Yes, they're awful. You can see their low-budget creative efforts and their cheesy production from beginning to end. I am thankful that hotels generally try to attract visitors from out of town; otherwise, we'd probably be watching ads screaming something like "What's it gonna take to put you and the Mrs. in this fine bed t'nite?!!" or "Our general manager has gone mad! He's slashing prices because we have too many rooms!!!" The point here is that unless you can do good television advertising, it is better not to do it. And good television advertising is not cheap. It doesn't necessarily have to be expensive, but it is definitely not cheap.

Which brings us to the crucial point about television advertising: production. Just as in movies, a good director with a good production crew will be able to add finesse and levels of emotion to your commercial that you never even know existed. So the message is: do not skimp on production, or, as the headline for Pepperidge Farm cookies states, "If you're going to have a cookie, have a cookie." Obviously, before you can move into production, you will have to approve story boards. This is a difficult task in itself because you'll have to visualize scenery, actors, expressions, sounds, special effects, and so on. When evaluating story boards, the two most important things to observe are the brand strategy and whether the story grabs you during the first few seconds. We are all easily sidetracked with funny and entertaining ideas, but if the story board is not on strategy or has a long overture, scrap it. Another important issue is the brand's personality; the story board must reflect it. Also, it pays to focus on one central message and avoid complicated story boards. You have 30 seconds; keeping it simple will pay off. Television is a great medium because it allows you to dramatize your product, so allow your agency to take full advantage of it.

Do you have a few favorite commercials? I do: Nike's soccer world cup commercial and the commercial showing athletes preparing before a race or game, with background sounds of musicians tuning their instruments before a concert; the Pepsi commercial featuring Ray Charles; some older Coke commercials; several European Levi's commercials from the 1980s and 1990s; several Target Stores commercials and, recently, a series of fabulous commercials of a dancing guy for Joe Boxer underwear at K-Mart. What do all these commercials have in common? They are 100% on target. They follow their brand strategies to the max. Their selling proposition is implied, not screamed. They make the viewer feel good. Their appeal is universal. Their execution is clean and lasts throughout the entire commercial (i.e., it doesn't wear off at the end). They are simple. And they are fun to watch over and over again. Have your commercials achieve 70% of these qualities, and you'll be in good shape.

RADIO ADVERTISING

Radio is a visual medium. The visual imagery is created by words and sounds in the listener's head. Take advantage of this because it provides limitless opportunities. Radio is also fairly inexpensive, and costs can often be negotiated for barter, which makes it even more attractive.

What to look for in radio commercials: The spot must capture listeners and set the tone during the first few seconds; there is no time for a long buildup. It must follow the overall branding strategy with an idea that works for radio. Just as in print, don't overexplain; let the listener reach his or her own conclusions. A good radio commercial will lead the listener from mental picture to mental picture by using a mix of words, sound effects, and transitions. Sound effects are wonderful as long as they are used sparingly and are relevant to the message and brand. Intelligent use of sound effects can evoke wonderful imagery. Unless you have a memorable phone number or Web address, providing a number to call is of questionable value, as many of your listeners will hear your commercials while driving.

Things to avoid: Don't change the tonality of your brand message just because it is for radio. The announcers in radio commercials do not have to sound elated. For some reason, many radio commercials sound as if the people in them are highly caffeinated screamers. This doesn't create the sense of urgency or excitement that it intends to evoke; it's just annoying. A radio commercial does not have to be funny either; the typical funny introduction, followed by a serious sales pitch, followed by a funny closing has been so overused that it's not funny. This approach works only if done extremely well, which is extremely rare. If you choose humor, the commercial must be funny from beginning to end; avoid using it to spice up an otherwise boring commercial. There's nothing more transparent and amateurish than opening with a blast of fun and closing with a pathetic sales pitch. Avoid boring listeners with a message that is long-winded and uninteresting; appeal to their self-interest. Unless you're poking fun at yourself, avoid boasting. Finally, avoid wasting half the spot on disclaimers.

You think that radio is not a good primary medium for hospitality or tourism? Consider Motel 6, whose declining business in the mid-1980s was revived by adjusting their outdated product and running a national radio advertising campaign. Their revenues almost doubled between 1986 and 1989, and their average occupancy rate rose from 66% to 72%.

A final advantage of radio is that the production is fairly inexpensive, so you don't just have to read the copy to approve it. You can actually produce a draft and listen to it.

OUT-OF-HOME ADVERTISING

Billboards are a fabulous medium for tourism products, especially if you are advertising a warm destination in a cold market. A 60-foot billboard showing mouthwatering Caribbean scenery has strong appeal for drivers working their way through gray, snowed-in Connecticut. My favorite billboards include the previously mentioned Virgin Atlantic board and a billboard for Chick-Fil-A, with two three-dimensional cows on a ladder writing "Eat More Chickin" on the board. Billboards can be used to dramatize the product, and due to their size they allow for spectacular visuals. Billboard advertising has one rule: don't use more than six words. The average driver will pass at a speed of about 50 miles per hour, so you don't have much time.

This rule doesn't apply to all out-of-home advertising vehicles, however. On the contrary, for ads in subways or trains, long copy is beneficial. The readers have plenty of time, and unless they have brought a book, magazine, or newspaper, they will read every single line of your copy. Take advantage of this unique circumstance.

Another subcategory of out-of-home advertising is point-of-purchase displays, posters, mobiles, and window displays. These work very well in travel agencies, as they serve both the travel agents and consumers. Travel agency floor space is limited, so it pays to design flexible displays that may be either freestanding or hanging. Posters can work extremely well, but they must depict spectacular visuals and not be too promotional (a logo and a destination are fine, but not much more than that). If you want to ensure that your posters will be displayed by travel agencies, send them already framed.

Outdoor advertising is not limited to billboards, public transportation, and point-of-purchase locations. There are literally dozens of outdoor vehicles, from imprints on the sand of beaches to sandwich boards. Make the creative choice of outdoor advertising part of your creative strategy.

INTERNET ADVERTISING

For more details on Internet advertising, see Chapter 11.

DIRECT RESPONSE

The biggest benefit of direct advertising is its measurability. The biggest disadvantage is its image as junk mail. Direct response mail used to be divided into direct advertising and direct mail, direct mail being advertising pieces created and mailed to the prospect on a one-to-one basis and direct advertising being ads designed to provoke an action such as an order. Today, especially in hospitality and travel, most advertising is a form of direct response, as most ads and commercials close with a call to action, such as a request for a brochure, a visit to the website, or a call to the reservation center. Yet most such ads have not been created as direct response advertisements. Here are a few tried-and-true rules for successful direct response advertising:

- Market a specific offer.
- Make the offer attractive to the target audience.
- The quality of the mailing list can make or break a mailing.
- Advertise the benefit, not the product feature—for example, a good night's sleep, not just a room (this rule applies to all advertising).
- Test a variety of different offers.
- Test all variables of the message (headline, price, type of mailing, media, lists).
- Don't shy away from long copy; in direct marketing, the more you tell, the more you sell (in mailings and advertisements).
- Ask for an action, and provide a sense of urgency with limited availability.
- Offer an added value as a reward for taking the action.
- Make it easy to respond.
- Base your media allocation and mailings on orders, not audience size.
- Measure every response and keep a detailed record.

In television, significant response levels will not be achieved with 30-second direct response commercials during prime time. Try different formats, such as 2- to 3-minute commercials or infomercials. Run them during off-peak hours and provide sufficient ordering information. Remember, you have to advertise a specific offer. Demonstrations work very well in direct response television, so an area that seems very appropriate for this approach is vacation property ownership.

Direct mail may also be used to build brand awareness, but that will be more difficult to measure. Unless it is directed to a targeted audience, other media will probably be more appropriate due to their lower cost.

THINGS TO AVOID IN ALL ADVERTISING

Avoid advertising multiple products. Nobody ever buys a product line (unless it's a corporate ad and you're trying to sell the company).

Avoid placing more than one logo in your ads (mergers, acquisitions, and their aftermath . . . you know what I'm talking about).

Avoid visual stereotypes (the chef coming out of the ocean in full attire carrying two live lobsters).

Avoid being perceived as stupid by trying to be funny (someone once said: "Dying is easy, comedy is hard." If you embark on this risky venture, make sure that your advertising is truly funny, not just trying to be funny).

Avoid using_____without brand connection or relevance (fill in the blank: "entertainment," "sex," "celebrities," whatever idea you're toying with).

◈ MEDIA ◈

MEDIA TERMINOLOGY AND BASIC CONCEPTS

There are several media terms and measurement concepts you'll have to know and understand to properly manage the media planning process.

First of all, the terms MEDIA and VEHICLE are not the same. While "media" refers to all media or a media category such as magazines, "vehicles" are individual carriers within a category, such as *Newsweek*.

Another term you will encounter is COST PER THOUSAND (CPM). This is a basic calculation that divides the total cost of media space or time by the number of readers or viewers. When discussing CPM, it is important to know the cost per thousand of the target (readers, households, women, etc.).

RATING POINTS represent the percentage of homes or viewers tuned in to a program within a coverage base (e.g., a program has a rating of 30 if 3 out of 10 homes are tuned in to it).

GROSS RATING POINTS (GRPs) the sum of all ratings for a commercial or media schedule. GRPs are calculated by multiplying reach by frequency, both of which are measured together over a specific period of time.

Similar to CPM is COST PER RATING POINT (CPRP), a simple calculation that measures the cost of broadcast spots by dividing the cost of a commercial by the rating value of that commercial.

REACH (or CUMULATIVE, NET, UNDUPLICATED AUDIENCE, or CUME) is the number of people or households exposed to a particular vehicle at least once. Keep in mind that reach measures exposure to the media vehicle, not to the advertisement or commercial. For example, if you're launching a new theme park and estimate that you'll need to reach 40% of households, you will not be able to do it if the reach is below 40.

FREQUENCY is the number of times an audience is potentially exposed to a media vehicle (heavy viewers will have a higher frequency than light viewers).

IMPRESSIONS indicate the total weight of the media plan (all the people who are exposed to the messages in all the vehicles).

DAYPART defines specific parts of the day for broadcast purposes. These include prime time, morning and afternoon daytime, and early and late fringe (pre and post prime time) for television and morning, daytime, afternoon, and evening for radio.

A B C D COUNTIES are classified by A.C. Nielsen as follows: A counties are the 25 largest metropolitan areas; B counties are all counties not included in A with a population of over 150,000; C counties are all counties not included in A or B with a population of over 40,000; and D counties are rural counties.

COLUMN INCH is a measurement for newspaper space (1 inch wide and 1 inch deep).

FLIGHTING is a technique of media scheduling that switches between periods of advertising and no advertising. It is used to maximize a limited media budget and retain a somewhat ongoing presence.

PULSING is an advertising scheduling method in which continuous advertising is supplemented with occasional increases or bursts (for special promotions, seasonal promotions, etc.). Pulsing ensures the best possible presence but requires large media budgets.

SPLIT RUN TESTING is a print media response measuring technique. It works by running two or more versions of the same ad that vary in only one element (the headline, price, special offer) in the same issue of a publication and measuring the response variance between the differing elements. Split runs can be done geographically or by running an ad in alternate issues of a publication.

OPEN RATE is the highest advertising rate in print media; it is equivalent to the rack rate.

RUN OF PRESS and RUN OF SCHEDULE are advertising space and time without a predetermined location in print or time in broadcast. This is the equivalent of run-of-house rooms.

STANDARD RATE AND DATA SERVICE (SRDS) is a service that publishes media rates and market research data.

CIRCULATION is a media vehicle measurement and has different meanings for different media categories. In print it is the number of copies distributed in an issue. In outdoor advertising it is the number of people who may see a billboard during a specific period of time, usually 24 hours. In broadcast advertising, it is the number of homes that tune in within a specified period of time, such as once a day.

PASS-ALONG RATE is the readership rate of a publication other than the subscriber or buyer. For example, a magazine may be bought by a mother but also read by her two daughters, thus increasing the overall readership.

AUDIT BUREAU OF CIRCULATION (ABC) is a nonprofit organization that verifies and reports the circulation figures of publishers.

AFFIDAVITS are notarized statements verifying the actual running of ordered broadcast advertising.

SHARE OF AUDIENCE is the audience of a program expressed as a percentage of total households using the medium at broadcast time.

SHARE OF VOICE is a measurement that shows a particular brand's share of advertising within a product category.

SPOT RADIO AND SPOT TV means usage of individual stations in select markets, regardless of their network affiliation.

MEDIA CATEGORIES

Planning and choosing media is difficult because so many media opportunities are available. While the number of main media categories is small, the number of subcategories and individual vehicles is staggering.

Consider the following example: The out-of-home media category includes billboards, posters, transit displays, point-of-purchase displays, airplane advertising, subway, bus, taxi, trains, boats, trucks, mile markers, bus shelters, phone booths, public restrooms, parking garage, tollbooths, train stations, mall displays, cinema screens, stadium advertising, theater, health clubs, hotels, gas stations, hospitals, airports, clubs, shelf talkers, table tents, mobiles, grocery carts, beaches, benches, sandwich boards, place mats—and more! Enough to give you a migraine. Now examine the other categories. They provide a maze of opportunities. So, in the hope of providing a modicum of help, Table 5.1 is a chart displaying the main advantages and disadvantages of the key media categories.

I guess the best plan to follow is this: as with your positioning strategy and creative efforts, avoid trying to be all things to all people. Also, look beyond the figures; one vehicle may deliver the largest audience, but another may carry prestige or more credibility. A good media planner and some common sense will help you develop a balanced plan (another compelling reason to track those ad responses), but you always have to remember that even if you have a $150 million media budget, the media plan will be a compromise.

TRAVEL AND HOSPITALITY MEDIA

Consumer travel media opportunities are vast. There are over 500 titles that are either exclusively travel oriented (such as *Conde Nast Traveler*, *Travel and Leisure*, and *Budget Travel*) or contain significant travel sections (such as lifestyle and special interest magazines, destination magazines, city guides, and coupon books) in the United States alone. Add to this every major newspaper's

TABLE 5.1   Media Categories

Media category	Advantages	Disadvantages
Newspapers	Excellent targeting—Sunday travel section; shopping environment; short lead time; timeliness; good local coverage and relevance; flexibility; believability	Poor reproduction quality, short life span; low pass-along audience
Magazines	Good targeting—travel publications and travel trade; geographic and demographic selectivity; high reproduction quality; long life span; high pass-along rate; special features such as pop-up ads or spectaculars; prestige	Long lead times; lack of immediacy; potentially wasted circulation; high cost for national publications
Television	Motion, sight, and sound quality; flexibility; good targeting with spot and cable; wide reach; large audiences	High cost of media and production; short message life span; not a shopping environment; clutter of channel and messages
Radio	Excellent regional and demographic targeting; relatively low cost of media and production; reaches mobile population; flexibility; excellent opportunity for promotions	Background medium/lower attention; short message life span; high repetition requirement; clutter of stations and messages
Directories	Long life span; reference quality; credibility; highly targeted	Relatively high cost; no sense of urgency
Outdoor	Excellent local coverage; size; visibility; reaches mobile population; high frequency; 24-hour exposure	Creative limitations; high cost of media and production; no audience selectivity
Transit	Excellent local coverage; high frequency; flexibility; message relevance	Space limitations; clutter; no audience selectivity
Point of purchase	Excellent targeting at point of purchase; accurate timing; immediacy	Space limitations; cost; clutter; location of display controlled by retailer
Direct mail	Excellent targeting with high audience selectivity; exact response measurement and tracking of results; personalization; flexibility	Junk mail perception; varying list qualities; cost
E-mail	Low cost; good targeting; interactivity; response measurement	Spamming; junk e-mail perception
Internet	Low production cost; measurability; good targeting; interactivity; flexibility; immediacy	Clutter; annoyance factor with pop-up windows
Telemarketing	Personal approach; high response rates; market selectivity; flexibility	Varying list qualities; high annoyance factor
Premiums	Potential for creativity	Perception of junk

travel section, travel directories, in-flight magazines, on-board publications, in-room publications, travel websites and travel sections within general websites, and travel shows, and you have a travel media overabundance. Obviously, media planning is the agency's responsibility, but your task is to approve the media plan, so it helps to be informed and knowledgeable.

The list of travel trade media (Table 5.2) is smaller than the consumer list, but it still remains quite large. It consists of national and regional publications that target travel agents, tour operators, groups, and meeting and incentive travel planners, as well as industry people such as hoteliers, recruiters, and so on. For reference, following is a table of most travel trade titles.

TABLE 5.2   List of Selected Travel Trade Publications

AgencyInc (myagency.com)
InsideFlyer (insideflyer.com)
Association Meetings (meetingsnet.com)
Association News (associationnews.com)
Bus Tours (busmag.com)
Business Travel News (btnonline.com)
Business Travel Planner (northstartravelmedia.com)
Canadian Travel Press (travelpress.com)
Caribbean Gold Book (caribbeantravel.com)
Convene Magazine (pcma.org)
Convention South (conventionsouth.com)
Corporate & Incentive Travel (corporate-inc-travel.com)
Corporate Meetings & Incentives (meetingsnet.com)
Cruise Trade (traveltrade.com)
Going on Faith (grouptravelleader.com)
Group Tour Magazine (grouptour.com)
Guest Informant (cityspin.com)
Hotels (hotelsmag.com)
Hotel Business (hotelbusiness.com)
Hotel & Motel Management (hotelmotel.com)
Hotel & Travel Index (htihotelink.com)
Jax Fax Travel Marketing (www.jaxfax.com)
Lodging Hospitality (lhonline.com)
Meeting News (meetingnews.com)
Meetings & Conventions (meetings-conventions.com)
Meeting Professional (mpiweb.org)
Meetings South/East/West (meetings411.com)
Official Hotel Guide (ohgonline.com)
Official Meeting Facilities Guide (omfg.com)
Premier Hotels & Resorts (premierhotels.com)
Recommend (recommend.com)
Small Market Meetings (smallmarketmeetings.com)
Special Events (primediabusiness.com)
Sports Travel (sportstravelmagazine.com)

(Continues)

TABLE 5.2   *(Continued)*

Successful Meetings (successmtgs.com)
The Group Travel Leader (grouptravelleader.com)
Tour Trade (traveltrade.com)
TravelAge West (travelagewest.com)
Travel Agent (travelagentmag.com)
Travel Agent Official Travel Industry Directory (otid.com)
Travel Courier Canada (baxter.net)
Travel Trade (traveltrade.com)
Travel Weekly (twcrossroads.com)
Travelweek Canada (travelweek.ca)
Travel World News (travelworldnews.com)
TRIPsouth (tripsouth.com)

MEDIA PLANNING

"Repetitio est mater studiorum" is a Latin proverb that, loosely translated, means "Repetition is the mother of learning." This is the key rule of media. Unless you have an earth-shattering message such as the famous 1984 commercial by Apple, which aired only once (in which case once was enough), you need repetition and plenty of it.

You, and every other advertiser in the world, have to decide the following: who, where and how many, when, how long, and how often?

Who are your primary and secondary audiences? They should be defined in full in your marketing plan. The definition of your audiences should include demographic factors such as age, gender, family, income level, and education level, as well as lifestyle, special interest, buying patterns, and consumption patterns. Try to be as specific as you can. Instead of saying that the target audience is female professionals; define them as follows: the audience is female professionals working in large metropolitan areas, between the ages of 25 and 49, and should be golfers or interested in golf. Your secondary audience may be travel agents who sell golf packages and perhaps golf equipment shops.

Where should you place your ads, and how many individuals within a certain audience do you need to reach? With an audience narrowed down to a manageable size, you can also narrow the various media opportunities. If your audience consists of commuters, two excellent media choices may be radio during drive time and train posters. There are special interest publications and associations. Perhaps direct mail is the best way to reach them. Another issue to consider is the purpose—personal use (vacations) or work (business travel)? Who makes the vacation purchasing decisions—the male, the female, the children, or jointly? Who makes the business travel purchasing decisions—the business traveler or the assistant? Perhaps the best media are not travel specific; perhaps they depend on lifestyle or special interests. With regard to how many persons to reach, you must evaluate quantity as well as quality. Perhaps the largest number of prospects will be reached by magazine X, but the best or potentially most profitable prospects read magazine Y.

When should ads be placed? This is an important consideration, as product usage may be ongoing, seasonal, or sporadic. While business travel may be a year-round activity, leisure travel is more seasonal. Thus hospitality, travel, and tourism companies need to evaluate the seasonality patterns of their product categories. Honeymoons are planned months in advance. Weekend getaways may be decided on the spur of the moment. Family travel usually coincides with school holidays and is planned in advance. Conventions and trade show travel may be planned up to a year in advance. Business travel is often decided at the last minute. It is important to know when the decision to travel is made so that you can allocate your media usage accordingly.

How long and how often should you run your campaign? Should it be ongoing or flighted? These are important questions that may be answered by observing usage and purchase patterns. For ongoing business travel, continuous reminder advertising may be necessary. For ski resorts advertising, year-round advertising is probably a waste of money.

On the other hand, use media to fortify your creative strategy. Why not be the only ski resort that advertises in summer? Why not advertise Christmas vacation deals in January? Why not target wives of frequent male business travelers in publications they (the wives) read or programs they watch? "Look, honey, Hotel XYZ will pick you up and press your shirts for free if you stay with them." Or why not create special packages for the spouses, which may influence the purchase decision? Or do the reverse: create come-along packages for husbands of female business travelers and choose media that target them. Media use may be as creative as the creative work itself. There are various nontraditional media vehicles at your disposal. You have to break through the clutter, and doing the opposite of what everyone else is doing may be just the creative touch that's needed.

Businesses with small budgets should choose one key media category and one or two key vehicles (publications, or stations, or any others) within that category, and then build up a continuous presence with those dedicated audiences.

For brand-building purposes, it is always better to reach one audience many times than many audiences once.

HOW MUCH IS ENOUGH?

Determining media budgets is difficult. There is no simple formula that will allow you to plug in some numbers and get a perfect answer. Some companies have a set amount every year, and that's the amount they can afford. Others try to reach optimal budget levels by varying the media mix and measuring responses. Regardless of your situation, before deciding how much to spend and allocate, it is helpful to answer these questions:

- What are the long-term and short-term goals?
- What market share do you wish to achieve?
- How much investment will it take to gain the desired market penetration?
- What budget limitations exist?
- Does your company have any set ratios for advertising spending (per unit or per sales figure)?
- Is your campaign primarily national, regional, or mixed?
- How many markets do you need to reach?
- How much do your competitors spend?
- What is their market share and share of voice?

Keep in mind that not only creative and media vehicles can be tested. Different spending levels can be tested in different markets to measure the cause and effect of media spending levels on sales, brand awareness, and market penetration.

USEFUL LINKS

- aaaa.org   American Association of Advertising Agencies
- accessabc.com   Audit Bureau of Circulations (ABC)
- adage.com   *Advertising Age* magazine
- adweek.com   *Adweek* magazine
- brandweek.com   *Brandweek* magazine
- dmnews.com   Online direct marketing newspaper
- mediaweek.com   Online media magazine

CHAPTER SIX

How to Create Better Brochures and Collateral Materials

God is in the details.
—Ludwig Mies van der Rohe

Regardless of the type, size, or location of your tourism or hospitality product, you need some type of collateral material to market it. This may be a simple black-and-white flier, a rack brochure, a one-page color shell, a multicolor, multipage brochure, an elaborate mailing piece, a video brochure, or a CD.

Coming from a packaged goods background, I have always seen hospitality and tourism brochures as the equivalent of product packaging. Yet, I am amazed at how many hospitality brochures look and feel generic and how few are designed to compete for shelf space (either actual, such as retail displays at travel agencies and trade shows, or mental—the "shelf space" in the travel agent's or consumer's mind). They don't differentiate the brand from the competitor. Why don't these companies study packaged goods? Just maintain your strategy, make the material attractive to the eye, focus on your key audience, don't forget your brand's personality, differentiate your brand, and remember the Bauhaus maxim that Form Follows Function. And the function of your collateral (packaging) is to brand and sell.

Here are 89 tips and a few additional comments about strategy, design, photography, copy, and production that will help you create more effective collateral materials and brochures. If you feel these are rules, I offer this solace from T.S Eliot: "It's not wise to violate the rules until you know how to observe them."

WHAT YOU CAN LEARN FROM PACKAGED GOODS

It's been said that one of the famous P's in marketing is packaging. Studies show that packaging impressions dwarf advertising impressions, and the packaged goods people know it well. If you're not on the shelf, you're not in the mind and you're not in the cart. Why don't hospitality companies follow their studious approach? Why not devote some time to research what grabs consumers' attention and what stays etched in their memories? Who are the leaders in packaged goods? Campbell Soup, whose packaging was immortalized by Andy Warhol. Absolute Vodka, whose packaging is the basis of a superb advertising campaign. Marlboro. Coca-Cola. L'Eggs. Why are they so strong? Partly because of the powerful imagery inherent in their labels.

Granted, applying this principle to hospitality is not a simple parallel, as more people frequent supermarkets than travel agencies or hotels. But do they? Well, perhaps some do and some don't. The ones who don't you are not going to reach anyway, so focus on those who do. A busy traveling saleswoman may stay at hotels almost weekly, while her stay-at-home husband does all the grocery shopping. Isn't she likely to be exposed to your hotel packaging more frequently than to your advertising? Quite likely. So create your packaging with that person in mind. Make it outstanding, differentiating, ownable, unique, exciting, interesting, category-shattering, funny, entertaining, whatever. Just avoid the generic look. And if you're confused about what I mean by "packaging," I mean your entire face to the public: your corporate directory, individual product brochure, environmental signage, in-room materials, the telephone directory in every room, the laundry form, the do-not-disturb sign, the menus. There are countless opportunities to stand out. Take them.

TYPES OF COLLATERAL

There are several basic types of collateral pieces. Each of them is briefly described here:

Fact sheets. Fact sheets are not necessarily collateral, but they are often the first piece of information given to guests, travel agents, meeting planners, and the media. Thus the importance of quality is paramount, including frequent product and service updates, correct spelling, crisp printing, and a simple, branded layout.

Fliers. Fliers are single-sheet promotional leaflets that can be either one- or two-sided. They are used for a variety of purposes, but most often to showcase a new offer and price and to promote a product or destination in large quantities. They can be distributed at trade shows, through mailings, by sales representatives, and through travel agencies.

Shells. Shells are similar to fliers; however, they contain only general information and some blank space for overprinting. They can be very effective, as they allow you to provide branded leaflets to wholesalers and travel agents for overprinting and distribution.

Postcards. Postcards are very inexpensive mailing pieces that can be extremely effective as reminders, teasers, or follow-up or introductory mailers. Oversized postcards provide sufficient space for nice graphics. Businesses with limited budgets can use postcards to run entire campaigns.

Self-mailers. Self-mailers are collateral pieces that can be folded, sealed, and sent by mail without using an envelope. They can be very effective in stimulating information requests or motivating action, as they can contain postage-paid reply cards.

Posters. Posters can serve two functions: decorative or promotional. Promotional posters should be created using the same strategy as for other out-of-home media. Decorative posters must use stunning images and minimal promotional information, usually just a logo, name, or destination.

Rack brochures. Rack brochures are the standard promotional materials for hotels and hospitality businesses. They can be trifolds, double-gate folds, multipanel rolling folds, or saddle-stitched booklets, all of which, when folded, measure $4 \times 8\frac{1}{2}$ inches and fit into standard envelopes and display racks.

Multipage brochures, booklets, and directories. Brochures are used to showcase individual products, product lines, or entire product portfolios. They can vary in size from pocket directories to tabloid-sized brochures. Multipage brochures provide an excellent opportunity to include plenty of images and product information. Also, due to their size and generous amount of space, they are very effective branding tools.

Videos. Videos are effective collateral materials, as they contain motion and sound. However, they can be quite costly to produce. If you decide to produce a video, make sure that it is of top quality; anything less (amateur or self-made videos, etc.) will reflect poorly on your product and brand.

CDs. CDs are exceptionally useful multimedia tools that can contain still images, sound, and video and hold plenty of information. Moreover, CDs may be created to be interactive and provide instant links to specific websites.

Other materials. Other items, include media kits, group sales kits, welcome packages, destination brochures, in-room information, and corporate information kits.

Collateral materials often provide the first contact with a prospective client, so it is imperative that they perfectly represent your product and convey the brand experience. Good collateral provides a balance of information, with product and guest experience photography and solid factual and branded copy.

WHERE TO START

Where do you start? Since you've done an excellent job of defining your brand, the optimal approach for your collateral material will be derived from you overall brand strategy. It will be an extension of your brand identity and must contribute fully to your positioning. Whether you have a strong strategy or are starting from scratch, the following points will help you initiate the process:

1. Define your strategy and objective. What is the purpose of the collateral piece—what do you want it to achieve? Do you want to attract more visitors, educate travel agents, or raise awareness?

2. Embrace your brand's personality and extend it to your collateral material. If you have a dude ranch and you've been positioning it as the best dude ranch for families, don't create a brochure that looks and feels like it's made for a business hotel.

3. Define your audience. For whom is your collateral piece created? Is it for meeting planners, end users, travel agents, a specific market segment, or a general piece for a variety of audiences? The more

Imaginative use of the company logo creates visual ownability
and recognition for Viva Resorts.
Source: Brandhaus and Viva Resorts. Used with permission.

narrowly you can define the target audience, the better and more focused your piece will be.

4. Define the usage. How will it be used? Will it be handed out at trade shows, sent out as a direct mail piece, used as a fulfillment piece, or all of these? Defining the usage will help you determine its size, shape, weight, content, and so on.

5. What is your positioning promise? Why should a consumer buy your product? Why should a travel agent sell your product? Make sure that the promised benefit is clearly defined and communicated.

6. Is your promised benefit backed up by facts? Don't promise anything you can't deliver.

7. Define your differentiation. What is unique about your product and/or your brand? Don't just create another standard rack brochure. Differentiate your product/brand by listing its unique features.

8. Before you create a new collateral piece, don't forget to check what the competition is doing. This will give you a good idea of what users will expect to receive as well as how to differentiate yourself. If your key competitors are producing elaborate pieces, creating just a simple flier will position you negatively.

9. KISS. Keep it simple, silly. Don't try to create unnecessarily elaborate and complicated pieces that will ruin your sleep as well as your budget. As Albert Einstein said, "Make it as simple as possible, but not simpler than that."

DESIGN AND LAYOUT

1. Keep it in the family. One of the most common mistakes is to create a "fresh new look" with every new promotional piece. This kills your brand positioning and recognition. Just think of your collateral piece as your best sales rep. Wouldn't you want all your reps to convey a consistent message (focused on your strategy) each time they interact with your clients?

2. Your collateral must reflect and reinforce your visual brand identity. Along with your advertising, point-of-sale displays, signage, collateral piece, business cards, stationary, and even invoices, your brochure must reflect that familiar branded look. The Coca-Cola Company employs an army of lawyers just to ensure proper usage of their logo.

3. Use colors to reinforce your brand's positioning and personality. Black and silver may be more suitable for a trendy Manhattan property than a California bed-and-breakfast place.

4. Own a color or element. Establish some ownable visual element with which your brand will be identified. After a while, your brand will own this element in the mind of the consumer, and it will help convey familiarity with the brand. Silversea Cruises does a good job of this.

So does Tiffany with their famous blue box, which has been their trademark for over 100 years. This element doesn't have to be a color, though. It may be another visual element such as Disney's Mickey Mouse ears, or some other visual brand print such as Burberry's famous plaid pattern.

5. Use the cover of your brochure to grab attention. The worst mistake is to have a cover without a message; that's like running an ad without a headline. Research studies show that as many as 80% of readers may never go past the cover; thus, you'll be losing a huge audience by not having a message there. Use your cover to convey your key point. This may be the destination and name, your positioning statement, or even a headline borrowed from your advertising.

6. If your collateral piece will be displayed in racks, put the key verbal elements (destination, brand, and message) in the upper third of the cover page, and make the type large and easy to read (even from several feet away). This is important, since the lower two-thirds may be covered by the display rack.

7. A single photograph on the cover will have more impact than a multitude of smaller visuals. If you use several, make one dominant. A collage of equally sized visuals will not draw the customer to anything specific. This recommendation also applies to inside pages.

8. Include detail shots. An architectural detail may better illustrate the overall ambiance than a whole building.

9. Use colors that will attract consumers. Your brochure must compete for their attention when displayed on a rack with 30 other brochures.

10. Make it look realistic. Unless this is part of your positioning strategy, brochure photographs depicting unreal-looking people, such as dancing cleaning ladies in miniskirts, look false and silly.

11. Use captions with photographs. Research suggests that on average, captions are read twice as often as body copy. Use them to your advantage to highlight relevant specific points.

12. Include some information for niche markets even if you have the budget for only one brochure.

13. Make it beautiful. Create a brochure that is too beautiful to toss, and you'll enjoy extended marketing impact. It'll give the client boasting rights and you word of mouth.

14. Use maps whenever you can. Travelers love maps; use them as selling tools. When appropriate, illustrated maps work very well.

15. Be aware of the ethnic, religious, and international sensitivities of your target audience.

16. If you don't have an advertising agency, work with a good designer. A seasoned professional will help you create a much better piece and save you time, energy, and money.

A great detail shot can capture the character of a location: a Chinese hotel.
Source: Corbis Digital Stock. Used with permission.

17. Beware of *artdirectoritis*. This is a disease that befalls otherwise intelligent, creative people when they forget that their job is to design material that sells. I once overheard an otherwise intelligent designer say that it is passé to include any product information in the brochure because the consumer is no longer interested in the destination or the product. Pure opinion, no facts, and the poor guy actually believed it. Have you ever seen a car brochure without pictures of the car?

18. Which brings us to the most important point: use stunning images. When you have outstanding shots, they will make a positive impression on the reader, regardless of whether they show a product, architecture, landscape, scenery, food, interiors, activity, or details.

It helps to use images that make your target market's mouth water.
Source: Bill Sumner. Used with permission.

COPY AND TYPE

1. Don't ramble and avoid stereotypes. For some reason, numerous hospitality brochures sound so similar that it's hard to distinguish one
   from another. Yet brochure copy can help establish the personality of
   the brand just as much as copy in an advertisement. Many brochures
   ramble on, line after line, making the reader work hard. Well-written,
   factual copy can be a feast to the prospecting customer. Make sure
   you're not saying more than you need to say. Avoid fluff. Although the
   statement has been overused and misused, less indeed is more. However, less doesn't mean less information than necessary. It means fewer
   words, less sales pitch, and simpler wording. Balance the use of pictures and words to "tell" the story. If you are showing something in the
   picture, you do not have to state it in the copy as well.

2. Involve the reader by including him or her in the story.

3. Be specific. Provide as much practical information as possible, such
   as available activities, local attractions, package inclusions, facility
   descriptions, and so on. Cruise lines are quite good at this. They provide
   a detailed description of how your vacation will be.

4. Avoid platitudes and excessive puffery. A little dress-up is expected,
   but pure puffery will not convince anyone to take a vacation.

5. Be honest. If you operate a budget bed-and-breakfast place, don't present it as a luxurious resort. If the cabins on your cruise ship are small, don't inflate the story by saying that you have luxurious and spacious staterooms. The worst thing you can do is to overpromise and underdeliver. It is not only unethical, but it will upset your guests, who were expecting a completely different experience.

6. Use type that is easy to read. If you think this is too obvious to be mentioned, check the multitude of marketing literature where the copy is too difficult to read. Serif type is easier to read than sans serif type, as most readers are used to reading newspapers and books using serif type.

7. Use type effects sparingly and for accentuation. The eye is a creature of habit. Long blocks of copy set in all caps or inverted copy (white type on a black background) and blocks of text shaped into design elements are all common effects that make copy difficult to read.

8. Think of your audience when choosing the type size. If a percentage of your clientele consists of senior citizens, use larger type.

9. If possible, try to include your pricing or at least price ranges. Consumers want to know how much to budget. Pricing information should be included as an insert, as prices change often and you don't want to have to reprint the entire brochure every time this happens.

10. Provide more information than consumers expect as an added value. What is there to be seen besides your product? Are there interesting local attractions, excursions, and activities? Can you list little-know facts?

11. Provide plenty of helpful specifics. Include the average temperatures by month or season. Tell consumers what type of clothing to bring. Tell them if they must bring hair dryers or irons or if these are provided.

12. Include information on how guests may best be contacted by family and friends in case of an emergency.

13. Make the brochure interactive by including a reply request. This may be a trivia quiz, a sweepstakes, a questionnaire, and so on. It will allow you to amplify your database and involve the guest with your brand.

14. Once the final copy is ready, have several people proofread it. You have read it so many times that you will probably not catch minor errors.

15. Make sure that you get sign-offs from anyone who has to approve the copy (such as the legal department). This will help you control costs by avoiding last-minute changes.

16. Finally, and most important: ask for the sale and make it easy for the client to buy. A call to action is crucial, and the more specific it is, the better the chance that your clients will buy. Toll-free numbers and web addresses are standard, but include any other information that may be helpful in the buying/reservations process, such as a list of preferred travel agencies.

The best photography documents the products in a way that makes them look like beauty shots: Dubrovnik.

Source: Getty Images Inc.—Image Bank. Used with permission.

PHOTOGRAPHY

Photography is the face your product presents to the world, so it pays to hire the best photographer you can afford. Also, make sure that the photo crew receives maximum support on location. A few days of dedicated support should not present a big problem, and it will ensure that the shoot runs smoothly. Photography is changing at an incredibly fast pace. While digital professional photography was inconceivable only a few years ago, it is definitely the wave of the future. But whether you shoot on film or digitally, here are some helpful tips:

1. Invest in good photography. Nothing will define your product and brand experience more completely. It is the most important marketing investment you can make. True, good photography is not cheap, but your photography is your product's face to the world, so don't skimp on it. Photography has a peculiar domino effect. If it's good, chances are that everything you'll use it for will be good, and vice versa. Good photography is created by good photographers. Seems simple enough, right? Wrong. Often lack of attention in finding a good photographer results in mediocre images. Take the time to review portfolios, websites, and slides. Remember, it always costs more to redo it. How can you recognize good photography? Because it simply is good, whether you depict rooms, buildings, cabins, restaurants, people, scenery, or action. You'll know it when you see it.

2. Make sure that the photographs you take are not just beauty shots. You must document the key points of your product. Hotel photography should show the building, the rooms, one or several restaurants, and public areas. You may also want to show meeting rooms and recreational facilities. Resorts should include the pool, beach, and special interest areas such as a golf course. People like to see where they are going, so it is important to provide them with enough visual information. The best photographs document the product in a way that makes it look like a series of beauty shots. A good photographer and art director will be able to deliver signature shots for any product.

3. Avoid visual stereotypes. Why do so many resort brochures use a similar shot of a dreamy girl standing on a cliff in a white bathing suit holding a white cape in the wind while waves crash at her feet? I've never seen anyone actually do this in her free time, so why use it in a brochure?

4. Create story appeal in your photographs, especially product shots. Pictures that tell a story sell better than pictures of the product alone.

5. Show people. People are interested in people. Don't just show an empty room, pool, or restaurant; show what the experience will be.

6. If you are selling a destination, show local residents. People interested in a destination want to know what the locals look like.

7. Choose the right models for your product based on the demographic, racial, and age profiles of your clientele. You're not being politically incorrect, just targeting your audience (this is the only area where racial profiling is a good thing).

8. Don't use supermodels. Unless you have a clientele of movie starts, don't use models who are too beautiful. Unrealistically gorgeous people may make the potential guest feel out of place. Instead, use models with a realistic look who reflect the target audience's real and aspirational traits.

9. Help prospective guests identify themselves in the pictures. Show models in activities that are interesting to your existing and target audience, such as playing golf on the actual golf course.

10. Show food. Research shows that the single most talked-about item after a vacation and even a business trip is the food. Whet the consumer's appetite before the trip. Detail shots work very well, and depicting prepared meals is more attractive than showing ingredients. Shots of food in motion (e.g., dripping chocolate) are particularly appetizing.

WORKING WITH PHOTOGRAPHERS

1. Some brands' campaigns have been defined by their unique photography due to the photographer who shot them. Like great writers or painters, great photographers have their own style, a sensitivity for showing objects and environments with a slightly different skew. You

will almost always be able to recognize the works of Helmut Newton, Annie Leibowitz, Ansel Adams, or Bruce Weber. Of course, these represent the pinnacle of photographic output and as a rule are prohibitively expensive. However, there are others with unique styles. So, if your brand strategy relies upon a unique visual look and you can afford to pay high fees, it may be worth the investment. A single unique and ownable photograph has often helped establish the look, feel, and personality of a brand.

2. All photographers are not created equal. Choose the right one for your project. Base the decision on the portfolio, experience, versatility, and uniqueness of the photographer, but also on his or her personality. When you have to spend 12–16 hours a day for several days together on a shoot, make sure that you can work with the person. The photographic genius may be a prima donna.

3. Plan your photo shoot well in advance. A photo shoot is one of the most exciting and challenging tasks of your job and can turn into a nightmare if not properly planned and organized.

4. Create a complete shot list and revise it on site. Once you arrive at the shot site, you'll see the need for various adjustments to the list.

5. Make sure that the photographer takes all the necessary shots. Photographers are notorious for wanting to shoot mood and beauty shots and avoid product shots. One way to ensure that you get the shots you need is by documenting all your product shots with a digital camera before the shoot begins; this way, you'll be able to avoid misunderstandings.

6. Always get full ownership and/or unlimited worldwide usage rights for all photography. Make sure that the photographer doesn't retain the right to resell usage of certain shots for stock.

7. Have everyone sign releases, without exception, even if you use local, residents, staff, or guests in your shots.

8. Always attend a photo shoot. You will be using these shots for various purposes, which makes you the best person to supervise the shoot.

9. When choosing wardrobe and props, use timeless pieces, colors, and designs. A pink polyester suit may be the rave this year, but it will certainly be outdated next season.

10. Make sure that out-of-pocket expenses are accompanied by receipts. This way you'll be able to control the budget for wardrobe, accessories, and other purchases.

11. If you can afford it, hire a production coordinator. These amazing people actually enjoy organizing photo shoots and will relieve you of a huge burden.

12. Hire a good stylist who will ensure that the models are prepared, the props are in place, and all details are taken care of. This will allow you and the photographer to focus on taking the right shot.

13. Buy wardrobe and props in your hometown. If you're shooting on location away from home, especially in foreign countries, you may end up paying three times as much for the same or inferior items.

14. In the model agreements, be specific on what expenses will and will not be covered. Long-distance calls and other charges can escalate very quickly.

PRODUCTION AND PRINTING

1. Even if you're product is coach, your collateral piece should be first class. Collateral material is not an item on which to save money. In addition to the layout, copy, and general aesthetics, the collateral will communicate with your audience on such emotional levels as warmth, feel, personality, touch, and quality, so make it outstanding.

2. Choose the paper quality appropriate for your product and use it for nonverbal communication. For example, Costa Rica, the eco-tourism destination, should always indicate that they use 100% recycled paper.

3. Standardize your paper size if you don't have a large budget. Again, for functionality, the standard 4 × 8½ inch rack brochures or the larger 8½ × 11 inch brochures are the most practical, as they can be mailed in standard-sized envelopes or displayed in standard-sized rack displays. If you create special sizes, you'll have to create special-sized envelopes as well. Make the content outstanding, not the shape. Conversely, if you do have the budget, use the shape as a differentiating factor.

4. If you are working with wholesalers and tour operators, create a piece that can be overprinted (by leaving a blank space) by them and distributed through mailings to travel agents. The most common (and economic) size for these pieces are one-page shells, but they could also be 8½ × 25½ inch trifolds. If you exceed a maximum flat width of 26 inches, most wholesalers will not be able to feed the sheets through their in-house printers.

5. Don't varnish the surface that will be overprinted. This will take the overprinted ink much longer to dry and may result in smudging.

6. When selecting a printer, don't base your choice on the cost alone. Quality is imperative, so always carefully review the printer's previous work. Keep in mind that printers are often print brokers who send out your bid to several printers throughout the country.

7. Always have your ad agency or designer supervise the print production process. They will charge you for this, but they have experience with print supervision and will ensure top quality.

HOW TO SAVE MONEY ON COLLATERAL MATERIALS AND PHOTOGRAPHY

1. Get at least three print bids. Even though you may print through your ad agency or your cousin is a printer, always get several bids for print jobs. This way you will keep your printing costs in perspective.

2. Plan production and printing well in advance. The most common reason for high printing costs is a rush charge. Always create a written production schedule.

3. Carefully choose the weight of the paper for your collateral material. A needlessly heavy paper stock may unnecessarily increase the paper price and your mailing costs.

4. Plan multiple uses for your piece. Create collateral that is flexible enough for a variety of uses and audiences.

5. Check, double check, and check again. Even if you are reproducing from the same file, *always* proofread and recheck the final printout before you go to press. Nothing increases production costs more than having to reprint brochures because of faulty information.

6. Slides reproduce better than photographs, which may minimize the need (and cost) for color corrections.

7. Keep in mind that every photograph needs color corrections and separations. Thus, a collage of many small photos will cost more than a large single photo.

8. If you have a tiny budget, you may want to try using royalty-free stock photographs or offer the job to not yet established photographers, photography students, or local photographers if your photo shoot takes place overseas.

9. Plan your photo shoot well in advance. A photo shoot is one of the most exciting and challenging tasks of your job and can turn into a budgeting nightmare if not properly planned and organized.

10. Make a contract with the photographer based on number of days of shooting, not your shot list. This way you can add necessary shots on the spot without incurring additional costs.

11. Plan your shoots for the off season. In south Florida, for example, summer is the low season for photographers and models. Use this to your advantage when negotiating fees.

12. Negotiate to pay for part of the contract in barter. With photographers you can sometimes pay part of the fee in trade credit. With models you can often barter for the entire shoot, (e.g., 4 days of shooting for 4 days of accommodations or a free cruise).

13. If you have to shoot more than one location, negotiate a packaged deal.

14. If you have to travel to the location, try bartering with airlines for seats or ask for an industry discount for the crew and models.

15. Shoot the entire shoot digitally. This will save money on postproduction items such as developing film, scanning, and duplication.

BROCHURE FULFILLMENT AND DISTRIBUTION

Cost, timeliness, and excitement are the three elements that define brochure fulfillment. If not planned wisely, the distribution of collateral materials via mail can take a large amount of money and effort. You have basically two ways of handling it: in-house or outsourced to a fulfillment house. Both have their pros and cons. In-house fulfillment is appropriate for smaller outfits that need customized replies. Even a small or medium-sized company can optimize in-house fulfillment by subcontracting metering and postage equipment from a vendor such as Pitney Bowes. A fulfillment house is usually the better solution for larger companies with large outgoing collateral requests. The way to optimize costs with both options is to create standardized mailing packages. If you have multiple brochures or audiences, create one standard package for each of the various types of requests. For example, all consumers should receive your corporate brochure and a CD. All travel agents should receive the corporate brochure and CD as well, along with agent-specific materials such as booking policies and reorder cards. Groups and incentive planers should receive a group and incentive kit. Using standardized packages, you will be able to reduce the postage cost and speed up the process.

Timeliness is the second key factor in fulfillment. In this age of instant gratification, timely delivery is crucial; you must respond with a shipment within 48 hours.

Lastly, the package's "excitement" factor should not be overlooked. What you send out is the most important thing. Someone who is interested enough in your brand to phone or visit your site and request additional information should be richly rewarded for his or her effort and interest. Invest in exciting brochures or video materials, and they will pay off.

However, collateral is not just distributed by responding to consumers' requests. Trade shows, road shows, product launches, proactive mailings, magazine and newspaper inserts, point-of-sale and point-of-use displays, and sales reps' handouts are additional ways of distributing it. Take advantage of all opportunities to distribute your materials.

There is a peculiar phenomenon that I call the "hamster paradox." Sometimes when smaller or inexperienced marketers invest in elaborate brochures, they are stingy about distributing them. They are very proud of their collateral pieces, showing them to everyone who visits their office and taking them to meetings. But when they do distribute them, they do so at a painfully slow and insufficient rate. Collateral is expensive to create, produce, and distribute and should not be wasted by distributing it blindly, but it must hit the market in sufficient numbers to have an impact on bookings. An intelligent approach calls for balanced order fulfillment and distribution through all available means. Remember, brochures on shelves attract dust, not customers.

FINAL COMMENT: POLICING PHOTOGRAPHY

There can be only one—original slide, that is. So, never give it away. Again: never give away original slides, no matter how urgent the need. Buying a lockable armoire for your slide library is one of the best investments you will ever make. Don't give anyone access to the key without your supervision. This will protect your only tangible marketing asset unless you scan your original slides and store them in digital format on CD, which I strongly recommend.

Keep the quality of your photography consistent. If you have shots from various photo shoots and one set is a fourth-generation duplication, you'll have a brochure with visuals of varying quality. Avoid this problem by retaining original slides at all cost.

Granted, photography is going digital and this advice may be obsolete by the time you read this book, but the same principles apply to your digital photography CDs. Make multiple copies of the master CD and keep them under lock and key.

CHAPTER SEVEN

Public Relations

"Would you tell me, please, which way I ought to go from here?"
"That depends a good deal on where you want to get to," said the Cat.
"I don't much care where," said Alice.
"Then it doesn't matter which way you go," said the Cat.
                    —Lewis Carroll, *Alice's Adventures in Wonderland*

A common problem with public relations is that it is not as focused as other marketing activities. While it generates results, it is often not driven by specific objectives. This is unfortunate, as it can be a tremendously effective marketing tool, providing credibility through nonpaid media coverage and motivating action when properly directed.

THE VALUE OF PR

Public relations can become one of the most powerful, valuable, and cost-effective weapons in your marketing arsenal. It can be used for generating awareness, building recognition, and creating a favorable image. For many new brands, it is publicity that creates the launch, not advertising. Why? Because in advertising you speak about your brand, and in publicity others speak about it. And when others speak, the brand's credibility is infinitely higher. Another great value of PR is that, unlike advertising, it is quite inexpensive. Not everyone has an advertising budget, but anyone can afford some level of public relations, even if it's sporadic and handled in-house. If you can come up with some unique, different, or newsworthy information about your product, brand, or company, media coverage will be easy to find.

A few years ago, when I was handling marketing for Allegro Resorts, we decided to start a weekly charter flight to Turks and Caicos from New York City, and I needed to launch the new program and inaugurate the first flight.

Together with our PR agency, JGR & Associates, we developed an unusual publicity stunt. Instead of the usual ribbon cutting, we promised 10 couples who showed up at the airport in their bathing suits a week-long all-expenses-paid vacation. Over 20 showed up (bathing suit clad in February at Kennedy Airport). This event was taped, sent out as a video news release over satellite, and picked up by over 365 news broadcasts nationwide, successfully launching the new destination. The whole publicity stunt cost less than $25,000. Buying the same air time would have cost millions. This is a good example of how combining public relations and promotion elements for the purposes of marketing can produce significant results when the goals are properly set and followed.

Public relations plays a very significant role in the communications mix of companies. It encompasses investor relations, employee relations, community relations, public affairs, government affairs, fund-raising, media relations, communications counseling, crisis management, publicity, and marketing communications. However, as this is a book on marketing, this chapter is devoted primarily to PR's marketing function. And the chief marketing function of PR is to generate positive publicity for your brand and company.

Willy Eiya, chief of the Huli tribe in Papua New Guinea, presents his new website on a laptop screen at the 2000 International Tourism Fair in Berlin.
Source: AP/Wide World Photos. Used with permission.

QUANTITY VERSUS QUALITY

One public relations theory is that the value of publicity lies in its quality alone; its quantity doesn't matter. In reality, you need a balance of both. To start with, quality is not a goal but a requirement. But without certain levels of quantity, you'll never achieve critical mass. It is somewhat like preaching in an empty church; your sermon may be exceptional, but if no one hears it, what's the point?

CHOOSING A PR AGENCY

As in choosing an advertising agency, the PR agency selection should be a process of in-depth evaluation. While some hold that the best public relations is done in-house, there are significant arguments for hiring a professional agency or consultant. PR agencies have a variety of trained professionals in communication and media relations, and while you can hire the same quality people, you will be limited to your few employees, who are likely to become involved in company issues and projects. Agencies, on the other hand, handle multiple clients and have a larger pool of ideas, experiences, and media contacts. In addition, they focus only on the PR.

There are large and small agencies, as well as PR consultants. Regardless of size, however, the two main factors to consider are communications creativity and results. Review samples of releases and press kits prepared for other clients and evaluate the clipping reports. Do these represent the kind of work you are looking for? Talk to some of their existing clients and call up staff writers for several industry publications. A few choice conversations will reveal the agency's reputation, knowledge, and creativity.

Some public relations professionals build significant personal relationships with writers and editors and use them as their key selling point. Keep in

Audience fragmentation is here to stay. That's the good news and the bad news.

mind, however, that while having extensive media contacts is good, no personal contact will persuade a serious editor to pick up a weak story. A newsworthy release, on the other hand, will be picked up regardless of personal media contact.

Another option is to have your PR handled by a division of your advertising agency. But look carefully at the pros and cons before you sign on. Their offer to integrate PR and advertising efforts may seem very appealing, but it must be more than just an attractive theory. Make sure that you are indeed getting a share of voice instead of a share of invoice. Ask to see samples of successfully integrated advertising, publicity, and promotional campaigns. Determine what results were achieved and what advantages the integration delivered.

HOW PR AGENCIES WORK

Highly newsworthy announcements, such as those concerning revolutionary new products, will require no pitching and will be picked up by multiple media. However, for most hospitality and tourism businesses, those events are quite rare.

All other stories have to be pitched by PR agencies to a variety of media. This is best done on a one-to-one basis, usually with a pitch letter, press release, and perhaps support material such as video footage and slides. Pitching media can quickly turn into the story of the boy who cried wolf. Good agencies know not to overpitch with insignificant story ideas, as the media will stop paying attention and often fail to pick up even a good story when one comes along. Good agencies approach pitching in such creative ways that they intrigue writers into wanting more information about the company or brand. Pamela Johnston, a PR expert, says that the best PR writing takes a step backward; it lets the writer come to the conclusion. One such example is a release for one of her clients, the last-minute Internet travel marketer Site 59. Instead of headlining a release "Cheap Travel Site" she wrote "Procrastinators Rejoice." Creativity is not limited to writing. For Vegas.com, another of Pamela's clients, the press release announcing some new illusionist spectacles was a blank piece of paper sent with a can of decoder spray.

HOW TO BE A GOOD PR CLIENT

Just like other creative companies, public relations agencies thrive on their ability to deliver great work for their clients. Yet it is often the clients who curb their agencies by having too many levels of approval or not understanding the process. You hired an agency because of their staff's expertise, experience, and creativity; now let them do their job. Here are some hints on how to be a good client:

- Trust your agency to do their job. There is nothing more frustrating for PR agencies than clients who nitpick at every detail and question every move.

- Provide sufficient information. One of the most important things for a PR agency is to receive continuous information from their clients. Instead of providing what you think is newsworthy, feed them all the available information and let them decide what is usable.

- Be open about taking chances and embracing nontraditional ideas. Great publicity is not created by sending press releases about product upgrades and personnel changes. Allow your PR agency to implement innovative ideas, as long as they are on strategy with your positioning.

- Trust their judgment. If your agency is telling you that an idea didn't work, trust them and move on to the next idea. Do not insist on something just because you like it.

- Avoid being process heavy. Big reports, heavy administration, and long meetings all occupy the agency's time. Instead of pitching stories to the media, they waste time on administrative tasks.

- Encourage spontaneity. Actions set in the PR plans should be followed, but some of the greatest PR opportunities arise out of nowhere. Embrace them—they are rare.

- Avoid approvals by committee. Just as with advertising approvals, too many people "correcting" releases will certainly make them weaker.

- Focus on the results, not the methodology. Often PR professionals need to take the writer's side to get things done. They know how media people work and think. Limit your approvals to press releases. Don't insist on approving the pitch letters.

- Appreciation goes a long way. Thank your agency when they jump through hoops and land some exceptional media coverage. People go the extra mile for clients they like.

CHURCH VERSUS STATE

Jefferson's principle of separation of church and state is often used to describe the separation of editorial and advertising departments in media. It serves as the covenant for editorial integrity and is highly regarded by all serious media professionals. While most reputable media maintain separate of advertising and editorial departments, there are some that favor advertisers in their editorial coverage. For this reason, some marketers are tempted to offer publications advertising only if it's accompanied by positive media coverage. This temptation should be resisted, as offering this to the wrong person may land you on the blacklist of an editor or writer. Besides, how valuable is media coverage that can be bought?

THE PRESS RELEASE AND PRESS KIT

The two basic public relations tools are the press release and the press kit.

The press release (or news release) is a written document that is used to communicate newsworthy information to the media. New releases are sent to the media via mail, fax, e-mail, or commercial newswire distribution (for more information, check out webwire.com, ereleases.com, internetwire.com, eworldwire.com, prnewswire.com, and internetnewsbureau.com). A good press release will spark writers' interest in intriguing copy or presentation. It will lead them to the story by making them think. A good release will be written in journalistic style and address the questions of who, what, where, when, and why. The most important news should be placed at the beginning of the release. Video releases are stories presented on video for use by broadcast media; they can be very effective for covering events or publicity stunts.

The press kit is the basic PR package, usually a folder containing a selection of releases, company fact sheets, biographies, brochures, slides, a CD with visuals, and video footage. Press kits should provide a writer with all the information necessary to cover a story. Many companies are posting their press kits on their websites, and some are presenting their press materials entirely in electronic format on a CD.

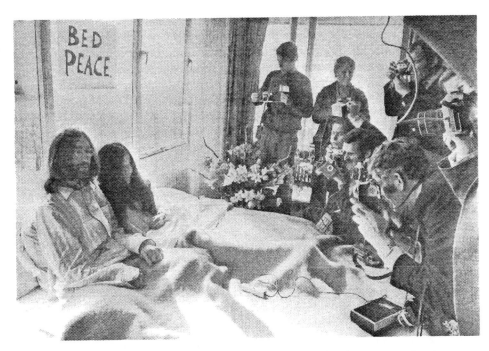

Sometimes great publicity just happens: John Lennon and Yoko Ono receive the press at their bedside in the Presidential Suite of the Hilton Hotel, Amsterdam.

Source: Getty Images Inc.—Hutton Archive Photos. Used with permission.

What makes a press kit and other press materials unique? Visual creativity is not limited to advertising. Innovative press materials should be designed in a way that will trigger writers' interest and spark their creative process. Check out what your competition is doing and create something totally different. Have your advertising and PR agencies work together on a unique concept.

PR TACTICS

Following are some proven public relations tactics that can help hospitality companies generate publicity and awareness:

Press conferences. These can be very effective for announcing to the travel trade significant news such as the launching of a new brand or product.

Press parties. Less formal than press conferences, parties can be used to deliver company news in a festive yet relaxed atmosphere.

Media visits and media trips. Individual or group media visits to locations can be valuable in generating interest in a new location or product. Be aware, though, that some media companies do not allow their reporters to go on media trips.

Interviews. Positioning key personnel as experts on certain topics and organizing interviews with them can help project a positive image for the organization.

Publicity stunts. Need to get TV coverage? Organize an offbeat stunt and send a VNR over satellite. Stunts must be unique to be picked up by the media, but they also must be related to your brand. Craziness for its own sake will do your marketing effort no good.

Newsletters. This is an excellent format to keep interested industry media updated about what's going on at your company. The newsletter must be professionally designed and written, contain real news and updates, and be sent only to media persons who are interested. Newsletters may be delivered inexpensively via e-mail.

Reprints. Reprints of articles that appeared in reputable publications can be used to establish credibility with consumer and trade audiences, depending on where the article was published. Some companies post all significant articles on their websites.

Sponsorships. Sponsorships and genuine commitment to a charitable cause or an arts and entertainment event can be used very effectively to generate publicity.

Demonstrations. Is your hotel restaurant operated by a famous chef? Is your bar famous for special cocktails? Organize an event for the chef or bartender to do some demonstrations or provide tips for the media. Their expertise will reflect positively on the host's location as well.

Company publications. Publish a series of how-to booklets on something pertaining to your product and use them to generate publicity.

Exhibitions. Hotels, cruises, restaurants, and even airports provide excellent locations for arts or photography exhibitions. Hire an artist, create an event, and invite local media to cover it.

Festivals. Organizing festivals or parties around holidays or celebrations can help you get media coverage.

Company announcements. Anniversaries, company milestones, significant achievements, and other company announcements can be presented in creative ways so that they get featured prominently in the media.

Photographs. Having a library of stunning images can help you land additional media coverage.

Trivia. Some companies collect interesting trivia and unusual facts and use those to hook writers. An example of such trivia is that all the olives served on a transatlantic cruise stacked on top of each other would reach the height of a five-story building (this is not a fact; I made it up).

Other promotional publicity. For other promotional activities, which can also be used to generate publicity, see Chapter 8.

HOW TO DEAL WITH THE MEDIA

Although most of the media contact on your behalf will be handled by your agency, interacting with the press will be part of your responsibility. It pays to become media savvy and appear confident when dealing with them. Following are some media relations basics:

- Don't circumvent your agency. They work hard to build your reputation with the media; circumventing them will make you look unprofessional and them unhappy.
- Don't lie. Reporters have a keen eye for dishonesty or attempts to cover up.
- Be media trained. Take the time to learn how to answer questions. The most common mistake is trying to answer all questions literally.
- An interview is an exchange, not a one-way street. Don't be afraid to ask questions.
- Take the time to prepare before an interview or press conference and know who you are speaking to. Mumbling or rambling will make you appear unprofessional or incompetent.
- Don't stonewall. "No comment" is very much a comment, one that implies that there may be something you are trying to hide. Let the reporter hear whatever news is available from you instead of from a source beyond your control.

- Don't make remarks off the record. Everything is on the record. Media people are not your friends; it is their job to report news. If something should be off the record, keep it to yourself.

PR COUNTDOWN FOR NEW PRODUCT LAUNCHES

When hospitality operators decide to launch new products, one of the key marketing tasks is to announce this to the media and start generating awareness of the new product with a variety of audiences. Following is a timetable summarizing the key steps involved in a new product launch.

Planning stage During the planning stage, the marketing department should start meeting with the PR agency to plan the strategy for the product launch. This should be presented in the form of a preopening plan and should include budgets, media targets, messages, and materials.

6 to 9 months before launch

- Start developing a specific preopening action plan (audiences, opening event, press event, launch tactics, set dates, and schedule).
- Start developing materials (renderings, photography, press kit, brochure, releases, virtual reality videos, model, invitations).

4 to 6 months before launch

- Send the first release to the media.
- Send the first project update to key trade and industry audiences.
- Finalize preopening materials.
- Finalize architectural models, model rooms, cabins, and so on.

2 to 4 months before launch

- Send the second release to the media.
- Start mailing the invitations for the launch press event and grand opening.
- Send the second project update to key trade and industry audiences.
- Organize hard-hat tours.
- Start organizing familiarization trips.
- Start promotional mailings to targeted consumers and agents.

1 to 2 months before launch

- Send the third release to the media.
- Send a brochure along with the final project update to key trade and industry audiences.

- Confirm attendance for the press event.
- Continue promotional mailings to targeted consumers and agents.

1 month before launch

- Host the press event.
- Send a press kit to media personnel who couldn't attend the event.
- Confirm attendance for the grand opening.
- Organize preopening tours.
- Continue promotional mailings to targeted consumers and agents.

0 to 3 months after launch

- Host the grand opening.
- Continue sending releases to the media highlighting the product's features.
- Continue promotional mailings to targeted consumers and agents.
- Host trade familiarization trips (travel agents, meeting planners, partners, etc.).
- Update photography, videos, brochures, and press kits with finished product information.
- Start an ongoing public relations and marketing campaign.

THE PR PLAN

Developing an annual public relations plan is very important in setting realistic goals for your publicity efforts. This should be done in cooperation with your agency and should contain:

Situation overview: an executive summary of the company situation, public relations update, and challenges.

Publicity objectives: a defined set of objectives that you want your PR campaign to achieve. The objectives should be qualitative (generating awareness of the brand, educating consumers, etc.) as well as quantitative. There is nothing wrong in setting specific placement goals, such as landing 2 cover stories in the trade press and 20 feature stories in consumer media.

Target audiences: an extensive list of the different audiences you want to reach with the campaign. These may include general consumers, niche markets, the travel trade, the travel industry, investors, and so on.

Target media: a detailed list of target media outlets (publications, associations, organizations, and websites) for each target audience segment.

PR strategies: a comprehensive description of strategies that will be employed to achieve the stated goals in the various audience segments. Each target audience segment will need a dedicated strategy; for example, attracting investors requires a different approach from launching a new niche market product.

PR tactics: a list of the different tactics that will be employed to reach different audiences. Again, these need to be carefully evaluated and chosen for each audience segment.

Key messages: even though messages will be developed as the campaign progresses, each company usually has one or a few core messages that should be the leitmotif for all PR communications.

Action plan and schedule: a comprehensive action plan that lists all campaign details—what is to be done, when, and by whom.

MEASURING PR

Public relations is an accountant's nightmare: pouring thousands of dollars into various activities without *any* guarantees of success or results. Since publicity depends on someone else's interest in what you have to say, it is impossible to set exactly quantifiable measurements. However, there are several techniques that can be used for measuring PR results.

To start, media placements are recorded via clippings, which document the appearance of the product and company in the media. It is important to keep in mind that clippings are a monitoring device, not a measurement.

The second, and most common, measurement technique is media impressions. This is an estimate of the number of people who are exposed to your message. For print, this is estimated by multiplying the circulation figure of a given publication by the average pass-along rate of 2.5. The flaw of this measurement is that the pass-along rate is an industry-accepted average, not a scientifically proven number. Print media impressions provide a good estimate but are hardly exact. For broadcast media, the impressions are simply the audiences that watch or listen to a specific show (these are measured by one of the rating companies, such as Arbitron or Nielsen). Another PR measurement is the calculation of advertising equivalency. This calculation is based on evaluating every editorial appearance based on media, space, time, and position and calculating how much it would have cost to place an ad or commercial of equal space or time in the same media. This measurement is flawed because it equates the value of editorial coverage with the value of purchased advertising space. Yet editorial coverage often holds more value and credibility for audiences than paid media.

A qualitative measure is the evaluation of key message points. Basically, before a PR campaign, you define your key message point and then determine how many times it has been mentioned in published articles. This technique is more valuable than the previous two, as it measures the quality of the message as well as the quantity.

Another way to measure PR results is to track sales generated through specific actions. This is virtually impossible to do for an entire campaign, but it can be very valuable for individual releases or publicity actions. Let's say that you want to promote a specific offer at your hotel and want to measure the sales generated through PR efforts alone. You could send a press release with the specific offer and provide a unique reservation number that will be used only in the release. All calls and bookings generated through this number will be a direct result of this action.

Finally, you can conduct target audience research to measure the effects of the publicity efforts. These include pretest and posttest audience polling, day-after recall, consumer surveys, and focus groups.

The bottom line is that public relations efforts are measurable to a certain degree. If you're looking for precise numerical accountability for every editorial mention of your brand, you're out of luck. Nevertheless, scores of cases demonstrate and prove that PR works when done consistently. What really counts is to set realistic goals in the public relations plan before the start of a campaign and use them to measure the achieved results.

CRISIS COMMUNICATIONS

Even though this chapter is devoted to the marketing function of public relations, one area that should be mentioned is crisis communications. Hospitality is a safer publicity environment than other industries, yet there are potential crisis situations that will require an immediate response. These may include anything from safety and security issues to on-location accidents to natural disasters. Whether you are retaining the services of a PR agency or not, here are 10 key points for handling crisis situations:

1. Have a crisis plan in place before disaster strikes.
2. React immediately. Don't let rumors gain momentum.
3. Don't avoid the media in a crisis situation. If they don't get the information from you, they'll get it somewhere else.
4. Gather the facts. Try to respond with as many facts as are available.
5. Be honest. Admitting responsibility will not make you appear weak. Trying to shift the blame will make you appear as if you're trying to avoid responsibility.
6. Turn a negative into a positive. If your company made a mistake, admit it and then immediately focus on how it will remedy the situation.
7. Guide your responses by long-term perception objectives.
8. Demonstrate genuine care and compassion.
9. If you don't have an answer, say so and then look for it. Never say "no comment."
10. In a time of crisis, you are the company. Stick with the facts and don't offer personal opinions.

USEFUL LINKS

• bacons.com	Media monitoring and other services
• burelles.com	Media monitoring service
• businesswire.com	News distribution service
• ereleases.com	News distribution service
• iabc.com	International Association of Business Communicators (IABC)
• internetnewsbureau.com	Online press release service
• niri.org	National Investor Relations Institute (NIRI)
• online-pr.com	Online PR resource
• prandmarketing.com	Online PR magazine
• prsa.org	Public Relations Society of America (PRSA)
• prnewswire.com	News distribution service
• prweek.com	PR industry magazine
• webwire.com	Internet press release resource

CHAPTER EIGHT

Promotions

An idea that is not dangerous is unworthy of being called an idea.
—Oscar Wilde

PROMOTIONS VERSUS ADVERTISING

Promotions are deemed the nemesis of brands because they frequently focus on discounts and deplete media advertising budgets. It does not have to be this way. Although it is dangerous to eliminate media advertising at the expense of promotions, promotions can be very good marketing and even branding tools. The key lies in developing promotions that are integral parts of advertising campaigns, support the brand message, and deliver added values instead of relying on price discounts alone. The key differences between promotions and advertising are:

- Advertising is usually long-term-oriented and ongoing, while promotions have limited life spans and require immediate action.
- Advertising is designed to create an image and build brands (and sales) over time, while promotions are designed to produce immediate sales.
- Advertising communicates a message, while promotions communicate an incentive for action.
- Advertising is better suited for building brand positioning, differentiation, and image; promotions are better for product sampling, launches, and initial trial.

PROMOTIONS OR DEMOTIONS?

Like all marketing activities, promotions must be managed as part of the overall marketing and brand-planning process. They should not happen randomly (e.g., let's run a contest) or because the CEO is a sailing fanatic (e.g., let's sponsor

Not just for ads. Why not strengthen an attractive promotional offer with
unique imagery for the target audience?
Source: Bill Sumner. Used with permission.

a regatta). It is important to ask how the promotion will be integrated into the
overall marketing campaign and how it will impact the brand. Since promotions are perceived to be sales-oriented, they are often implemented as sales
projects instead of marketing projects. Yet they are such an integral part of the
marketing process (and budget!) that unless they are branded and generate
brand value, in addition to immediate sales results, they may be more detrimental than beneficial.

THE LIMITATION OF PROMOTIONS

There are certain limitations on what promotions may achieve. Following is a
list of what promotions can and cannot do.

Promotions Can:

- **Stimulate trial.** Since many promotional offers are designed to provide incentives for purchasing (consumer pull) or selling (wholesaler
and retailer push), they can be effective in stimulating the trial of a new
product or offer.

- **Generate sales.** Attractive discounts can help generate short-term sales.
- **Help motivate distribution partners.** Incentives to wholesalers, retailers, and other trade partners, as well as promotions that refer consumers to designated distribution contacts, can be excellent channel motivators.
- **Support the brand message.** Promotions that are strategically creative, brand relevant and unique, or tie into the advertising campaign can help support the intended message in the market.
- **Help increase the size of the order.** Promotions can be used effectively to move a client to a more expensive product or increase his or her purchase. Examples include a hotel offering added values to stimulate bookings of a higher room category or a business hotel offering attractive add-on weekend packages to weekday bookings.
- **Combat competitive offers.** Sales promotions can be very effective in neutralizing competitive offers in the market, especially for companies trying to protect their customer base (i.e., prevent switching).
- **Generate initial awareness of and traffic to a website.** Smart, unique, campaign-driven promotions can greatly enhance the launch of a campaign by generating awareness and prompting audiences to visit a designated website.

Promotions Can't:

- **Build a brand image.** A brand image is built through brand identity, advertising, and usage. Promotions can stimulate trial and increase usage but cannot communicate brand value or image.
- **Substitute for advertising.** While sales promotions can provide short-term purchase incentives, they cannot compensate for insufficient advertising support; it takes advertising to communicate benefits and values and build a brand image. Optimal results will be achieved through a balanced approach in which advertising and promotions are planned and executed together as part of the overall marketing strategy.
- **Sustain long-term sales growth.** Sales promotions, discounts, and special offers can be very effective for short-term sales spikes, but they cannot sustain sales over the long term. Continuous sales are generated through product quality, service, value perception, branding, brand loyalty, and ongoing marketing.
- **Build brand loyalty.** Loyalty is a relationship built over time and based on trust, comfort, value perceptions, and usage benefits. Promotions may build loyalty to discounts but not to the brand.
- **Make up for product deficiencies.** No amount of discounting or creative promoting can cover product flaws. In fact, promotions often help

accelerate the demise of flawed products, as the increased usage generated through promotional offers will expose more users to their flaws.

PLANNING PROMOTIONS

The success of promotions depends on proper planning and execution. To start the planning process, it is helpful to ask the following questions:

What is the objective of the promotion? Before implementing a promotion, start with the most important issue: what is its objective, that is, what outcome is sought? This may be increasing sales, launching a new program, stimulating trial, enticing past visitors, creating awareness, supporting the brand message, keeping the brand strongly in mind, building consumer lists, or generating traffic to a website.

How is the promotion relevant? Running a sweepstakes or contest to "just do something" is hardly a business-building strategy. The strategy behind a promotion is as important as the strategy behind an advertising campaign.

Does the promotion add value to the campaign and the brand? Promotions must be exciting to get noticed. They should be tied into your overall campaign and reinforce the key message. Good promotions will help maximize campaigns with sampling, events, merchandise, point-of-sale displays, and publicity.

Is the promotion simple enough? Elaborate promotions may sound good in the board room but seldom work in the marketplace. The most successful promotions are completely "packaged," and can be explained in a few sentences and understood by a widely varied audience.

Can the promotion involve the distribution partners? Some of the best promotions involve the strategic distribution partners, and some focus entirely on generating traffic to third-party retail outlets (e.g., travel agencies). If you have preferred retail partners, why not run a promotion to entice customers to visit the designated retail locations? For example, you could send a regional mailing with an added-value offer that is redeemable at one of your top-producing travel agencies. You'll make sure that the agencies are ready to take the reservations, that they will earn extra commissions or a booking bonus on those reservations, that every customer who calls with a promotional code or comes in with the mailing piece will receive a collateral piece, and that your displays are properly and prominently set up. This promotion will yield multiple benefits: incremental sales, reinforced commitment to your top producers (traffic and booking incentive), awareness, prominent display setup, and multiple points of contact for customers (mailing, display, collateral piece, and bookings).

Does it have longevity? Some companies run promotional campaigns on a monthly, quarterly, or seasonal basis year after year. These become events in themselves, and consumers grow to expect them. Even if you can run only one promotion a year, make it so unique and exciting that the market starts associating you with it over time.

Is the name or concept of the promotion too gimmicky or overused? A common mistake is to run promotions with overused concepts or gimmicky names (names that rhyme or use alliterations: March Madness, September Specials, December to Remember, Summer Sell-A-Thon, One-Two-Free). There is no need to use them, even if the concept is a regular summer sale. Invest time in developing a unique, ownable name or just use something as straightforward as "Summer Sale." Hey, it's still an alliteration.

Can it achieve multiple results? As mentioned earlier, some promotions may be executed in such a way that they achieve multiple results such as generate bookings, fortify the brand message, and create a mailing list. Look for opportunities to maximize promotions for multiple benefits.

Can the results be measured? One of the big advantages of promotions over advertising is that they can be measured more accurately and rapidly. Yet, after many promotions are executed, often nobody takes time to tabulate the results. Also, promotions that are aimed at the trade (e.g., booking incentives aimed at travel agents but run through wholesalers) are more difficult to track. Nevertheless, the extra effort of tracking results pays off handsomely. By analyzing success factors over time, you'll be able to see patterns and use that knowledge to improve future projects. Make sure that you plan for measurement from the beginning.

TYPES OF PROMOTIONS

Price Promotions

This is the simplest and most common form of sales promotion. Price promotions come in different packages, but the common expectation is that they will increase sales. The five basic price promotions are:

1. Limited-time price offers (e.g., book before this date and receive an extra discount)
2. Discount coupons (rate discounts redeemable through retailer, wholesaler, or direct bookings)
3. Sampling (e.g., Burger King's Free FryDay sampling promotion, which gave free french fries to over 15 million consumers; hotels, cruise lines, and other hospitality providers can provide certificates for free stays, food, or services to stimulate trial)
4. Refunds (cash returns after consumption with proof of purchase)
5. Bonus deals (e.g., reserve for 6 nights and get the seventh free)

There are several situations, such as stimulating trial, adjusting price levels to market conditions, or combating competitive offers, in which a strategic price reduction presented in the form of a promotion may be necessary and beneficial. However, price promotions that are too frequent will have adverse affects on your business and brand because you may be building loyalty to discount offers instead of to the brand. Keep in mind also that low prices may be attracting the wrong audience, one that will disappear as soon as the pricing returns to regular levels.

Conversely, nondiscounted pricing can be used as a positioning tool. For example, in certain situations, not discounting may actually be used to communicate the superiority of your brand. As mentioned earlier, pricing per se sends a very strong marketing message, and changing that message too often will damage the image of your brand.

In an age when commodities such as water and milk have strong brands and product features are hardly a differentiating factor, competing on price alone is a losing proposition. Occasional price promotions may be good to supplement sales and marketing efforts, but a heavy emphasis on discounting does nobody good.

Added-Value Promotions

Infinitely better than lowering price is adding value. While discounts say cheap, added values imply appreciation. These may be in the form of an extra service such as breakfast in bed, a gift certificate for the spa or a round of golf, small personalized gifts or free usage of some property services, free tickets to shows or events, and so on. The best added-value promotions are the ones that are relevant to the campaign and reinforce the positioning of the brand. For a romantic resort, a good added value would be a free romantic massage for couples; for a family cruise, free ice cream for children throughout the stay; for a luxury hotel, personalized stationary; for a business hotel, free laundry service. The idea is to offer something that is enticing enough but will not break the bank. And by adding value instead of discounting, the rate levels will be maintained so that the incremental costs of these items will be easily absorbed.

Contests and Sweepstakes

Contests and sweepstakes can generate tremendous consumer interest if they are exciting and offer attractive prizes. But while they certainly have the ability to create awareness, the question remains whether consumer contests and sweepstakes affect sales. It is therefore crucial to carefully plan them (concept, communication, execution, prizes) in such a way that they tie into the brand message and sales offer. Sweepstakes attract larger audiences (an estimated 5–10 times more) than contests; besides building awareness, they are excellent ways to build databases. Before embarking on a million-dollar sweepstakes, check with your legal counsel, as there are federal regulations that stipulate a variety of requirements.

Contests can be interesting promotional tools if they strategically tie into the brand or the campaign. For example, a good contest for a family resort can be a family vacation photo contest. Contests can create excellent opportunities for interaction with consumers. Or if a company runs advertising with a theme of fun vacations, a contest could involve searching for the most fun vacationers based on set parameters and organizing a final voting event with the final 10 contestants and a panel of observers. The event could be used for additional exposure through publicity. When I was working at a New York brand consulting firm, one of our clients was Boston Beer Company, which owns Samuel Adams beer and started the micro-brewing trend. One of their promotions, called Longshot, was a contest that invited home brewers to participate in a beer-brewing contest. The grand prize was that the winning beer would be commercially produced by Boston Beer and marketed under the Longshot brand name. The contest was a great success, and Boston Beer benefited in several ways: building awareness, generating a lot of publicity, and fortifying their core message of being beer-brewing experts.

Different from contests aimed at consumers, contests for the trade, such as travel agent or reservation agent booking contests, are based on actual sales results, leaving no doubts about their potential impact on sales. Trade contests, however, are not an easy substitute for marketing and agent education, as agents will make an effort to push a certain brand only if they feel comfortable selling it in the first place.

Consumer Promotions That Make Money

Hospitality companies have a unique opportunity to run promotions that generate awareness for their products, brands, or destinations and even charging for them. One such example is selling come-along packages for radio and television remote broadcasts. Here is how this works: in partnership with a radio or TV station, you organize a live remote broadcast with a local on-air personality to be hosted at your facility. This is usually done during the summer months or can be even organized around a popular holiday or event. In partnership with the station and other necessary suppliers (transportation company, etc.), you create a limited number of guest spots and invite consumers to come along and be part of the on-premise live audience. These come-along spots are sold during the course of the promotion to help offset the organizational cost or even to generate extra revenues. Other examples include tournaments, seminars, events, and contests.

Co-Branding

Co-branding is a good way of achieving several brand objectives. For one, it can help multiply your brand's exposure, thus increasing awareness of your brand while lowering marketing costs by pooling resources. But more important, for smaller brands, co-branding creates an opportunity to project a certain image and establish the brand in the market by aligning it with a strategic

Logical co-branding partners.
Source: Dorling Kindersley Media Library. Used with permission.

partner brand. Before embarking on a co-branding campaign, you have to ask several crucial questions: (1) does the partner brand project the right image? (2) does the partner brand have a good reputation? (3) is the partner brand a good strategic fit? and (4) what is the objective of this co-branding effort? As in any good partnership, there can't be just one winning party; each partner must contribute and receive according to its contribution.

A good example of a successful co-branded promotion (that also made money) was a project called Bacardi-Allegro Adventures. In 1998, to supplement the main vacation market, Allegro needed to develop niche products at several properties and position itself in several niche markets including windsurfing, scuba diving, and deep-sea fishing. We realized that it would be too costly to launch campaigns for several markets on our own, so we decided to look for strategic partners that could benefit from a unique promotion. One partner was World Publications, which publishes magazines in all the different target niche markets, as well as *Caribbean Travel and Life* and American Eagle's *Latitudes*. The second partner was Bacardi, which acted as the main sponsor. The promotion consisted of a series of week-long vacations specifically created for the different niche markets and hosted by the editors of the respective niche market publications. Advertising was placed in the niche publications, and readers could sign up (for a fee) to go fishing, windsurfing, or scuba diving

If you can't bring your audience to your location, take your promotion to your audience.
Source: Peter Arnold, Inc. Used with permission.

with their trusted editors, which was a special treat. Bacardi sponsored the advertising, and Allegro provided accommodations and operational logistics. The promotion was very well received and sold out rapidly. The fees charged helped offset the cost of the promotion, and each of the partners benefited: Allegro launched their niche products at a reduced cost, Bacardi maximized exposure in several key markets and destinations, and the different World Publications magazines made some money through the advertising and positioned themselves even more solidly as authorities in their fields.

Opportunities for great co-branding promotions are out there, from joint mailings and event sponsorships to co-branded credit cards. Discounting need not be the only approach. It just takes some time and dedication to come up with the right ideas.

On-Premise Promotions

Most hospitality products, including hotels, resorts, cruises, and even destinations, have an opportunity to organize promotions on premises. These include presentations, games, parties, performances, concerts, and raffles, and may be directed at existing guests or organized as events to entice new visitors. While on-premise promotions can be very successful, they take proper planning and execution. Unfortunately, they often lack a clearly defined marketing objective or are not perfectly coordinated and end up resembling weak entertainment efforts. Also important is to make sure that the promotion itself is sufficiently promoted.

For hospitality companies with multiple locations, each location should be used for cross-promotional efforts. Lobby displays, closed-circuit television, interactive kiosks, company brochures and directories, and destination publications, as well as certificates for return stays, are all ways to familiarize guests with the entire product portfolio.

Sponsorships

The advantage of sponsorships over other marketing actions is that they reward consumers with something of interest beyond the sponsor's commercial message: a concert, for instance, or a cultural, charitable, or athletic event. The commercial message, while undeniably present, remains implied. The intended commercial effect, along with mere brand presence, is the creation of a positive association with the sponsoring brand, the so-called halo effect. However, sponsorships are big business, and unless sponsoring a particular event fits with your corporate or brand strategy and you can measure the return on investment, it is probably wiser to avoid them. Randomly sponsoring events just to have your logo printed on the invitations is not a convincing reason to participate. On the other hand, well-chosen sponsorships can help put your brand on the map. When considering sponsorship, start by asking the following key questions:

1. What is the reason for sponsorship and what is the expected outcome? Is your company considering sponsoring the tennis tournament because it will create tremendous awareness for the brand and its tennis camps or because the GM is a tennis enthusiast?

2. Does the event or organization perfectly suit the corporate culture or brand strategy? A golf resort sponsoring a golf tournament is a good fit. A conservative business hotel sponsoring a heavy metal concert is not.

3. Is the event relevant and does it add prestige or esteem to your company? Some events may be a perfect fit and follow a fine marketing strategy, yet they are not exciting, recognized, or relevant to the public. Choose events or causes that will add extra value to the effort.

4. How many co-sponsors will be participating? If you're 1 of 30, how likely are consumers to pay attention to your brand?

5. How much time, effort, and money can be allocated to promoting the sponsorship? It is not enough just to become a sponsor. To take maximum advantage of your sponsor status, you have to market it vigorously.

6. How will you measure the return on your sponsorship investment? Sponsorships can yield various returns: the increased perception value by being associated with a prestigious event, the number of sales leads generated, the returns on using the venue for entertaining key clients, and the additional publicity.

Celebrity Endorsements

Using celebrities has been a much-debated marketing ploy. There seem to be more cons than pros, as consumers seem to have become indifferent to celebrity spokespersons. Especially for high-profile celebrities who endorse a variety of products, their credibility as endorsers seems to be low. And advertising research shows that consumers often remember the celebrity but not the advertised brand. Another problem is that if celebrities run into trouble, they end up tarnishing the image of the endorsed brand.

If you must do it, determine if a celebrity endorsement fits your overall strategy, and make sure that the celebrity of choice is relevant to your product category and believable as a user of your brand (how realistic is multi-million-dollar-income-a-year Kathy Lee Gifford as a $999 Carnival cruiser?).

There is one effective and believable way of using celebrities: have them use your product as real customers. If you have the appropriate product (hotel, cruise, restaurant, destination), extend complimentary invitations to celebrities and have their visit covered in a few choice media. It will be believable because the celebrities used the product. And even though their stay or visit was free, the consumer's perception will be that they were not paid for saying nice things about the brand. Best of all, this marketing approach will cost only a fraction of the cost of an endorsement contract.

Product Placements

Another way of getting additional exposure is by placing your product in magazines, catalogs, reports, and movies. On-premise catalog or magazine shoots will obviously be much easier to obtain than movie placements. Nevertheless, if your property has a beautiful beach, stunning architecture, landscaping, or any visually appealing setting and background, you may get lucky. With catalog and magazine shoots, you should receive credits in the publication in exchange for room and board for the crew. Some may even include a photograph with information about the location. For movie placements, unless you are just hosting the crew in exchange for a mention in the credits or you have the perfect property in the perfect location, you will normally have to negotiate a fee agreement.

Sampling

While sampling is a widely used promotional tactic for consumer products, hospitality companies can also use sampling as a promotional tool. Vouchers for free food and services, free nights, or tickets are all ways for hospitality companies to offer potential customers a chance to try their product before purchasing.

Trade Promotions

It has been reported that trade promotions consume approximately two-thirds of all promotional budgets. In hospitality and tourism, trade promotions include various promotions aimed at wholesalers (coop marketing, sales incentives, etc.) and retailers (booking contests and incentives). These are covered in Chapters 9 and 10.

USEFUL LINKS

- maaw.org   Marketing Agencies Association Worldwide (MAAW)
- pmalink.org   Promotion marketing association
- promomagazine.com   Promotion industry magazine

CHAPTER NINE

25 Proven Ways to Reach Travel Agents

Oh, I didn't know you have properties in the Dominican Republic. That's in Costa Rica, right?
—A travel agent at the 1996 World Travel Market, London

The Internet has changed the way travel is distributed. Whereas only a few years ago volume travel sales were generated by large traditional agency chains, nowadays new players such as Expedia and Travelocity are taking the lead. Nevertheless, while it may be true that some agencies are going out of business and many are trying to move from brick-and-mortar to click-and-mortar operations, large-volume sales for many hospitality products are still generated through travel agencies, regardless of the booking vehicle used. The Internet will perform a valuable service for the retail travel agent community: it will weed out the order takers and force the remaining agents to become true travel specialists and counselors. In order to fulfill these roles, agents will have to specialize and educate themselves profoundly on the products, destinations, and brands they are selling. They will achieve this by using the Internet as a learning and sales tool.

Agents get relevant travel information from a variety of sources. With the proliferation of hospitality and travel products and the inconsistent knowledge level among agents, one of the most important tools of marketing to this segment is and will remain educational marketing (see the quote at the beginning of the chapter). Whatever your overall marketing strategy for this segment is, you will not go wrong if you start with an educational effort because travel agents who are not knowledgeable about your product will not sell it. Brad Tolkin, former CEO of Travel Impressions, stresses this point: "There is nothing more powerful than a person confident about what they are selling. People sell products they know at the expense of better products they do not know, even if the products they do not know are a better fit for the customer."

Below, then, are 25 proven methods for reaching travel agents, starting with four essential educational tools.

FAMILIARIZATION TRIPS

Travel agents will not sell a product with which they are not familiar. Therefore, familiarization or "fam" trips are a staple in the quest for reaching and educating travel agents. Fam trips are an excellent marketing tool, as they allow the selling agents to actually experience the product and destination and establish a relationship with your brand firsthand. There is no activity that can produce immediate sales results as well as a perfectly executed fam trip. And "perfectly executed" means just that, as any glitches or mishaps will be happening right in front of a live audience.

The best fam trips have an activity program that starts with the welcome greeting and ends with the good-byes (and follow-up mailings). The secret lies in creating an activity schedule that will not appear as a military exercise but will cover all necessary elements with a light flow and an entertaining atmosphere. If you plan team activities, don't make them obligatory and always include enough time for agents to experience the product (hotel, resort, cruise, attraction, theme park, or destination) as if they were clients. They will appreciate it, and if they have a good time (which is up to you), they will surely recommend it to their clients. Also, make absolutely sure that all the food you serve is superb, and if your fam trips are hosted at your overseas locations, ensure that the hosts are fluent in the language of the participants. Finally, have outstanding information materials for all participants, either as handouts or as follow-up mailings.

A last word of caution: in travel, as in any industry, you'll encounter people who will want to take advantage of you. Therefore, make sure that you create a good preselection mechanism to weed out freeloaders. One way of doing this is by charging a participation fee and making it refundable from the first booking.

SALES TRAINING MANUALS

A well-developed and -presented sales manual is always a very helpful educational aid. Keep in mind that most sales manuals are just that—manuals, and rather boring. Take the opportunity to differentiate your brand by creating a sales manual that is interesting, creative, and unique. It will become an important branding tool, producing a marketing value well beyond its intended usage.

Keep this potential extra value in mind when developing the manual. It is very easy to develop a generic manual that provides basic information and ignores your branding. Beware of this mistake. A manual doesn't have to be presented in the usual form. You may present it in a form that is interactive and involving for the reader. Why not present it in the form of a board game, with a system of rewards for correct answers necessary to proceed? Think outside of the box and make it fun for the audience. It will repay your effort many times.

EDUCATIONAL SEMINARS

Educational seminars are a unique method of bringing the product, brand, or destination experience to a significant and captive audience. Breakfast or lunch seminars are popular and commonly accepted forms of presenting your message to travel agents. Organize the seminars at a time that doesn't coincide with the agent's busy time of day (i.e., early in the morning or during lunch hour), and make it convenient and easy to access.

Most travel agents have been to a variety of seminars, and they will get easily bored if you talk for 2 hours and show a few slides. Add some fun or excitement to your presentation. Make it interactive by involving the audience. Instead of just reading from a script, use the training manual you have developed to organize your presentation in the form of a game, ask questions, and reward the correct answer with a small prize. Use anything that is specific to your product—a special type of entertainment, an ownable piece of music, a signature spa treatment, or a unique food—and make it an integral part of your seminar. Also, try to bring a key person from operations, if possible, the GM. Travel agents will pay more attention to a message from an operations person than from someone in the sales department.

Research shows that people will have the most positive associations for messages delivered together with food. Aim to deliver the key points of your presentation during the food service period.

CERTIFICATION PROGRAMS

A travel agent certification program is the ultimate educational marketing tool: you are creating certified experts on your product and company. Certification programs basically consist of (a) the development of sales training manuals; (b) educational seminars or classes; and (c) a certification test packaged in the form of a branded certification program. As a financial incentive, offer participants who successfully complete your certification course incentive pay in the form of a higher commission level. Also, provide each successful participant with a framed certificate of completion. A prominently displayed certificate will serve as reinforcement to the certified agent and will communicate to customers that he or she is qualified and knowledgeable about your product.

With the availability of the Internet, you have the opportunity to offer certification programs on-line. If you don't have the time or staff to develop such a program yourself, travel agent publications such as *Travel Weekly* (twcrossroads.com), Travel Agent (travelagentcentral.com), and Recommend

(recommend.com) offer customized certification programs. For more information, visit the website of the Institute of Certified Travel Agents (icta.com).

FAXING

One of the quickest and most cost-effective marketing tools is the fax. Every travel agency has one or more fax machines, and they expect to receive a daily variety of offers via the fax. Unless your fax volume is extremely small, you'll need to get an outside supplier for transmitting your faxes. There are many good fax broadcast service companies. Request proposals from at least three and compare pricing, on-time delivery track records, and so on.

Do not send too many faxes, as they will be considered junk mail and end up in the trash. If you send an entirely different offer, you can send several each week, but do not send the same fax more than once a week. If you do not fax too often, agents will know that whenever you do fax, it is because you have something important to communicate. Also, make sure that your fax broadcast company has a way for agencies to unsubscribe; if you keep sending unwanted faxes, you are creating a negative image.

In terms of design, since faxes are such a simple medium, you are probably better off buying simple layout software such as Printshop and creating the faxes in-house. If you pay your advertising agency for each fax, you'll be paying through the nose. If you cannot do it in-house, one way to avoid repeatedly paying high design charges is to incur a one-time cost and have a variety of fax templates created. You can use them over time by overprinting the offer. Use the fax to reinforce the message and offers from your newspaper advertising.

Keep in mind that the fax is a black-and-white medium, so shades of gray, elaborate graphics, or very small print will not transmit well. The best faxes are simple and straightforward, focusing on one or two key elements (product/destination and price/special offer). Make sure that each of your faxes contains a different offer, not just the same offer packaged or worded in a slightly different way.

Finally, don't forget to use the fax to fortify your brand strategy by including your logo and tag line and/or by creating a signature ownable layout. Every point of contact is an opportunity to drive home that branding message.

DATABASE MARKETING AND DIRECT MAIL

Database marketing and mailings are very effective tools for reaching travel agents on a one-to-one basis. Travel agent database mailings may be divided into two main segments based on contact information: mailings to agents whose contact information you collect yourself and mailings to agents on rented mailing lists.

Let's start with your own list. As you collect travel agent contact information at trade shows, seminars, and fam trips, through collateral requests, and so on, start a database with this information. Make sure to also request the agent's home address or personal e-mail address, as travel agents often move or work from home. In a short period of time, you will have an excellent proprietary mailing list. Depending on the amount of information you collect, you can use the database for mailing anything from birthday cards to special offers or marketing materials. Simple, friendly follow-up mailings are a powerful and underused marketing tool. Remember, however, that if you are sending a birthday card or thank-you note, don't try to sneak in a sales pitch. Agents will appreciate a genuine gesture but will resent an underhanded sales attempt.

Besides including some personal information, enhance your database by creating travel agent profiles, which may include a history of the transaction, the type of product most often booked, the destination, and so on. This will give you a powerful source of information and a precisely targeted audience for future activities, from new product launches to agent surveys. Finally, make sure that you clean and update your list regularly, as travel agents are a mobile group and many agencies are going out of business or consolidating.

With regard to renting travel agent lists, a variety of mailing lists are available, such as the ASTA list (astanet.com) as well as others. The advantage is that when you subscribe to a yearly list service, they will do the cleaning and provide you with updates every few months. The disadvantage is that it is a general list, unlike your proprietary database. If your marketing budget allows, the optimal solution is to use both.

E-MAIL MARKETING

E-mail is a very convenient, fast, effective and—best of all—inexpensive marketing tool. For a detailed discussion of e-mail marketing, see Chapter 11.

TRADE SHOWS

Trade shows are a crucial part of your travel agent marketing activity. Working with wholesalers, you will be invited to participate in a series of seasonal trade shows, road shows, or product launches that are used to launch the new product line for each season. Granted, once you've done a few, they all start resembling one another. Nevertheless, if you use trade shows not just to launch the new season but also to bring your brand experience to the travel agents, they will be an excellent marketing tool.

First, participate only in the trade shows that are appropriate for your product and attract a targeted audience. General shows may attract agents who specialize in business travel, while you may need to promote vacation packages to Europe. Choose carefully, as trade shows may turn into prohibitively costly venues where you hand out brochures to relatively small audiences.

Second, be sure to design the booth and display as part of the overall brand identity. It is surprising how many companies use displays that say nothing about their brand, product, or origin or do not resemble in the slightest the rest of their materials and visual identity.

Third, always try to get a high-traffic location. If you can't, create activities that will draw people to your booth. One of the best ways to attract agents is to serve food. You can also give away free gifts, play music, and organize games, contests, or raffles. One year at the World Travel Market in London, we hired a Michael Jackson look-alike and spread the word that he would be performing and signing autographs at our booth. It created a major buzz, and the traffic was immense. The key is to generate traffic, and it all depends on your creativity.

Fourth, have the visitor experience your brand right there and then. If you represent a destination, create a virtual tour or organize lectures with a famous local resident. If you operate a spa, offer free massages. If you operate a business hotel, offer free messaging service at your booth for all trade show attendants.

Fifth, properly train the staff attending your booth. It is imperative that they are knowledgeable, friendly, and always smiling, that the booth is never left unattended, and that there are plenty of materials.

Sixth, have innovative giveaways. Pens and key chains are standard, expected, and boring. Differentiate yourself by putting your logo on items related to your product or by distributing them in an innovative way. When we launched Allegro Essentials, the all-inclusive package that included resort wear, our giveaway items were logo T-shirts. Every hour on the hour, we had a mini-fashion show to present the package's clothing. And immediately following the show, we blasted our theme song for 5 minutes and threw the T-shirts into the crowd. The giveaway item was fairly common, but the way we handed it out was different. Do not, however, give anything away without getting information on the agent in return.

SALES REPRESENTATIVES

If your budget allows it, sales reps are a good investment. They become your company's face to the retail travel agent community, and they provide a good local contact for the agents. You can contract either full-time reps, shared reps, or multiline reps.

The advantages of employing full-time reps are evident. They are devoted exclusively to promoting your product and brand. They are perceived as steady employees of the company. With sufficient time, training, and effort, full-time reps will become experts on your product and assets in your marketing arsenal. On a daily basis, their work will consist of visiting travel agencies, pushing the product, providing information and updates, handling complaints, and maintaining a personal relationship with the agencies. Sales reps will be of great value when you need a special push for a certain product, such as a product launch or a sales blitz. Before you employ full-time reps, you must create guidelines, procedures, and training for conduct and presentation, as well as controls for tracking travel agent visits. The only disadvantage of a full-time rep is the cost.

An alternative is to split the cost of a full-time rep with a noncompeting travel company. This will reduce the cost by 50% and still allow you to train the rep extensively.

The third option is to hire multiliners. These are reps who handle various product lines, and their advantage lies in their lower cost. The challenge is to make sure that enough of the multiliner's energy and time are devoted to you, both in acquiring knowledge about your product and in delivering your message.

Whether hiring full-time, shared-time or multiline reps, you want to buy the rep's existing recognition in the marketplace, so look for reps who have been around for a significant period of time and have built a great reputation in the local retail community. Always check references and ask for referrals. Keep in mind, however, that experienced and well-recognized reps know their value, and hiring them may be quite costly.

Finally, it is most important to have a mechanism that will allow you to track and measure production per travel agency. Only in this way will you be able to assess the effectiveness of your reps per assigned territory.

SALES BLITZES

Sales blitzes are basically a large number of quick, precise travel agency visits and can be an excellent tactical tool for reaching a large yet targeted audience in a short period of time. They can be used to push the sales for a particular product, create awareness for a new program, introduce a new product or destination, promote a new service, introduce a special offer, or distribute a new piece of collateral. Depending on the geographic location, one person should be able to complete up to 10 quality agency visits per day.

Even though you may not have sales reps or enough regular sales or marketing staff, blitzes can be organized by using operations staff for a few days to blitz a strategic area. If you do this, keep in mind that operations staff is not trained in sales. It is advisable to invest the time and energy to prepare a sales-blitz manual and to train everyone on the objective, strategy, and basic sales and presentation skills necessary for this action. The last thing you want is to have a sales blitz fail due to the poor presentation skills of the staff.

It is crucially important to have a "blitz master," someone who will plan and orchestrate the whole campaign, from defining the agency locations and preparing the routes to organizing all the necessary materials. The optimal blitz is focused on a single message, such as the launch/opening of a new property, location, or brand. If you have more than one offer to promote, however, limit your blitz to two or three offers. If you try to push more than that number, no single message will be received completely and you will end up with a lot of confused agents.

To make your blitzing more effective, consider the following techniques: Sponsor a meal for the entire agency. This forces agents to take a break for a few minutes and pay attention to your message. Or show up at the end of a work day and offer to take the staff out for drinks. The best companies invest time in getting to know their customers, and both of these techniques are effective ways of creating relationships and getting the agents' undivided attention.

BOOKING BONUSES AND INCENTIVES

In this time of commission cuts and caps, any extra cash is highly appreciated by the travel agent, so booking bonuses, incentives, and booking contests can be a good way of enticing agents to sell your product. They can also work very well with noncash rewards. If you have an attractive product, a free stay will be a sought-after reward.

Booking bonuses are usually cash rewards for each booking a travel agent makes. They are a good way of pushing sales without reducing the price to the public. The bonus, which usually ranges from $10 to $50 per booking, can be worked into the package price from the beginning and discounted with the commission so that it will not affect your average daily rate. If you make the benefit nonmonetary, you can state that for each cruise of 5 nights or longer, the agent receives 1 free night at your establishment. You can also barter with local merchants, gas stations, or movie theaters for free product and award it (merchandise, movie tickets, gas cards, etc.) as booking bonuses.

Incentives are slightly different from booking bonuses, as they may be monetary or nonmonetary awards and are given only after a certain preestablished number of bookings have been completed. Again, you can use your product (free tickets, vacation nights, meals) instead of cash as the incentive or you can offer tangible goods such as television sets, VCRs, or household products.

Whether you use bonuses or incentives, don't reward just any booking; use them strategically. Reward the sale of more profitable products, such as higher room categories or packages, or bookings for periods that are more difficult to sell, such as the low season.

BOOKING CONTESTS

Unlike bonuses and incentives, which reward either every reservation or a preestablished number of reservations, booking contests reward the agent or agents who book the largest number of a designated product during a limited period of time. When you organize booking contests, always set a minimum to qualify the winner, because if nobody makes a booking except for one agent who makes a single booking, that agent will win. If you set a minimum, you will avoid having to award a prize if the desired number of bookings has not been attained. A realistic calculation is to estimate the cost of the award in the range of 5–10% of the projected sales.

Regardless of which incentive approach you use, make sure to check all legal and financial implications, specify time and participation limitations, and have a tracking mechanism in place before starting the program. Also, keep in mind that travel agents are bombarded with similar programs, so create programs that are simple to promote, simple to implement, and simple to account for. Some extremely attractive and rewarding programs fail simply because they are too complex for the travel agents to track and claim. If you need more than one sentence to explain the program, it is too complicated.

Finally, don't expect miracles from any of these sales aids. If you have not done your marketing job properly, educated the agents, and familiarized them with your brand and product, no booking bonus or incentive will be able to save your production. On the other hand, if you present your booking bonuses, incentives, or contests as part of your training seminars, the response rate will be significantly higher.

GDS PROMOTIONS

Global distribution systems (GDSs) are reservations networks that give travel agents direct access to specific hotel chains, as well as airline and car rental companies. Their purpose is to allow travel agents to book complete travel packages or itineraries all at once. The main GDSs are Sabre, Apollo/Galileo, Worldspan, and Amadeus. They all offer a variety of marketing opportunities for suppliers. Most of them provide sign-in messages and a variety of promotional messages.

Log-on messages, as their name indicates, are messages you can post that the travel agents will see when they log on to a particular GDS. They may be used as a good tactical tool to announce special new pricing or products and to tell the agent where to find more detailed information.

Promotional messages are basically electronic messages posted within certain areas of the system. For example, if a New York–based agent is researching flights to Las Vegas, on the page listing the available flights, your promotion of your Las Vegas hotel could be displayed in the form of a promotional message.

The great thing about GDS promotions is that you can target specific travel agencies in terms of date, geographic segmentation, and booking patterns. In addition to these electronic promotions, all GDSs provide an array of promotional opportunities through their custom publications, newsletters, and training seminars. Research the available opportunities and incorporate them in your marketing plan.

Keep in mind, however, that agents are becoming less dependent on these systems as airlines are distributing products directly on their own websites, so evaluate the cost–benefit ratio carefully.

POINT-OF-SALE DISPLAYS

While point-of-sale displays are not primarily designed to reach travel agents, they can be surprisingly useful in creating a strong brand support environment inside the travel agency. Great displays will stop passers-by and draw their attention to a particular destination or brand. With a well-designed and -presented display system, most agency managers should not object to your setting up a branded display. Create displays that the agency manager will want to display, such as ones with a store calendar or clock or seasonal displays. Don't be surprised, though, if the manager or owner asks you to pay a fee for the floor space of your display. Agencies are strapped for income and are becoming savvier in generating extra revenues.

What makes for a good point-of-sale display? Even the simplest displays can be very effective if they are nicely designed and produced. Clean, bold letters and graphics combined with good production quality will make displays communicate rapidly. Displays will be even more effective if they have an interactive feature. From a simple brochure holder to an elaborate touch-screen display, interactivity is a great branding device. The best point-of-sale displays will communicate the nature of your product and help establish a connection with your brand through design and interactivity. For a golf resort, the display could consist of a golf simulator and panoramic shots of the golf course. The handout could be a brochure containing all necessary information on the resort and course, as well as an interactive CD that includes a golf game played on the course. Compare this with the standard rack brochure prepared by a golf resort.

TRAVEL TRADE ADVERTISING

Advertising in the travel trade publications is a valuable tool for maintaining your presence among travel agents across the nation. The key to advertising in the travel trades is consistency, continuity, and differentiation. Use your advertising to position your specific offer and sales message, as well as to keep driving home that brand message. Beware of the sameness trap: generic photograph (e.g., a couple on a beach for a beach resort), generic headline (e.g., "We Offer Great Accommodations"), and generic copy (e.g., "Stay with us because we . . ."). Avoid this or risk wasting your media dollars. Differentiate yourself. Take some risks and make statements that will make an impact. Use photography and artwork that will stand out. Allow your ad agency to think outside of the box and be truly creative (without forgetting to deliver that branding message). What should you do if your product is not outstanding and you have nothing to differentiate your brand? Come up with creative ways of positioning yourself in the mind of the agent: offer creative commissions, develop added-value gifts for your guests—the opportunities are limitless. Use the trade publications to educate the agents on your product, provide specific information, and do it in an exciting way. With regard to frequency of advertising, if you don't have the budget to run a continuous campaign, it makes little sense to advertise in the trade publications at all; a few small ads here and there will not have a significant impact.

The travel trade publications are listed in Table 5-2. Other media for travel agents include directories such as the *Official Hotel Guide* and the *Hotel & Travel Index* (see Table 5-2) as well as consortia guides. Keep in mind, however, that travel agents also frequently use other publications for travel and product information. These include a variety of wholesale brochures, cruise directories, destination directories, travel guides such as the Michelin guides, the OAG Business Travel Planner, or one of many online information services. It pays to research what your agents use for reference and increase your presence in those publications.

TRAVEL TRADE PUBLICITY

Travel trade publicity is a good and inexpensive way of establishing a presence and communicating news and information to travel agents and the travel trade community. The best way of getting maximum exposure is by developing strong personal relationships with the trade publication editors who cover your segment (you, your PR agency, or both) by supplying them consistently with valuable news, updates, and information on your company, brand, products, destinations, educational programs, commission structures, and so on.

There are many ways to generate publicity. One strategy may be to create a travel agent recognition program. A recognition program is designed to track measurable performance according to preset parameters (anything from top producers to charity work). The important point is to create a rewarding environment and then periodically recognize the agents for their performance or contribution. The purpose of this program is to establish a relevant and consistent stream of information about your brand or company by associating with agents. The publicity will help you establish goodwill in the agent community.

NEWSLETTERS

Publishing a regular newsletter for travel agents can be a valuable communications tool. It gives you an opportunity to provide agents with updates and news, as well as trivia on your company and product line. In terms of frequency, a quarterly or bimonthly mailing seems about right. More frequent mailings may be too costly and probably won't have sufficient meaningful information and real news.

Also, consider sending digital newsletters via e-mail. The major advantages are low cost and flexibility. Do not, however, send them too frequently because the method is inexpensive. The newsletters will become junk mail.

AGENT LOYALTY PROGRAMS

For a detailed discussion of loyalty programs see Chapter 12.

TRAVEL AGENT CLUBS

A travel agent club is not a loyalty program but rather an affinity club organized to serve agents with a variety of benefits. The basic purposes of a travel agent club are to build a dedicated database, develop a platform for personalized communications with agent members, and thus create a stronger bond between them and your brand and organization. Your company must have a certain size for a formal travel agent club to make sense. But even if you are a small supplier, you can employ certain elements of a club and use them to differentiate your brand. The benefits for travel agents who join your club should be special member services such as:

- A travel agent hotline. By providing a dedicated travel agent hotline for club members, you are sending the message that they are special. They know that they will have instant access to information on your product and the status of their reservations, commission payments, updates, and so on.
- Member travel benefits.
- A special club member check-in area.
- Exclusive member fam trips and educational seminars.
- A members-only section on your website.

These and other special services will let agents know that you care for them and that they are valuable to you. Nevertheless, offering all these services will require a large commitment on the part of your company. So before you launch a club, make sure that you have buy-in from all departments and that all logistical issues have been ironed out.

Lastly, since you will have no way of measuring production as closely as with a loyalty program that tracks each booking, try to create a system to avoid freeloaders. One way to do this is to charge a nominal annual membership fee that will be refundable from the first booking of the current year. This way you'll make sure that only agents who know they'll produce will sign up. And members who produce are members who should have an interest in belonging to your affinity club.

TRAVEL AGENT EVENTS

Unlike educational seminars and presentations, travel agent events are more loosely organized, with the sole purpose of entertaining them and thanking them for their business and support. These events can be organized relatively inexpensively and can yield excellent results.

Some companies organize thank-you events for agents in their key markets on a seasonal basis and create a theme for each event, either around a destination (e.g., a Mexican fiesta, Caribbean party, or Hawaiian luau) or around activities. They bring staff from the actual locations and involve the agents in enjoyable games and activities. This not only helps agents to interact with the staff and have fun, but also brings the product experience to them.

Before you invest significant resources in organizing multiple events, make sure that you are inviting the biggest actual and potential producers.

SALES SUPPORT MATERIALS AND COLLATERAL

Besides making sure that your agencies are always stocked with current collateral materials, having branded support materials that the agents can give or send to their clients will always be welcome. For example, you can create a series of branded sales materials such as postcards, chocolates, candy, guides, and maps that the agents can distribute. These will help them support their sales efforts and reduce costs, and you'll have an army of ambassadors distributing materials containing your logo.

PREMIUMS AND GIVEAWAYS

Distributing premiums and giveaways to travel agents is a tried-and-true branding tool. These items are a sign of appreciation and will often be welcomed. The challenge is to create giveaways that are creative, meaningful, and communicate something about your brand. For standard purposes, nice logo pens, key chains, mugs, calendars, T-shirts, and letter openers are fine. However, they are rather boring. Differentiate yourself by putting your logo on items related to your product or use the premiums to create a promotion. You could, for example, distribute logo caps to agents and launch a mystery shopper campaign where agents who are discovered wearing the cap win a prize.

DEDICATED TRAVEL AGENT WEBSITE AND HOT LINE

Creating a dedicated travel agent website or an area within your existing website gives you the opportunity to establish one-to-one communications with your travel agents. This dedicated agent area may contain special destination information, travel agent specials, incentives and contests, updates on fam trips, a calendar of events, interactive sales manuals, an online learning center, educational seminars (webinars), and travel tools such as currency converters. It will give you an opportunity to create a proprietary database of interested travel agents that you can use to send updates on special offers, new products, or periodic newsletters.

If you are doing a lot of direct business, a dedicated hot line for travel agents may be an extremely helpful branding tool. It will convey the message that they are special and that they have a dedicated line for handling issues such as commission payments or agent vacation reservations.

AGENCY DECORATIONS

Another way of showing your appreciation is to sponsor office decorations for the travel agency. These may be short-term, such as flowers, or long-term in the form of plants, furniture, or artwork such as posters, prints, or maps. The airlines have done a nice job of creating destination posters (with rather subdued brand insignia) that many agencies are happy to display. Agency window decorations are particularly good, as they serve a dual audience: the agents and the passers-by. Remember to make it branded or brand related, but without being overly promotional.

TRAVEL AGENT PANELS AND ADVISORY BOARDS

Travel agent panels and advisory boards are organized for the purpose of establishing a forum that may help deal with a variety of travel trade–related issues such as regulations, travel trends, product development, industry reviews, strategic planning, and corporate communications. While your company may need to be of a certain size to establish an agent panel of your own, there are a variety of independently organized panels in which you can participate. Panels are a great way of keeping abreast of the industry and networking, as well as showing industry commitment.

FINAL COMMENT

Treat your travel agents as partners and pay their commissions on time—or, better yet, early. This will pay off handsomely. Use the commission payments to drive your brand positioning. Don't just send a check; send it in an amusing branded package or a money holder with a thank-you note. You will be surprised how details like these can create goodwill. Remember, you are your brand's evangelist, so use every point of contact with your agents to evangelize.

USEFUL LINKS

- astanet.com — American Society of Travel Agents (ASTA)
- iatan.org — International Airlines Travel Agent Network
- icta.com — Institute of Certified Travel Agents (ICTA)
- nacta.com — National Association of Commissioned Travel Agents (NACTA)
- pata.org — Pacific Asia Travel Association (PATA)

CHAPTER TEN

Coop Marketing: How to Get the Best Results from Marketing Through Wholesalers and Tour Operators

It is hard to catch large fish in small waters.
—Latin Proverb

As in other industries, many leisure hospitality and travel suppliers distribute product in volume through wholesalers. This works as a follows: a wholesaler or tour operator contracts the individual vacation product elements with a variety of suppliers: air seats with airlines, transfers with ground handlers, accommodations with hotels and resorts. These elements are packaged and sold through travel agents to the public. The product is displayed in the wholesaler's annual (or seasonal) brochure, which is distributed to a multitude of travel agencies. The travel agencies use the brochures to showcase available products to their clients, the end consumers. In addition to the brochure, the product is marketed through a multitude of marketing activities.

The main distinction between wholesalers and tour operators is that wholesalers work mostly with scheduled airline contracts (and seat inventory), while tour operators fly their own charters. Thus wholesalers have no risk and tour operators have full risk on the seats of the planes they use to package their offers. This is not a clear distinction, though, as wholesalers may operate charter flights and tour operators also have scheduled airline contracts. For the sake of simplicity, the terms "wholesaler," "tour operator," "operator," and "account" are used interchangeably.

Since travel is a product that generally consists of several components (transportation, accommodations, ground transfer), in leisure travel the operators control the distribution. They sell what they consider is appropriate and accepted in the marketplace based on their experience, which is usually good. And while many travel suppliers complain about the wholesalers' distribution control, they fail to realize that their presence can also be a blessing, particularly for smaller suppliers. How? Because no other industry allows a small regional product to be present along with the big brands. How much money would it take to gain distribution for, say, a new can of soup? Millions of dollars. But a 100-room hotel with a good product, good service, and some marketing can achieve nationwide U.S. distribution from one season to another, thanks to travel wholesalers. The answer lies not in bypassing distributors, but rather in generating such strong demand through product quality, marketing, and branding that they will have no choice but to push your brand through their network. Yes, the answer once again lies in branding.

This said, it must be noted that for some hospitality companies, up to 100% of sales may be generated through wholesalers and tour operators, so marketing through them (coop marketing) becomes a crucially important, if not the most significant, marketing activity. This chapter examines the main coop marketing issues, as well as ways of maximizing coop marketing for the purpose of brand building.

WHAT IS COOP MARKETING?

Marketing with or through partners is called "coop" (for cooperative) marketing. And while this chapter focuses on coop marketing with wholesalers and tour operators, many of the activities and concepts described are applicable to coop marketing with other strategic partners, which may include transportation providers, local attractions, entertainment venues, destination marketing organizations, or convention and visitors bureaus.

In coop marketing, you are basically using the wholesaler's marketing infrastructure and distribution, as well as knowledge and experience, to sell and market your product. Coop marketing may be as simple as distributing a flier or as complex as developing a variety of annual marketing plans that include media schedules, training seminars, use of sales reps, and so on.

Regardless of the extent of your activity, coop marketing is an excellent way to sell your product and promote your brand in a variety of markets. Savvy marketers use it not just to sell (i.e., advertise the product and price), but also to reinforce their image and consistently drive home their branding message.

THE COOP MARKETING BUDGET

The extent of your coop marketing plan with any operator will depend on the available coop budget. The industry average for a coop budget is 3–6% of sales per operator. The five key factors determining your coop marketing budget with a given operator should be:

1. The operator's annual production
2. The operator's market potential
3. Your profit margins with the operator
4. Your relationship with the operator
5. Your overall marketing budget

You can also use the coop budget as a strategic sales tool by tying the amount of coop support you are willing to allocate into an escalating sales incentive structure. For example, if a certain wholesaler traditionally sells 1 million of your product a year and you think that they can sell twice as many, you could create the following incentive: for all sales up to $1 million, the coop budget is a standard 3%; for sales between $1 million and $1.5 million the budget grows to 4%; and for sales between $1.5 million and $2 million it increase to 5%. For any sales over $2 million, you could increase the coop budget to 6%.

HOW TO PAY FOR COOP MARKETING

You have three basic methods to pay for coop marketing: (1) cash, (2) invoice deduction, and (3) barter credit (also know as "trade credit"). Let's analyze all three briefly.

1. **Cash** Paying cash is the straight and simple method. You create the coop marketing plan, approve a coop budget figure, are billed for it, and pay. The advantage is that you have a clean, simple accounting procedure with minimal room for errors. The disadvantage is that you're paying cash for something that could be handled differently.

2. **Invoice deduction** With this method, you're still paying cash, but you are linking the marketing investment to actual sales production. This is how it works: you estimate, for example, that next year's sales for a particulart operator will be $1 million. You agree to a 3.5% coop marketing plan based on invoice deductions. Thus, you estimate a total marketing investment of $35,000. Then the operator deducts this coop participation from the invoice payment. It's fairly simple.

   Yet, you have to consider the following issues: (a) Base the agreement on a percentage and prorate the deductions throughout the coop period to make sure that the percentage is applicable per invoice or time period. Otherwise, the operator may deduct a lump sum from their first payment. (b) Consider if you want to cap the coop budget at the estimated figure—$35,000 in our example. Alternatively, do you want the operator to apply the 3.5% deduction even if production exceeds the estimated sales level? Perhaps you want to create an incentive system that grants the operator a higher deduction percentage once they surpass the estimated sales—by increasing the coop deduction to 4.5% on all sales over the estimated $1 million. (c) Conversely, make sure to discuss what will happen if the estimated sales level is not reached. Let's say that annual sales reach only $700,000; thus, a 3.5% coop deduction would equal only $24,500, yet the operator spent the full $35,000. Who is responsible for the $9,500 difference? You, the operator, or both in equal proportions? Define these issues beforehand.

3. **Barter** Barter credit is financially the most advantageous way of paying for coop marketing. Why? Because you are not paying with cash, but with empty rooms, cabins, tickets, or whatever your product may be. You are bartering. Let's illustrate by using a hotel example: you operate a luxury hotel, and each year the wholesaler Happy-Go-Lucky Tours sells 16,000 of your hotel rooms at an average daily room rate of $125, for a total of $2 million in sales. Since they are a preferred partner, you have a 5% coop agreement. This means that their annual coop budget equals $100,000. However, instead of paying cash, you have agreed to pay them with $100,000 worth of free rooms. At an average daily room rate of $125, Happy-Go-Lucky will be able to sell 16,800 rooms and will not have to pay for 800 of them, thus collecting their full $100,000 coop budget (800 rooms × $125 = $100,000), while you collect your total of $2 million in sales. Your advantage is that you will receive your coop budget value based on the rate contracted with the operator. Internally, however, you will account for these rooms at a lower operational room cost.

The disadvantage is that your accounting becomes more complicated. You will have to create a procedure for your accounting department to work with the operator's to make sure that all rooms that need to be paid are paid and all rooms that are free are not invoiced for payment.

It is recommended that you allocate the free rooms from February through November (vs. January through December) so that you have 1 month at the beginning and end of each fiscal year for budgetary adjustments. This would give you 10 months to prorate the free rooms monthly. In our example, this would equal 80 free rooms per month. Also, remember to include blackout periods so that you can maximize revenues during peak seasons and holidays.

Is barter more complicated than paying cash? Definitely, but considering the cost advantage of this approach, especially when multiplied by a multitude of operators, the extra accounting effort becomes well worth it.

IF THIS IS COOPERATION, WHAT'S THE OPERATOR'S CONTRIBUTION?

Another issue is how much the operator will contribute. Coop marketing, in its purest form, means that all coop partners allocate matching funds; in other words, two coop partners would contribute 50% each, three partners 33.34% each, and so on. In reality, however, the "matching" budgets vary by wholesaler. Some contribute and others let you pay for the whole thing. Exactly how much you will be able to negotiate depends on your relationship, their size, and production volumes as well as politics. You should never give up without trying, though. Often the operator may not be able (or willing) to contribute a cash budget, but they may contribute in the form of activities such as offering you free on-hold messages, free sponsorships of consumer events, travel agent seminars, booths at trade shows, or arranging dedicated presentations that will help you get your company's name out.

BUDGET ALLOCATIONS: HOW TO SLICE IT

Now that you have a merry little budget (with or without the operator's contribution), it's time to slice it and dice it. How much should you allocate for each activity to achieve optimal results? There is no set formula, but an acceptable general guideline is to allocate a larger portion (30–50%) of the overall coop budget for newspaper advertising and use the remainder to cover brochure participation, trade shows, travel agent faxing, direct mail and collateral distribution, Internet marketing, and promotions. Finally, leave 10% for miscellaneous activities such as fam trips, booking incentives, and contingencies. Some operators offer coop advertising in the trade publications, but you're better off doing that on your own. Obviously, this is a very general guideline. You should analyze each operator's marketing strengths and allocate funds according to your overall marketing strategy and the operator's market realities.

CAUTION: OBJECTS IN PROPOSAL MAY APPEAR LARGER THAN THEY ARE

Operators operate on slim margins, and some may try to use the coop as a supplemental source of revenue. Costs such as those for printing, media contact, and creative work are easily inflated, and you may be contributing to the operator's bottom line without knowing it. Some operators even base part of their employees' bonus on how much coop funding they can obtain. A fair markup to cover handling, time, personnel, or out-of-pocket expenses is fine, but keeping an unprofitable operator afloat through excessive coop costs is not. So be careful. Ask for a commitment to be billed at cost, require preapprovals on printing bids, ask to see their media contracts, and get media rates yourself. You will probably not get all (or any) of these requests, but you'll be able to benchmark at least part of the market cost and make the operator aware that you're keeping a close watch. Remember, it is your budget, and it is your job to get the most bang for your buck. On the other hand, don't nickel and dime each operator to death. Focus on obtaining optimum production from each operator, not on trivial budget issues.

THE KEY ELEMENTS OF A COOP MARKETING PLAN

Now that we have discussed the basics of coop budgeting, we arrive at the fun part: the coop marketing plan. The key elements of this plan are listed and briefly described below.

Brochure Participation

The brochure is a staple in wholesalers' marketing plans and the way they seasonally display their product line(s). The bigger the wholesaler, the larger the brochure and the greater the number of brochures produced. Small wholesalers may produce a single annual brochure, while large ones may create over a dozen brochures each year or season. The theme of these brochures may be a region such as the Caribbean, Las Vegas, Florida, Hawaii, or Europe; the type of product, such as all-inclusive resorts, city vacations, or beach vacations; or a market niche such as honeymoons, family travel, golf, or skiing.

The key parts of the operator brochure are the product section, where the contracted properties are depicted and described; the advertising section, which contains brand advertising; and the pricing section.

To offset the cost of creation, production and distribution, wholesalers will charge you to display your product in their brochure. Brochure participation may be as simple as a property description and a small property picture placed in the product section of the brochure or as extensive as a multipage ad insertion. If you place brand advertising, the product description and display will usually be included free of charge.

Nowadays, some hotel and resort companies place large inserts of 5–15 pages in the advertising section. This is a rather questionable practice, driven more by politics than by the return on investment. The brochure ads should provide supplemental factual information that could not be included in the product description section, presented in a branded single-page ad or double spread. As with all media placements, the same general rules apply. Try to get premium positioning, such as a back or inside cover or the beginning of your destination section. Always keep in mind your brand's positioning. Do you have a strong presence in a certain destination? Try to negotiate an official sponsorship of that section. Don't just settle for what the operators offer. There are always creative ways of getting extra mileage out of your brochure participation.

Finally, perform the standard media-buying measurements for brochure advertising, just as you would for any other media buy, since the value of tour operator brochures is changing with the declining number of retail travel agencies, which are the main recipients of these brochures.

Product Launches

Every season, once the contracting period is over, operators present (launch) their product lines in a series of trade shows or road shows. Most of them will invite you to participate with a booth and display your product. These trade shows are a great opportunity to showcase what you have to offer, interact and network with travel agents, receive feedback, and fortify your brand message. (See also the section on trade shows in the previous chapter.)

Since you'll probably be working with many operators, avoid being bombarded with individual show participation requests by getting all of their product launch schedules beforehand and including them in your overall coop plan and trade show schedule. This way, you'll be able to plan costs, materials, and staff travel to the events. Signing up for participation early will also allow you to pick better locations for your booth and may help you minimize costs, as many operators offer an early sign-up discount.

Newspaper Advertising

Newspaper advertising is the way wholesalers promote travel offers to the public on a weekly basis. Newspaper advertising in the Sunday travel section is one of the most important elements of any coop marketing plan. Most wholesalers place corporate "menu" advertisements, either themselves or through their retail travel agency chains, in key gateway and feeder markets. They pass on the media cost to their coop marketing partners in exchange for their presence in these ads.

Before allocating a large portion of your coop budget to newspaper advertising, evaluate the operator's newspaper presence and strategy. Do they have a permanent location in key newspapers? Are their ads prominently displayed? Are the ads well designed? What is their call to action? Is the operator well known in the advertised markets? Do they provide destination exclusivity in their menu ads or will you be listed among many direct competitors? How much are they charging you for the media space?

It is very important to communicate a consistent brand look throughout all the coop advertising. The best way of doing this is by creating templates of your coop advertising presence in a variety of sizes and supplying them on disk to all operators. This way, you'll ensure proper usage of your key brand identity elements such as your logo, typography, and photographs.

If your budget is sufficient, supplement the menu ads by allocating money for some dedicated stand-alone ads with the operator. Since the menu ads offer a multitude of destinations and products, your presence will be somewhat lost among a variety of offerings. Thus, stand-alone ads will be very valuable in creating stronger brand recognition and will communicate your alliance with the operator in the markets.

Travel Agent Faxing

This is the same activity described in the previous chapter; however, it is done through the wholesaler on your behalf with their pricing and call to action. Again, take advantage of this medium to communicate your brand. Study the fax formats of your operators and supply them with branded artwork that can easily be used. This will help you differentiate your product from the crowd of line-item/price-point listings.

Shells, Fliers, Newsletters, and Other Promotional Materials

Operators produce a huge number of fliers each year and distribute them at trade shows and through mass mailings. These fliers supplement their brochures and can be very valuable for placing your product and price in front of travel agents. They may also be very helpful in launching a new product in mid-season. As many tour operators' fliers are rather generic in design, you have a good opportunity to set yourself apart from the crowd and use them as branding vehicles by creating branded shell templates and providing them to the operators.

Create one or several single-page color shells that adhere to your brand identity standards and have a large area for overprinting. Make sure that you don't include a call to action such as a toll-free number or website, since the operators will want to direct the calls to their reservations center, not yours. For little money, you can produce tens of thousands of these fliers and offer them free to the operators. The only expense they will have will be for overprinting and distribution. An added value of doing this is that since your insignia will brand the shells, this will prevent the operator from including any competitive product.

If you need to work with simple black-and-white fliers, you can still use them to your branding advantage. Follow the same brand identity guidelines you have used in the creation of newspaper ad templates and faxes (both black-and-white media), and you will get extra mileage from their usage.

Some operators produce newsletters that they distribute to travel agents, clients, or employees. Often they will offer to include updates or news on your product free of charge. At other times, they may offer you advertising participation at cost. Treat it like any other media buy. Research publication frequency, circulation, CPM, and so on, and base your decision on the data. Don't participate just because you believe it may be politically beneficial. On the other hand, if you think it is a decent marketing opportunity, the political benefit may be an extra value.

Other promotional opportunities you may want to discuss with the operator include branded stuffers for the travel documents sent to the operator's clients and the creation of branded ticket jackets, luggage tags, or other travel materials. Discuss with each operator the variety of opportunities that may be available.

On-Hold Messages

Many operators offer on-hold messages as part of the coop plan. These are pre-recorded messages that are played whenever a travel agent calling the operator's central reservations number is placed on hold. Some operators swear by them and try to charge a premium for them. Will *not* using on-hold messages reduce your sales? No. However, these massages are good reminders of currently available packages and pricing. They also provide an extra way of pushing your brand by including your tag line or brand statement. And since the production cost is virtually zero, these messages are a good negotiation point for added values provided by the operator at no cost.

Reservation Staff Training and Familiarization

Important as it is to train and educate travel agents, it is also important to familiarize the operator's reservation staff with your product offering, company, and brand. Make sure to schedule regular presentation seminars with your operators. This will help them sell your product to travel agents and keep your brand constantly present. Also, considering the rather high turnover of reservation staff, regular presentations will ensure that all staff will be properly trained to sell your product. In order for your reservations staff training to be truly effective, periodic fam trips for the staff will be invaluable. It is fine for them to learn about a product or destination in a classroom, but it is even better to experience it for themselves. When scheduling presentations and fam trips, though, you must take into account that many operators have certain peak booking activity periods during which they won't allow their reservation staff to attend any training presentations or fam trips. Finally, consider extending your travel agent certification program to reservation agents and reward each agent who completes the program with a free stay.

Booking Contests and Reservation Incentives

Booking contests and reservation incentives for the operator's reservations staff may be a good supplemental tactic to achieve an extra sales push for a new product or in the low season. Some operators have limitation policies concerning the type of incentive their reservations agents are allowed to receive, so be sure to consult your account manager. For a more detailed discussion of booking bonuses, contests, and incentives, see the previous chapter.

Appreciation Events and Activities

There are two types of appreciation events: those organized by the operator and those organized by you. Regardless of the organizer and venue, an appreciation event can be organized for a variety of purposes and audiences; the operator's sales staff, top-producing travel agents, top-producing reservation agents, and so on. These events can be valuable for forging a stronger bond with the invited audience as well as for networking.

When operators hold these types of events, they often provide an opportunity for sponsorship or participation. Take advantage of it. If you don't have the budget to be a sponsor, at least make sure to participate. It will pay off in the long run.

The second type of appreciation event is one organized by you. You can do it at a local venue in the audience's market or on location.

Regardless of the type of event, who organizes it, or where it takes place, there are always opportunities for branding. Even if you're just participating as a guest, you can bring small tokens of appreciation for all invitees, using branded items or nonbranded items in branded packaging. They don't have to be expensive gifts, but make sure that they are meaningful and associated with your brand. If you sponsor or organize the appreciation event, do it well and create an unforgettable experience, again keeping your brand identity in mind. Are you famous for on-board entertainment? Bring the entertainment to the events. Or perhaps your hotel has a famous bar. Bring the bartenders to serve your signature drinks and do a cocktail-mixing performance. The opportunities for establishing a stronger bond, differentiating your brand, and creating lasting impressions are endless. Be creative. One final comment: make sure that your appreciation dinner is not a training seminar in disguise. There's a time and place for both. A short video or slide presentation is okay, but an in-depth presentation of your entire product line is not.

Other related activities that can help you build your relationship with the operators include establishing a special rate for the operator's employees, creating a mailing list for all employees and sending them small tokens of appreciation such as birthday cards, or providing them with desk calendars. There are many inexpensive ways of strengthening your bond with the operator and its employees. Not many companies are doing this well, so take advantage of the opportunity.

Familiarization (Fam) Trips

Operators, especially tour operators with charter programs, are very interested in organizing or participating in fam trips for travel agents as well as their reservations staff. Often operators are willing to provide complimentary seats on their planes if you provide complimentary accommodations. Also, you can agree with an operator that a number of seats on every non-sold-out flight will be provided for travel agents. This way, you'll ensure a continuous stream of agents visiting your property. Whatever your agreement, check to ensure that the operator has a selection process in place to avoid hosting freeloaders (see also Chapter 9).

Travel Trade Advertising

Sometimes operators will place ads in the travel trade publications and invite you to participate. The ads are usually in the operator's format with your logo or menu ads with price point and logo inclusion. If you can't afford trade advertising on your own, this may be an interesting way to increase your price, product, and brand presence with agents. But, unlike newspaper ads, these ads are generally not run frequently enough to have a significant impact. If you can afford it, keep the coop budget for other activities and run your own ads in the travel trade publications, focusing on building equity for your brand.

One benefit of coop advertising in the trade publications is credibility. Agents will feel more comfortable recommending and selling a product or destination they see advertised jointly with a reputable wholesaler. This will indicate a certain stability and will help communicate your positioning.

If you do decide to participate, differentiate and brand your offering or you will go unnoticed. If you flip through the trade publications, you'll be amazed to see how many companies and destinations use boring, generic, run-of-the-mill ads with the same basic underlying message: we offer something for everyone. Avoid the sameness trap by inspiring your advertising agency to communicate genuine brand differentiation.

Radio and TV Advertising

If your budget allows it, it may be beneficial to participate in the wholesalers' TV or radio campaign. Again, treat it as you would any other media buy, and make sure that your message is branded and delivered in the correct way. Ask to approve the creative before it runs.

Internet Presence

Most operators have Internet presence and will offer you some sort of participation, from simple product listings to extensive promotional packages. As with all Internet data, use caution when you are presented with the numbers of unique visitors, click-throughs, audiences, and so on, and evaluate them as you would any other media offer. Request that the Internet promotions be paid on the basis of performance.

Joint Promotions

Most operators have a firm hold on one or several key metropolitan or regional markets. They will often receive promotional opportunities from local radio stations, TV shows, sports teams, retail stores, celebrities, and even businesses. Take advantage of their regional strength and presence by participating in such promotions. You can gain serious market penetration for your brand in strategic markets at a fraction of the cost and effort of doing it on your own.

Popular joint promotions may include live remote broadcasts of local radio stations (often with come-along packages), the local sports team's or their cheerleader's photo shoot, a variety of sweepstakes with retailers in which your product is awarded as a prize, and so on. The opportunities are extensive. It is up to you to seek them out and take maximum advantage of them.

Frequently you'll be able to participate by providing free product in exchange for promotional exposure or using coop funds. Once you have an understanding with an operator, it pays to establish a "bank" of complimentary product that will allow the operator to participate in these promotions. The use of the comps must be subject to your approval.

Price Promotions

Rate discounts, early-booking bonuses, last-minute offers, and added-value promotions are common tactics to boost sales through the distribution channels. Nevertheless, good wholesalers should not focus exclusively on price. Instead, they should help you maximize your marketing presence and promote the value of your offer. Remember that too frequent price promotions will have a negative effect on your brand.

Direction and Control

The two final elements of the coop marketing plan are direction and control. While they may not be marketing actions per se, they are crucial operational elements. The coop marketing plan will be incomplete if you allow it to be handled by the operator without proper supervision—that is, if you do not direct its implementation and control its execution. Is it a policing job? Absolutely. Will the operator complain? Perhaps, but it is up to you to do it in an amicable manner that matches your relationship. On the other hand, the operator will appreciate a partner who knows what he or she is doing and will respect the diligence. Exercising direction and control will also give you an excellent opportunity for relevant ongoing interaction and strengthening of the partnership. But be sure to do this from the beginning. If you create monitoring mechanisms and manage the process continuously, it will become an integral part of the coop process. If, however, you are lax from January to November and turn into a control freak in December, you are not doing your job.

Once you have determined how much money you wish to allocate to a particular account, request an annual marketing plan. Revise it together with the operator and agree on the media schedules, promotions, events, and so on, and all corresponding costs. Now you have to start controlling implementation. If you have a large media plan, it is advisable to monitor all newspaper advertising yourself. Sometimes the operator will advertise an incorrect price or fail to include you in a scheduled ad. By monitoring, you'll know when to request price corrections and make-up ads in future insertions.

Another crucial area to control is pricing. For what price is your product being advertised? Is it equal to, higher than, or lower than that of the competition? For what price is your competitor's product being sold? Have the recent discounts you've given the operator been reflected in the new advertised pricing or is the operator advertising the old price and pocketing the difference?

For budget control and accounting, request that all invoices be backed up with tearsheets, photocopies, or affidavits. You should agree with the operator that no invoices (for cash, deduction, or trade) will be paid unless accompanied by proper backup.

Brand execution is the most difficult area to control. Except for brochure participation, newspaper ads, and TV commercials, monitoring all faxes, fliers, radio commercials, promotions, and so on will require quite an effort. Make no mistake, though. Distorted logos, misspelled tag lines, and low reproduction quality will eventually take a toll if you don't take control. Your brand is your destiny and investment. You must make a conscious effort to protect it.

Beyond Coop Marketing

Apart from managing coop marketing, optimal wholesale production will be achieved only by developing a strong relationship with the operator through sales account management, a consistent quality product, reliable inventory control, and swift handling of complaints.

FINAL COMMENT: TOUR OPERATORS AND BRANDS

Most U.S.-based operators do not represent strong consumer brands. Yes, travel agents know them, as do the airlines and other travel suppliers, but operator brands do not mean much to the average consumer. Some operators are consolidating their product portfolios, which is good, but few are investing in themselves. In other countries, tour operators have achieved very strong brand recognition in their own light. In Germany, for example, TUI (a large, vertically integrated operator) is a key travel consumer brand. TUI stands for high-quality, reliable vacations. German consumers know that if they buy a TUI vacation, their risk of negative surprises and spoiled vacations is minimized. In addition to promoting special offers, TUI advertises their brand on television. I predict that U.S. wholesalers will start integrating vertically and subsequently start pushing aggressively for consumer brand recognition, which will result in even stronger control of product distribution. So, only hospitality companies that manage to build solid consumer demand and strong brands will have leverage in dealing with distributors. For more information on wholesalers, contact the U.S. Tour Operator Association at www.ustoa.com.

CHAPTER ELEVEN

Internet Marketing

Imagination is more important than knowledge.
—Albert Einstein

The Internet is the greatest platform of equality. You do not need to have a large company or a huge budget to have a meaningful Internet presence. It just takes imagination, dedication, time, and some knowledge. Sure, large companies have a stronger Internet presence due to their sheer size. But what other medium allows a small company to have a virtually equal or, better yet, a smarter presence than the big boys? Network television and radio are out of reach and nationwide print is prohibitively expensive, but on the Internet, the only difference is what's between "www." and ".com."

Companies know that they need to be on the Internet, but often they don't know enough about it and as a result, more often than not, end up wasting resources, time, and money for various unnecessary services and consultants. It doesn't have to be that way, for in essence, the Internet is a media outlet. Granted, it is one with significant advantages over traditional media, and hence a fabulous sales and marketing tool, but a media outlet nevertheless. The smart marketer will take full advantage of its benefits:

- **It is a commerce tool.** Unlike any other medium, the Internet is a means in itself, with a sales transaction capability that directly contributes to the bottom line.

- **It is a marketing tool.** It provides an excellent environment for marketing and branding by educating and involving the visitor through meaningful content.

- **It is interactive.** It allows you to communicate with your visitors by giving them an opportunity to provide you with feedback, answer questions, participate in surveys, sign up for memberships, join clubs, participate in contests and promotions, and so on.

- **It is ongoing.** Your site is available 24/7, giving your visitors the opportunity to access information at their own convenience.
- **It is expansive, instant, and flexible.** Unlike any other marketing tool, your website gives you the facility to make constant adjustments, which are effective immediately and are not confined by space or time (unlike ads, commercials, or printed materials).
- **It is measurable.** You can measure the number of visitors, click-throughs, and responses to promotions, special offers, sweepstakes, and so on. Thus, you can assess the effectiveness of your marketing actions faster and at lower cost.

For all its advantages, however, the Internet is not a perfect environment. Consider banner advertising, for example. People visit a site because they are interested in something that site has to offer. So, clicking on a banner ad that takes them to another site raises the question of the effectiveness of that approach; that is, why would they want to leave the site they chose to visit in the first place?

By the time this book is published, chances are that some of the information in this chapter will be obsolete. This is why I have limited it to the key

Why should travelers not make use of their time during the ride from the airport to the hotel?

Source: AP/Wide World Photos. Used with permission.

points, many of which will remain valid even through technology changes. There are many factors in having a presence and conducting business on the Internet, but from a marketing standpoint, the following are the most important issues you will have to deal with in developing a successful Internet strategy.

THE IMPORTANCE OF AN INTERNET PRESENCE

The impact of the Internet on hospitality, travel, and tourism is undisputed. Some of the largest travel distributors today are Internet-based retailers. Airlines have totally eliminated commissions for travel agents by selling tickets directly on the Web. And various studies show that the Internet is the first source of information for business and leisure travelers, with destination, airline, and lodging information being the most frequent types of online travel information accessed.

It is virtually impossible to compete in today's marketplace without a solid Internet strategy. This chapter discusses the key areas of online presence and marketing.

TERMINOLOGY

Before delving into the details of online marketing, it is helpful to be familiar with the key terminology:

AUTORESPONSE is an automatic e-mail message sent as a reply to incoming e-mail.

BANNER ADS are Web-based advertisements that link to specific sites when clicked.

BROWSERS are software (such as Internet Explorer or Netscape Navigator) used to view Internet content.

CLICK-THROUGH RATE is the rate of click-throughs generated by a banner ad.

COOKIES are messages sent to an individual browser by a server. They are used to store user data such as preferences or login information for return visits.

COST PER CLICK is the rate charged for each click on a banner ad.

DIRECTORIES See portals.

E-COMMERCE is online commercial transactions.

FIREWALLS are programs designed to protect information on a server or network.

FLASH is a programming language that allows web pages to include animation.

FTP or FILE TRANSFER PROTOCOL is the method of moving files between computers through the Internet.

HITS are an inexact measure of site visitors. If a page contains five graphics, a visitor who request that page would have six hits, one for the page and one for each graphic.

HTML or HYPERTEXT MARKUP LANGUAGE is the coding used for creating Internet documents.

HTTP or HYPERTEXT TRANSPORT PROTOCOL is the protocol used for moving files over the Internet.

HYPERTEXT is text that is formatted (usually underlined) to be clickable and therefore requires minimum effort to provide links to specific sites or pages.

JAVA is a programming language that allows web pages to include animation by using Java programs called "applets."

META TAGS are pieces of HTML information developed for the purpose of including specific information about a web page without affecting the look of the page. There are description, keyword, and title tags.

NETIQUETTE is the user etiquette for the Internet.

OPT-IN E-MAIL LISTS are e-mail address lists of users who opted to be included on the list.

PERMISSION MARKETING is a way of online (and offline) marketing whereby the marketer asks permission before sending information.

PORTALS are large websites (Internet directories), such as Yahoo, that provide a multitude of information on a variety of topics and are used as the default sites for multiple users.

SEARCH ENGINES are programs, such as Google, that allow users to search the Web by keywords.

SPAMMING is unsolicited Internet marketing (e-mails, pop-up windows).

SPIDERS are programs that automatically index site titles and keywords.

SITE TRAFFIC is the measurement of traffic to a website.

UNIQUE VISITORS are visitors to a website who are counted only once, regardless of how many times they visit.

CREATING A WEBSITE

Website Design

As with any design project, the design of your website should stem from your branding and start with a strategy. The Web strategy should address your Internet project's core objective. Do you want your site to provide information, educate, strengthen the brand connection, process reservations, communicate with guests, handle special requests, or all of these? Your objective will also define the necessary sections of the site, as well as its intended audience(s): end users, repeat customers, travel agents, meeting planners, or all of them.

Regardless of who your audience is, design your site with the user in mind. The first element of any website is its domain name. The simplest approach for hospitality companies is to use the company, brand, or destination as the domain name. Why create additional mental steps that require customers to memorize a different domain if you can have a simple solution? You can check the availability of domain names at register.com and godaddy.com

More important than a fancy design is a site that is user friendly, has convenient navigation, and loads quickly. Too many graphic elements and pictures will make it slow. Your home page must grab the visitor's attention in the first few seconds. The look and feel of the site must be in sync with your branding. It should use the same colors, typefaces, graphic elements, and overall tonality. All pages should follow a consistent layout and overall design. It pays to use dark-colored text on a simple light background; dark copy is easier to read, and a simple background loads more quickly. Splash introductory pages are quite popular, but many people don't like them because they add an involuntary additional step for the site visitor. Web animation, such as Flash, can add excitement to the site but should be used for accentuation, not to dominate. Images, especially for hospitality and travel websites, are very important. They should be used in moderation throughout the website and provided as thumbnails in a dedicated section. Streaming video and virtual tours can also increase the versatility of the site.

It is important to carefully choose the sections (menu items) of the website. Too many sections will make it seem cluttered, and too few will require visitors to search extensively. When deciding on the individual menu items, it pays to group the submenus under logical main headings. The "About Us" section has become fairly standard, and most visitors expect to find company information, news, employment information, and an address list in this section. Look for similar patterns. Some sites are designed to be so unique they are not user friendly. Instead of "About Us," they say "Soul"; instead of "Contact Us," they say "Touch." While this may seem hip, many visitors will find it quite annoying, for it will make them go through unnecessary steps to reach their destination. Also, to help visitors navigate faster, always include buttons that allow quick returns to the top of a long page, redundant main menu links at the bottom of each page, and a prominent link to the home page.

Besides company information, some businesses include so many different options on their sites that they start resembling portals. This is seldom a good strategy, as real portals require significant resources in which most companies are not willing to invest. And having anything but a real portal will be more detrimental than beneficial. Yet there are some additional sections that are worth exploring. If a lot of your business is generated through travel agents, a good idea is to provide an agent referral section on your site. This tool can also be used as an incentive for agents or included as part of your educational and loyalty strategies. Another useful option for hospitality companies is to provide a link to the individual properties that allow communication with

Not just for customizing sneakers and cosmetics. Why not allow guests to customize their next stay via the Internet?
Source: Getty Images Inc.—Taxi. Used with permission.

the staff prior to departure about special requests or inquiries. Providing local weather information may be another good idea for companies with multiple locations.

The temptation to overload websites with unnecessary information is largely due to the limitless space available. But visitors want information fast, so page after page of unnecessarily long copy will actually produce negative results. It pays to design for simplicity, limit the content to the necessary minimum, and avoid anything that requires visitors to work harder than is absolutely necessary. The most frequently visited sites, such as Yahoo, use simple backgrounds, simple type, sufficient but few images, and links to more information for whoever wants it. They recognize that visitors have limited time and ensure returns by facilitating usage.

Bells and Whistles

Some additional features such as streaming media (audio and video that don't need to be downloaded but are transmitted directly over the Internet), real-time animation, and virtual reality are growing in use and with faster connections will surely become even more popular. They should be used in moderation and according to your visitors' connection speeds. What good is an exciting animation sequence if it takes forever to load? Also, don't just use these features for effect; use them to emphasize and reinforce your product and brand. Web cams can be used to show the actual product and also to boost traffic to your site. For example, if you offer weddings at your location, by using Web cams you can offer the service of a live Internet broadcast for friends and family. This will not only provide an additional service (added value or added revenue) but also reinforce your positioning as a wedding specialist.

Site Elements that will Help Achieve Better Search Engine Rankings

Chances are that you are going to hire a professional company to develop your site. Nevertheless, it is helpful to know what elements should be incorporated to achieve the best possible search engine rankings.

The proper use of Meta tags is crucial, as they are used for identifying and indexing websites by search engines. Meta tags include the title, keywords, and site description tags.

For search engines that do not use Meta tags, a descriptive paragraph should be included at the top of the home page. This way, those search engines will have a source of information for indexing.

Another important element for search engine prominence is the keywords used on your website. These are word combinations that describe your site, business, and purpose and should be limited to around 15 carefully chosen combinations. Besides Meta tags, keywords can be used in paragraph headings, and image source tags, as well as in the page text.

Two other components that need to be kept in balance are graphics and copy. A home page that has too many graphic files or mostly long text will be ranked lower by many search engines.

Many sites use text embedded in images for page headings. This is a huge mistake. Most search engines cannot read embedded text and will therefore not use this information when indexing your site. Instead, use a larger, more prominent heading font for paragraph headings, as many search engines assume that text that is emphasized contains more important information.

Maintaining and Managing a Website

The biggest challenge for companies is not the creation of a website, but its continuous maintenance and management. Once the initial site is live, the task of updating and managing the content must be assigned to a dedicated person. There's no way around it. A site that is not periodically updated and refreshed may serve its most basic function as an online brochure, but it will not be very interesting, invite repeat visitors, or rank highly with the search engines. The best way of keeping a site updated is by using software that allows simple text and graphics changes to be made without the need for a webmaster or programmer. These programs are readily available and should be built into certain sections of the site, such as those providing product updates, news, company information, and contact information. They will allow the basic changes to be made daily, with product updates, posting of news releases, and updating of new images. One key section to keep updated is an area with special offers and hot deals. This section will allow you to keep relevant information fresh and give a reason for visitors to return to your site or subscribe to e-mail alerts or newsletters. Depending on your specific product category, you may also be able to provide a variety of relevant updates on your website, ensuring new content.

Taking Reservations on a Website

E-commerce is the ultimate objective of a website, and in the case of hospitality sites this means taking reservations. In their most basic form, the reservations on a site will be handled through e-mail. On an advanced level, the reservations will be made in real time through a web user interface into the actual inventory of a central reservation system. Another option is to use a third-party reservation system and just provide an embedded link to that system within the frame of your own site. Do not lose the opportunity of turning some of your visitors into actual customers. If nothing else, provide links to your preferred Internet travel retailers and negotiate extra credit for the referrals.

GENERATING TRAFFIC TO THE WEBSITE

Many companies believe that by having a website, they are marketing on the Internet. Actually, the Internet marketing process only starts when a site goes live. The website is a necessary first step, but perhaps the easiest one. Marketing on the Internet has many different levels, but we will concentrate on the generation of traffic to your site. People find websites through word of mouth, articles, search engines, online and offline advertising, links, and e-mail. The easiest, as well as costliest, way of generating traffic is by investing in advertising campaigns. Nevertheless, there are other ways that are either less costly or may be managed on a performance basis.

Search Engines and Directories

There are literally billions of web pages on the Internet, and search engines sift through them in an effort to provide direction when users search for specific information. Search engines use different technology and thus a variety of criteria to rank websites. Some use Meta tags, others look at keyword frequency, and still others look at the location of keywords on a page, that is, headings or body copy. Large search engines include Google, Lycos, Excite, Altavista, Infoseek, Metacrawler, Hotbot, AskJeeves, and others. Some search engines are accepting bidding for keywords, as well as premium or sponsored positioning for a fee.

On the surface, there is no visible difference between directories and search engines. The difference is that directories use a more intricate process managed by human administrators for evaluating websites. As they are not driven purely by technology, the submission process is more complex and requires more work and time. Directories can be huge sites such as Yahoo and MSN or specialized sites such as floridahotels.com or resortsandlodges.com.

The key to achieving consistently good rankings is to keep up-to-date on the submission requirements and changes in the subscription procedure for each search engine and directory (at least the top 12) and to keep resubmitting. This is a time-consuming process, but there's no way around it. You can do it yourself or outsource the task. Sites that may provide helpful information on the submission process are searchtools.com, searchenginewatch.com, and searchengineworld.com. To check your and your competitors' Meta tags for free, go to bcentral.com/products/metatags.asp. There are also sites such as submit-it.com and addme.com that offer submission services to multiple search engines for a fee. To check for the optimal keywords, most common misspellings, and most frequently searched words, visit wordtracker.com.

E-mail

E-mail has been hailed as the killer application of the Internet. No wonder. Over 95% of Internet users use e-mail to communicate, it is virtually free, and it is the most time- and cost-effective communication vehicle available. Its applicability for marketing purposes is evident, yet e-mail marketing has some limitations or "rules" that should be observed.

Just as with traditional direct mail, you need a list to launch an e-mail campaign. Unlike traditional mail, e-mail cannot be unsolicited; that is, you should send e-mail only to users who have opted to receive it. These opt-in lists may be generated through your own efforts, such as by collecting data on your website (which is highly recommended), rented from qualified list brokers, or both. Following are some tips for using e-mail as a marketing tool:

- Use auto responders for standardized replies; most types of software have those options built in.
- Use subject lines creatively.
- Do not use ALL CAPS; it is the equivalent of shouting.
- Be short and concise; e-mail readers are used to brief messages.
- When including a web address, always type "http://. . . " as some e-mail programs may not recognize web addresses without this and thus won't permit the reader to click directly on the link.
- Use HTML e-mails instead of plain text when appropriate for greater impact.
- Do not attach large files to marketing messages.
- Always review and spell-check your e-mail message before sending it.
- Again, send e-mail only to users on opt-in lists. Do not send unsolicited e-mail; spamming will do more damage to your brand's reputation than you can imagine.

E-mail may be used for sending a variety of messages, from special offers and last-minute discounts, to company and product updates, to more creative messages such as newsletters and digital brochures. If you do not want to handle it in-house, there are companies that can assist with various aspects of e-mail marketing, from capturing data on your site to managing your lists to creating newsletters and digital brochures. Some websites that may be helpful for developing an e-mail marketing strategy are postmasterdirect.com, 123promote.com, and roving.com. If you would like to create and send digital brochures, check out worldtravelvision.com.

Affiliate Programs

If you are trying to boost sales on your e-commerce site, affiliate marketing may be an interesting way to do it. This basically consists of paying other businesses (affiliates) a referral fee for each customer who was referred to by that site and completes a transaction on your site. It takes some coordination, but since it is performance based, it is virtually risk free. Things to consider for a successful affiliate marketing program include offering competitive referral fees, finding the right referral partners, and continually signing up new partners. To find affiliates, you can advertise on your own website, contact potential affiliates, or get listed on affiliate directories such as associateprograms.com, clickquick.com, and referit.com.

On the other hand, if you do not have transaction capacity on your site but do enjoy significant traffic, you can sign up with a variety of travel providers (and nontravel providers, for that matter) to become their affiliate and earn commissions on transactions that originate from your site. Most travel retail sites (including Expedia, Travelocity, Priceline, and Site59) have a section with information about becoming an affiliate.

Links

Having your web address (URL) featured on noncompeting hospitality-, travel-, and tourism-related sites can help you generate additional traffic. When considering links, you must be selective and ascertain that the links are relevant to your customers. This will ensure that the provided links are perceived as an extra service and added value.

The key to a successful linkage campaign is reciprocity; you cannot expect to get your site's link listed on various other websites without offering the same service to them. Link reciprocity has two benefits; your link on other sites will deliver traffic to your site, and the presence of links on your site can improve some search engine rankings (e.g., that of Google). When listing links to related sites, make sure that they are either organized under a separate section or appear a few pages into your site; never place them on your home page. This will ensure that your visitors will visit your relevant pages before clicking on a link that will take them away. Also, make sure that you link with sites with similar or higher traffic. Finally, a key maintenance task is to check occasionally for dead links.

How should you go about linking? First, check where your site and your competitors' sites are linked. You can do this for free at bcentral.com/products/link_finder.asp. You can also check on who links with whom by using Alta Vista or Google. In either of these search engines, in the search area, type "link:" before a URL to check which sites link to a particular site. (For example, to see who has links to hilton.com enter "link:hilton.com" and click "search.")

Second, make a list of potential link partners. For example, if you have properties in various destinations, you could link your site to all the relevant destination sites, such as the convention and visitors bureau, the chamber of commerce, city, state, or regional sites, tourism office, and various community organization sites, as well as local businesses and special interest sites. Other companies to consider for linking are suppliers, wholesalers and retailers, companies that offer complementary products and services, and even companies in fields unrelated to yours that target the same audience. Another good place to search for link partners is the Open Directory at dmoz.org.

Third, evaluate potential link partners. As mentioned, Google uses the number of links on a website to approximate its popularity, so one way of checking a site's ranking based partly on this parameter is to install the Google toolbar (toolbar.google.com) on your computer, which will provide you with a "page rank" for each site you visit. The page rank is Google's evaluation of that page. It is a good indicator of the site's quality and thus of its potential value as a link partner.

Once you have evaluated and chosen the appropriate sites, contact their administrator regarding linking. You can either look for the webmaster contact on the site itself or, if you can't locate it, the administrative contacts for websites may be found at register.com in the "whois" section.

Advertising on the Internet

The objective of Internet banner advertising is to have someone click on it and get connected to your site or a specific section of your site. As with all advertising, the key to a successful banner campaign is developing a strategy that addresses the objective of your campaign, the intended audience, the creative approach, and the expected results. The beauty of banner advertising is that it is fully (and rapidly) measurable and can be used for a variety of purposes, from building traffic and interest for your site, to generating brand awareness, to building a mailing list or pushing specific offers.

Good banner ads (just like regular ads) appeal to the self-interest of viewers and arouse their curiosity strongly enough to lead them away from their current location. Travel sites are particularly suitable for banner advertising, as most travel products can promote sweepstakes and giveaways with free trips, stays, and vacations.

It goes without saying, but I'll say it again: the design and tone of your banners must stem from your overall branding; avoid the temptation to try "something different or fun" (you know, irritating blinking and similar gimmicks) just because the Internet is a different medium. Branding is branding, regardless of the medium. Banners have often been compared to billboards, as they share both limited space and limited viewer attention. And while this is true, banners have one great advantage: interactivity. But it does make sense to use the same guidelines for creating banners: keep them short, interesting, and relevant. To get started, you can play around with various online design elements and create banners at animationonline.com, and mediabuilder.com. But for running a serious banner campaign, it is advisable to use professionals for the creative work. Banners can be simple and static or expandable and contain animation. Nevertheless, keep in mind that one of the key features of banner effectiveness is how quickly they load; more complicated banners will load more slowly.

Finally, in terms of media planning, make sure to fish where the fish are. Many media offers boast impressive visitor numbers, but thousands of generic visitors may have zero interest in your specific product or offer. If you want to promote vacations to retired people, you'll get better responses by targeting them on specific sites such as retired.com, aarp.org and fifty-plus.net than by placing expensive banners on a general site such as AOL. Besides special interest sites, other options are the various special interest web magazines called "e-zines;" to search for different e-zines, visit magatopia.com.

A key benefit of Internet advertising is the instant measurability of its effectiveness and therefore a better gauge of the expected return on investment. If you want to manage the campaign based completely on performance, valueclick.com provides a variety of purely performance-based online advertising options. Also, there are some banner exchange sites that let you place your banner ads in exchange for accepting banners on your page. Check out the opportunities on bcentral.com and bannerswap.com.

Traffic Analysis

One of the key benefits of Internet marketing is the analysis of traffic that is generated to your website. By reviewing statistics, traffic analysis tools can determine where visitors came from, where they entered and exited your site, which pages they visited, how long they stayed, to what promotions they reacted, which browsers they were using, and when they visited. All of this incredible data will give you a better understanding of your visitors and allow you to develop more targeted marketing strategies. Traffic analysis software needs to be installed on the server where your website is hosted. So, unless you host your site on your own server, the statistics should be available from your hosting facility, either for free or for an additional charge. If you cannot get this information through your Internet service provides, you may track part of it for a fee from thecounter.com or check out sane.com and test their Nettracker software for free.

Offline Marketing

In addition to all of the above-mentioned activities, the web address and its Internet contents (promotions, special packages, updates, news) must be included and, when appropriate, emphasized in all offline activities, from advertising to public relations. Only by integrating all online and offline activities will you be able to maximize the use of the Internet as one of your most powerful marketing tools.

Spam and other Fare you must Avoid for a Healthy Online Diet

As mentioned before, "spam" (inspired by the famous Monty Python song) is a term used to describe unsolicited Internet marketing, including bulk e-mail and pop-up windows, and should be avoided at all costs. But there are also a few other questionable techniques that are sometimes used by sites in an attempt to trick search engines into providing more prominent positioning. One technique is key word spamming, which involves repeating keywords over and over in the Meta tags or at the bottom of the document, or hiding keywords by using a very small font or by making them the same color as the background. Other techniques include constantly changing the titles or starting the site name with the letter A or different characters. Avoid all of them, as the search engines will recognize them and penalize you. Besides, they are considered shady business practices that will reflect negatively on your brand.

PERMISSION MARKETING

The final word on online (and offline) marketing is permission. Unsolicited e-mail, pop-up windows, and tricky data collection are becoming the devils of Internet marketing. Rightly so. They are the equivalent of the old bait-and-switch technique, and clients should not be subjected to them. Asking customers for permission before sending them information or special offers not only initiates a positive relationship but also helps the marketer weed out unqualified prospects.

USEFUL LINKS

- bcentral.com — Internet resources, marketing, and development
- catalog.com — Domain registration and hosting
- godaddy.com — Domain registration and hosting
- groups.google.com — Internet discussions and user groups
- internet.com — Internet resources
- netb2b.com — Business-to-business marketing
- register.com — Domain registration and hosting
- verisign.com — Online transactions and payment

CHAPTER TWELVE

Loyalty Marketing

An ounce of loyalty is worth a pound of cleverness.
—Elbert Hubbard

All customers are not created equal. According to the famous Pareto rule, 80% of any business is generated by 20% of its clients. With a little variance, this is true in any industry; and so in hospitality and tourism. And for some companies, the ratio may even be as high as 95:5. Airlines recognized this years ago by introducing frequent flier programs. These have become an industry standard. Then hotels followed with frequent stay programs and car rental companies with their own version. The problem with many loyalty programs is that they are not true loyalty programs but merely repeat purchase/discount programs. This is unfortunate because loyalty programs, if done well, can be a unique differentiating factor and yield a significant competitive advantage.

Studies show that it costs up to five times as much money to attract new customers as to maintain existing ones, yet many companies perpetually chase after new business and, in the process, neglect existing customers because they erroneously believe that revenues will be generated only by a stream of new customers. Studies further show that a decrease in customer defection can increase profits by 5 to 15 times. Loyalty programs address these issues by focusing on the best customers. They involve heavier users with the brand through rewards, interaction, and recognition, and in the process create loyal users. They maximize the value of customers by increasing the share of those customers.

Nonetheless, although this chapter discusses loyalty programs as marketing tools, the concept of loyalty goes much deeper than running repeat-customer programs. Various reports show that a vast number of CEOs list increasing customer loyalty as one of the top three corporate objectives, yet they fail to realize that creating loyalty (like building brands) must start at the top long before the launch of a formal loyalty program. A company that is promiscuous with its clientele and employees will have an extremely difficult time building loyalty just by implementing a frequency program. That's because loyalty is not something that can be acquired; it has to be earned. In addition, loyalty is mutual, so it's foolish to expect it before demonstrating it. This would be the equivalent of a philandering husband trying to buy his wife's loyalty by giving her gifts. It just doesn't work that way. In business, as in life, loyalty is a mutual commitment and investment. Its equation is quite simple: (1) start with your employees; protect them, nurture them, involve them, and make them feel appreciated (financially, professionally, etc.), and they will become loyal. (2) Loyal employees and a corporate culture of loyalty will, in turn, generate loyal customers, and loyal customers will generate continuous and profitable business as well as powerful word of mouth, which will attract more customers. (3) This will attract long-term (loyal) investors, who will remain investors throughout the company's short-term financial fluctuations because they will know that in the long run the loyalty will pay off.

Since this is not a book on corporate management but on marketing, the focus of this chapter remains on the operational and marketing aspects of loyalty programs. But the point needs to be made that companies that nurture a

Casino loyalty card.
Source: Dorling Kindersley Media Library. Used with permission.

culture of loyalty to customers and employees will reap tremendous financial and brand equity benefits in the long run. For such companies, a loyalty program will be a natural extension and a vehicle to formalize their commitment to loyalty. Just as advertising must be driven by a brand strategy, a loyalty program should be driven by a corporation's commitment to loyalty.

TYPES OF LOYALTY PROGRAMS

In hospitality there are two types of loyalty programs, differentiated by the segment to which they are geared: customer programs for end users and business-to-business programs for travel agents.

Customer programs directed to the end user—the frequent traveler, flier, overnighter, driver, and so on—are designed to entice the frequent user to stay with a particular brand or group of brands. These programs are widespread and somewhat commoditized. Companies in each travel and hospitality segment offer loyalty programs. All major airlines offer frequent flier programs. Hotel program examples include Starwood Preferred Guest, Hilton Honors, Best Western Gold Crown Club International, Red Roof Inns' Redicard, Marriott Rewards, and many more. Cruise program examples include Royal Caribbean Cruises' Crown and Anchor Society, Norwegian Cruise Lines' Latitudes, and the Cunard World Club. Other hospitality and travel examples include restaurant programs such as Idine, Hard Rock Café's All Access, TGI Friday's Gold Points; rental car programs such as Budget's Perfect Drive, Hertz's #1 Club, Avis' Preferred or Alamo's Business Benefits program; travel programs such as Abercrombie & Kent's Marco Polo Club; and many others.

Business-to-business programs, on the other hand, are directed to the retailer, and are designed to motivate retail travel agents to make as many bookings as possible of a particular brand and receive rewards for each of those bookings. In addition, a good travel agent program will serve as a platform for communicating with and educating travel agents and turning them into brand ambassadors. Travel agent loyalty programs are rarer than consumer programs, and since they are directed to limited audiences, they are much more obscure. Examples of travel agent program include Sol Melia Amigos, Apple Vacations' Royalties, SuperClubs' SuperAgency, and Thrifty Car Rental's Look to Book program.

Further segmentation of loyalty programs is based on the way programs are organized: either as point-system/reward-for-usage programs or as affinity clubs. While point-system rewards programs are mostly used for frequency programs, affinity clubs can be excellent vehicles for building brand loyalty via common interests when the transaction frequency is low or sporadic. The most successful loyalty programs combine elements of both frequency programs and affinity clubs to achieve a strong rational and emotional bond with their members.

Finally, loyalty programs may be organized with open or limited membership. Open programs have no membership prerequisites and allow anyone to join. This type of program is more suitable for reaching a wider audience and when a company doesn't have much specific knowledge about its customers. Open programs require bigger budgets and are more suitable for consumer programs such as frequent flier programs. Limited programs, on the other hand, are designed to attract a highly targeted group of members. They are more suitable for business-to-business clubs because they are more focused and geared to a smaller, well-defined audience.

THINGS TO CONSIDER BEFORE STARTING A LOYALTY PROGRAM

There are certain prerequisites that should be evaluated for the operation of any loyalty program.

First of all, a point-based loyalty program will work only if there is sufficient frequency of transaction or usage. A typical frequency program, for instance at a remote resort, where the incidence of travel may be once a year (for the same person), doesn't make much sense. In that case, an affinity club may be a better idea. A point-based program is suitable when the usage frequency (e.g., business travelers) or transaction frequency (e.g., travel agents) is high.

Second, the brand and product must be relevant for the intended market. Some products are purchased routinely, and some brands are perceived as generic. The existing customer base may just not have enough interest to warrant a loyalty program.

Third, there must be enough product locations in the portfolio. Without the necessary portfolio, the program's fulfillment may be difficult, the scope too limited, and therefore the interest too low. While a loyalty club based on a single hotel or cruise ship may be possible, you may have to consider signing up a few club partners to expand the scope, relevance, and appeal of the program.

Fourth, the intended customer base must be large enough to justify a significant investment such as a loyalty program. Loyalty programs are usually launched when the existing market is large enough to support them. For a company that is still struggling to build occupancies and increase production momentum, a loyalty program may be more of a headache than a marketing tool. The company should consider postponing the launch until this critical mass exists.

Fifth, brand awareness—or the lack thereof—may be another point to consider before launching a program. Some programs are launched prematurely and suffer accordingly. Companies may fare better if they concentrate on other marketing activities to build up brand awareness prior to launching a loyalty program.

Nonetheless, except for the first point, none of these should be considered absolute requirements. Perhaps starting a new brand with no existing business and a strong emphasis on loyalty is just the strategy that will allow you to differentiate your brand. It is crucial to know why certain steps are taken, not just to take them because everyone else does.

LOYALTY LINGO

Like any other specialized activity, loyalty marketing has several specific concepts and terms:

RECENCY, FREQUENCY, MONETARY VALUE (RFM) measures the historical purchase or transaction behavior of a customer.

RECENCY shows the timing of the last transaction and may uncover potential changes in the customer's behavior.

FREQUENCY shows the incidence of transaction, that is, how often it occurs during a specific period of time.

MONETARY VALUE calculates the total transaction value of a customer expressed in monetary units.

CUSTOMER LIFETIME is the calculation of a realistic customer life span for a certain brand or family of brands. The lifetime commences with a customer's first transaction. One of the goals of loyalty programs is to extend the effective lifetimes of its customers.

CUSTOMER LIFETIME VALUE (LTV) is the measurement of the potential total value of a customer over the customer's realistic life span. For example, if a travel agent books an average of 16 cruises in any 12-month period, each cruise is on average valued at $2,000, and the estimated lifetime of that travel agent is 17 years, the LTV of this travel agent is quite significant. However, to calculate the real net present LTV of a customer, the calculation should factor in a discount rate on future earnings and take into account the value of word of mouth and referrals a loyal customer will produce (average or estimated), as well as the marketing cost of retaining a loyal customer (since all customers are different, this calculation is not exact but an approximation).

A MOST VALUABLE CUSTOMER is a current loyal customer with the highest possible LTV. These are the customers most worth keeping.

CUSTOMER POTENTIAL is a term used to describe the potential value of current customers who have not yet reached their full potential. This is the customer group most worth increasing.

LEAST VALUABLE CUSTOMERS are customers who actually cost more to service than they generate in revenues. Those are the customers most worth eliminating.

SHARE OF CUSTOMER is the percentage of business a brand receives from a customer within a certain category. For example, for a business traveler staying for 15 nights per year at Marriott, 20 nights at Hilton, and 15 nights at Hyatt, the share of this customer for each brand is 30%, 40%, and 30%, respectively.

ACQUISITION COST is the total marketing cost it takes to gain a new customer.

RETENTION COST is the total marketing cost required to retain an existing customer.

DEFECTION RATE is the percentage of customers who stop doing business with your company.

AVERAGE TENURE is the estimation of the average length of time a customer does business with your company.

ATTRITION is the process of customer loss.

PARTICIPATION RATE is the rate at which new members join a program. A healthy program should maintain a high participation rate even after the initial launch period.

BREAKAGE is the number of awards earned but unclaimed by program members. Some breakage is good, as it helps lower the cost of redemption, but high or growing breakage rates may be indicators of declining interest in the program.

THE KEY ELEMENTS OF A LOYALTY PROGRAM

As mentioned, whether directed to consumers or travel agents, loyalty programs are organized either as reward-for-usage programs or as affinity clubs. While the former are based on the frequency of transaction, the latter are based on the affinity with the brand, product category, or market segment. Nevertheless, both types have similar key elements, so we'll discuss them together.

Objectives

The loyalty program must have a set of defined objectives. These may include customer retention, reduction of attrition, brand differentiation, increasing the share of customer, increasing the market share, attracting new customers, and so on. Without highly defined objectives, it will be impossible to plan and organize a well-executed program or measure its success. The program should also have specific objectives such as membership goals, annual growth rates, and so on.

The Membership Concept

Any loyalty program must be organized around a membership concept. Usually the concept is repeat behavior, which may be anything from a simple coffee shop "loyalty" card that is stamped each time the consumer buys coffee to a complex frequent flier program.

In an affinity club, membership may be based on the interest in coffee instead of the repeat purchase.

The Member Database

The foundation of any loyalty program is the database of program members. Along with basic member information, a good loyalty database should contain transaction and usage records, preference profiles, contact records, awards status, and redemption records. All of this information will be used to run the program, as well as to establish member profiles based on which patterns of behavior may be analyzed and the LTV of members calculated. Ultimately, this information will allow you to create cloning profiles that you can use to attract new members with similar preferences.

Promotional Currency

In the case of point-based programs, a point system such as airline miles, dollars spent, or rooms booked will track the usage frequency and level and convert them into a (preferably unique, branded) currency. This currency will be usable later for redemption of rewards by members of the program.

Member Rewards and Benefits

Two of the key elements of any loyalty program are member benefits and rewards. These may include merchandise, special services, club events, educational seminars, VIP services, member packages, upgrades, club or program merchandise, special branded benefits, trips and vacations, program partner or sponsor programs, and so on. All of these are exchangeable for the earned promotional currency. The most important thing here is to create a set of rewards that is compelling enough for members to stay loyal, yet economical enough to be financially viable.

Club Communication Channels and Materials

Communication with members starts with their enrollment in that club and continues throughout the membership period. Communications vehicles include the membership kit, club catalog, member website, newsletters, e-mail, mailers (statements, postcards), member hot line, club meetings, and events. Communication materials are key in building and maintaining a dialogue with the members. In addition, they are an excellent vehicle for further brand building and differentiation, which is why it is imperative to have all club communication pieces designed as part of the overall brand identity.

Club Infrastructure

Each loyalty program is in essence a club, and the club infrastructure should be organized as a service center. It should be a dedicated entity that handles all coordination and management of the program, such as communications, reward redemption, account maintenance, accounting, procurement of rewards, contracting with partners and sponsors, and overall program administration.

Budget

The loyalty program or club must be managed as a separate business unit with its own operational, administrative and promotional budget.

BENEFITS AND REWARDS

Regardless of corporate objectives, smart strategies, or warm and fuzzy intentions, without the right set of member benefits and rewards your loyalty program will not succeed. A unique set of awards and benefits will be the key differentiating factor for the program, and if the benefits are also unique to your brand, the loyalty program will not only be perceived as more valuable, it will generate additional goodwill for the brand.

A good loyalty program will offer its members a balanced selection of hard and soft benefits. Hard benefits are tangible, financial, repeat-purchase rewards such as miles, points, member discounts, and reward merchandise. Soft benefits are added-value items that could include special products and services such as free upgrades, member-only updates, special events, and other member services. The benefits must be compelling enough to have genuine (real and perceived) value for the members and unique enough so that they can't be easily copied by the competition; in addition, they should not only have intrinsic value but also reinforce your brand's positioning. For instance, a loyalty club for adventure travelers should have a reward program that includes adventure travel–related merchandise, publications, services, and events. Such a program would generate no interest if its rewards included regular merchandise such as toasters and free tickets to the Ice Capades. Actually, those types of rewards would be detrimental, not just to the success of the program but also to the image of the brand. The balance between soft and hard benefits must be well defined, as programs heavily weighted on either side will not be perceived as valuable. To illustrate this, here is a personal example: I belong to American Airlines Advantage and have the status of Gold member, which means that I fly more than 25,000 miles a year. I earn bonus miles on every flight, and I've used my miles to fly for free to Europe and the Caribbean, which was enjoyable. Occasionally I have had a chance to upgrade to first class, which was also enjoyable. What really makes me appreciate the program, however, is the fact that as a Gold member, I have the privilege of checking in at the first-class counter even when I fly coach. This helps me avoid the long lines in coach class, which costs American nothing extra and makes the program truly worthwhile for me. There's a lot to be said about paying attention to the right balance of benefits.

A market study conducted by InsightExpress, an online research company, revealed that over 30% of respondents claimed that the main reason for not joining a program is that the benefits lacked real value. This is no surprise. Most programs are copies of each other with slight variations. Customers' tastes, needs, and wants change over time, and it is wise, both for existing programs and for new launches, to conduct market research and collect feedback from current or potential members about what would constitute compelling benefits.

Table 12.1 lists selected hospitality loyalty programs and the hard and soft benefits they offer. This information was taken from the companies' websites.

TABLE 12.1 Select Loyalty Programs

Company			
Celebrity Cruises	**Requirements**	**Hard benefits**	**Soft benefits and communications**
	$35 enrollment fee *Must sail once with Celebrity Cruises	• One-category upgrade	• Complimentary custom air arrangements • Presailing specialty restaurant reservations • Priority embarkation (where available)—Founder Classic members only* • Exclusive Captain's Club party • Benefits for Classic members, including welcome amenity, gift with purchase at the AquaSpaSM, and certificates for the Celebrity casino • Golf clinic and Classic member rate for Golf Simulator • Complimentary wine tasting • Preferential debarkation (where available)—Founder Classic members only • Reunion cruises • Quarterly newsletter with exclusive offers
Royal Caribbean Cruise Line			
Three levels of benefits	Must be 18 or older Gold Level after first cruise *Only offered on sailings of 7 nights or longer Platinum Level after fifth cruise	Gold Level • Gold Ultimate Value Booklet Platinum Level • Ultimate Value Booklet • Special rates on balcony and suite staterooms	Gold Level • Complimentary wine tasting* • Welcome-back party* • Crown & Anchor magazine—new for 2002 • Members-only web page • Members-only sweepstakes • More member cruises Platinum Level • Gold benefits, plus: • Private departure lounge • Exclusive onboard event • Robes for use on board • A special number to call for precruise benefits

	Diamond Level after 10th cruise	Diamond Level • Diamond Ultimate Value Booklet • Special rates on balcony and suite staterooms	• Complimentary custom air fee • Priority check-in (where available) Diamond Level • Platinum benefits, plus: • Priority wait list for sold-out shore excursions/spa services • Concierge service on select ships • Priority departure • Priority wait list for dining room seating

Norwegian Cruise Line

First cruise	• Members-only savings and discounts • Onboard booking discounts and credits	• Specially designated Latitudes Member cruises with exclusive members-only amenities and events onboard • Special check-in at select ports • Latitudes onboard liaison • Complimentary subscription to Latitudes' quarterly magazine • Members-only cocktail reception hosted by the captain • A Latitudes membership card • Members of NCL's Latitudes Club are also entitled to Polo Club past-guest benefits when sailing on Orient Lines' *Marco Polo* or *Crown Odyssey* • Special discounts at the Internet Café

Silversea Cruises

First cruise	• 5% savings on any future cruise for those with 100 days or more of cruising • 10% savings on any future cruise for those with 250 days or more of cruising	• One $250 shipboard credit for shore excursions, spa services, or boutique purchases • 5% or 10% savings for friends who join the member on a cruise • Credit to member account with the number of days friends sail with member

(Continues)

TABLE 12.1 (*Continued*)

	Requirements	Hard benefits	Soft benefits and communications
Silversea Cruises		• 7-day complimentary cruise for those with 350 days of cruising • 14-day complimentary cruise for those with 500 days of cruising • After 500 days of cruising, a 7-day cruise for each additional 150 days sailed	
Holland America Cruise Line	First cruise	• Preferred pricing on many Holland America cruises	• Mariner bag tags and buttons to identify you as a member of the Mariner Society during embarkation • An invitation to the Mariner Society champagne reception and awards party, hosted by the captain • Lapel pins and medallions acknowledging your Holland America cruise history • Surprise pillow gift • A complimentary subscription to *Mariner*, a full-color magazine featuring news and Mariner Society savings
AAA Diamond Rewards	Automatic enrollment with AAA Platinum Plus Visa card	• One point for every dollar charged to the AAA Platinum Plus Visa card	• Free supplemental car rental insurance when rental is paid with AAA Visa card • Statements • Online account access

Program				
Vail Resorts Peaks Program	Automatic enrollment with purchase of certain type of pass	• Free lift tickets • Ski and snowboard school lessons • $50 off dining bill at participating restaurants • $50 off lodging during peak seasons at participating properties • Free 1-hour ski bike tour for one person at adventure ridge • Free 1-hour snowmobile tour for one person	• $40 voucher for every 5,000 points, to be used at any AAA branch	• Credit card link for charge privileges • Members-only special offers • Member area website
Six Continents Hotels	Three levels of benefits Free enrollment	Club member benefits • Free hotel stays • Single rate for double-occupancy rooms		• No blackout dates for reward nights • Points purchase or transfer between member accounts • Points never expire • 3,200 locations to earn and redeem points • Custom rewards with the Personal Shopper program • Online personal account access • Complimentary weekday newspaper • Extended checkout

(Continues)

TABLE 12.1 (*Continued*)

Six Continents Hotels	Requirements	Hard benefits	Soft benefits and communications
	Gold membership requirements: • 15 qualifying nights per year • 20,000 points per year • Purchase Gold status for $50 U.S. dollars per year	Gold Member benefits • All Club-level member benefits plus: • 10% point bonus on base points	Gold Member Benefits • All Club-level member benefits plus: • Priority check-in • Access to the exclusive Gold Elite phone number
	Platinum membership requirements: • 50 qualifying nights per year • 60,000 points per year	Platinum Member benefits • All Gold-level member benefits plus: • 50% point bonus on base points	Platinum Member benefits • All Gold-level member benefits plus: • 50% point bonus on base points • Priority check-in • Complimentary room upgrades available at check-in* • Guaranteed room availability (72 hours in advance) • Access to the exclusive Platinum Elite phone number
Howard Johnson	Free enrollment	• Hotel stays—free and half-off HoJo stays for up to 7 consecutive nights • Airline tickets—round-trip coach ticket anywhere within the continental United State • Free Avis car rentals • Retail gift certificates worth $25 or $50	• Frequent flier miles—members can supplement their frequent flier accounts by earning miles on Continental and American Airlines • Toll-free customer service number and website for account and program information
	Awards depend on point level		

Best Western

Free enrollment Three levels of membership Member status and awards depend on point level	• Global free room nights • Complimentary room upgrades • Variety of merchandise and services including automotive, travel, dining, shopping, entertainment, and savings bonds	• Quarterly recognition gifts • Exclusive offers • Dedicated level-exclusive priority service • Early check-in, late check-out privileges, upon availability • Point pooling for individuals at same address

TGI Fridays

Member of Carlson Marketing's Gold Points program Free enrollment Awards depending on point level	• Free food • Merchandise and service certificates valid for redemption with Gold Points partners	• Bonus points for occasional partner promotions • Website

Burger King Big Kids

Free enrollment for children aged 4–12	• Birthday coupon for free kids meal	• Website and mailings

Chart House Restaurants

$25 enrollment fee refunded in the form of a $25 welcome certificate	• $25 reward certificates for each $250 points (1 point = 1$ spent)	• VIP reservations • Account status with receipt • Birthday and anniversary mailings • Double Viewpoints for every dollar spent on Mondays and other special days

(Continues)

TABLE 12.1 *(Continued)*

Chart House Restaurants	Requirements	Hard benefits	Soft benefits and communications
			• Members' hotline • Online account status
Harrah's Entertainment	Must be 21 or older Gold-level requirements: no minimum reward credits	Gold level • Ability to earn comps and cash, based on play	Gold level • 10% discount at Harrah's-owned gift stores • Priority access to rooms, shows, and events when you call • Offers and discounts in your mailbox
	Platinum level requirements: 3,000 annual reward credits	Platinum level • Ability to earn comps and cash, based on play	Platinum level • All Gold-level member benefits plus: • Preferred restaurant reservations and seating • Priority check-in at company hotels • Special 800 number for priority service • Exclusive travel service, plus benefits with select airlines and other travel partners
	Diamond-level requirements: 10,000 annual reward credits	Diamond level • Ability to earn comps and cash based on	Diamond level • All Platinum-level member benefits plus: • Members-only access to Harrah's VIP lounges (where available) • Personal VIP hosts at your service • Free room upgrades and tickets to Harrah's shows (where available) • Exclusive hotel check-in area • Invitations to Diamond-only special events and tournaments

DIFFERENTIATION

Differentiation is one of the most important aspects of any loyalty program. It can mean the difference between success and failure. The problem is that once one company launches a program (e.g., American Airlines Advantage), others are quick to follow with their own copycat versions. This makes most programs me-toos, and after a while, instead of being differentiators, they become industry standards. How can you differentiate? First, take a look at what your competition is doing. Is everyone offering a point per dollar, a 10% discount on the next transaction, and free coupons for a car wash? Offer something completely different. Is everyone stipulating redemption restrictions? Break that rule. Is everyone trying to reach everyone? Focus on a select segment of the market. Is everyone mailing quarterly statements and a newsletter? Send postcards. The point is, if you take enough time to find out what the competition is doing and what customers really want and need, you will have a good idea of how to make your program stand out. You can use almost any element of your loyalty program for differentiation, including member awards and benefits, program communication, member interaction, point structure, and redemption.

I have said it several times throughout this book: dare to be different. Be unique. If everyone is zigging, zag. Don't just follow the crowd. If you created a strong and differentiated brand strategy, some of those traits can easily be extended to your loyalty program.

One such example is Starwood. First, they have an exceptional portfolio of brands. Second, their Preferred Guest loyalty program is differentiated from the main competitive programs, and they make no little fuss about it. They even have a comparison chart on their website to showcase the advantages of their loyalty program in contrast to those of their four closest competitors.

THE BENEFITS OF HAVING A LOYALTY PROGRAM

Loyalty programs hold tremendous value for their companies. The previously mentioned InsightExpress study indicates that 50% of U.S. consumers belong to at least one loyalty program, with the strongest participation in the credit card industry (27%) and the travel industry (airlines 19%, hotels 12%). The study further shows that, among program members, over 55% claim that membership does influence their purchase behavior. This is extremely valuable, but the cumulative value and impact of loyalty programs goes even beyond the behavioral influences:

> **Identification and segmentation of customers.** A loyalty program allows members to be identified as individual clients and segmented based on their consumption (consumers) or production (travel agents) levels, usage behavior, interaction, and transaction history. This provides invaluable input for a powerful proprietary database.

Knowledge. A rich proprietary database provides a new level of market knowledge through data mining and member profiling. Based on this knowledge, existing members can be turned into loyal customers and loyal customers into brand ambassadors. And new members can be targeted and acquired based on existing member profiles.

Cost savings. As mentioned at the beginning of the chapter, various studies show that it costs up to five times as much money to acquire new customers as to retain existing ones. A loyalty program communicates only with members, thus delivering communications to a captive and highly targeted audience. The levels, the frequency, the type, and therefore the cost of communications can be tailored to different tiers of members. Wastage is reduced to a minimum.

Sales growth. Executed properly, a loyalty program will become a crucial sales tool. The key objectives of any loyalty marketing strategy are to increase sales per member (share of customer) and expand the database of members (increase market share). Also, loyal customers tend to be more profitable and less discount driven.

Relevant brand involvement. A loyalty program creates a reason for members to get more involved with the brand based on their self-interest. This is done through the creation of relevance, because instead of selling to a generic customer, a loyalty club will identify individual members and reward them in a variety of ways for each transaction. This provides the opportunity for meaningful one-to-one communications versus mass communication, strengthening the involvement with the brand through every interaction, both planned and spontaneous.

Promotional relevance. Loyalty programs provide an opportunity to market more powerfully. All of a sudden promotions become relevant, as there is something extra in it for the customer besides the promotional offer.

Referrals. Loyalty programs provide an excellent platform for referrals. Members can be given incentives in the form of bonuses or special offers for referring new members.

Adding value versus discounting. Instead of constant discounting and price promotion, a loyalty program gives members a reason (self-interest and brand relationship) to buy, even though the competition may offer lower prices.

Measurability. Unlike other marketing actions, promotional campaigns run through a loyalty program are measurable at the individual member level. For example, for a launch of a new hotel, all member agents are sent an educational brief about the property along with an incentive (double or triple points) to book during a booking window. After the booking window is over, the exact number of bookings received can be tallied by member, region, type of booking (demographic), length of stay, and so on. This is powerful data to be collected after each promotion. Imagine the cumulative market intelligence obtained after tracking various promotions for 2 or 3 years. Achieving this level of accuracy with traditional marketing is impossible.

Feedback. Collecting meaningful feedback from the marketplace is one of the most important elements of marketing. Yet, it is also one of the most misleading ones, mostly because feedback collection can be sporadic, quite costly, and often from questionable target audiences. Loyalty programs create an opportunity to collect quality feedback, data, and opinions from actual customers. It can be done quite inexpensively and will not only provide invaluable market insight but also create additional opportunities for brand involvement.

BENEFITS OF HAVING A LOYALTY PROGRAM FOR TRAVEL AGENTS

In addition to all the benefits listed in the previous section, travel agent loyalty programs deliver the following benefits:

Education. Travel agents sell the products and brands they know. A loyalty program provides a powerful platform for educating agents on the company, brand, products, destinations, updates, news, offers, promotions, and so on. With time, agents will seek to become brand experts so that they can earn more rewards. The membership allows for dedicated agent communication and involvement, as well as a database of agents for a sales specialist or certification course.

Promotional relevance. Agents are inundated with faxes, e-mails, and mailings. However, for member agents, a fax is perceived not just as another promotion or special offer, but rather as an opportunity to earn something extra for themselves. Response times to special offers are often significantly reduced.

Competitive advantage and differentiation. Through education, incentives, and special treatment, a loyalty program will create the perception of higher brand/product value for agents. Innovative programs create differentiation and potential extra income for agents. From a corporate standpoint, an innovative program will strengthen any company's position as a market leader and innovator.

Organized incentives. Instead of frivolous bribes with staggering commission levels, agent loyalty programs provide for a way to organize and structure the payout of commissions and incentives.

Enhanced agent satisfaction. Loyalty programs recognize the agents as individual producers and reward their loyalty, thus enhancing their satisfaction with the brand.

Control of performance of sales reps. A travel agent loyalty program is also an invaluable tool for tracking sales rep performance by measuring the regional production of travel agents and agencies by location.

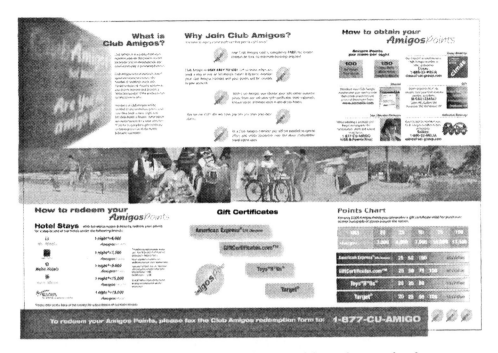

Brochure interior of Club Amigos, Sol Melia's successful travel agency loyalty program.
Source: Sol Melia Hotels & Resorts. Used with permission.

HOW TO CONTROL THE COSTS OF A LOYALTY PROGRAM

Operating a loyalty program is not an inexpensive proposition. Here are some ways to help offset the costs:

Membership levels. "Primus inter pares," or first among equals, as the Latin saying states, is the best way to approach the creation of tiers in a loyalty program. Most point-based programs have at least three levels of membership. This helps define and tailor the benefit structure, administration, and communication based on preestablished and calculated usage levels. For example, after the initial sign-up, entry-level members may qualify only for Internet-based communications, thus eliminating large mailing and postage costs for low-frequency customers.

Membership fees. Programs with high perceived value or limited programs may include membership or processing fees. These should be realistic so that the program is not perceived as a profit center. They could also be refundable from the first transaction or returned to members in the form of welcome reward certificates of equal face value.

Expiration of currency. The promotional currency should have a limited shelf life to entice usage and help maintain inventory control. The life of points should be long enough for members to earn sufficient rewards yet short enough to eliminate procrastination and "hamstering." A good rule of thumb is to maintain the validity of points for 18 to 36 months.

Redemption. Some experts recommend that rewards should be redeemable only for even amounts. This prevents members from ever cashing out completely and thus lengthens their involvement.

Expiration of membership. Members who remain inactive for longer periods of time should be dropped after attempts to re-activate their patronage. Maintaining inactive accounts just increases the administrative and communication costs.

Partners and sponsors. Strategic partners and sponsors can substantially lower the operational cost of loyalty programs by providing free rewards in exchange for exposure, sponsoring club events, seminars, or presentations, as well as by offering various co-branded activities.

Promotional currency. The sale of promotional currency can be a lucrative proposition. American Airlines Advantage miles may be earned through a variety of merchants or even bought in the form of certificates.

Merchandise sales. Club, limited edition, member-only, or program partner merchandise may be sold for profit to help offset operational costs.

Advertising. Selling advertising space in a club brochure, magazine, or the website, as well as organizing mailings for sponsors, can help generate additional revenues.

Research. For programs with highly defined audiences, conducting proprietary member research for third parties may be another way to supplement the program budget.

BEFORE YOU LEAP

Before launching a loyalty program, it is wise to formally review the objectives, market segments, internal capabilities, and infrastructure requirements. This should be done in the form of a complete business plan with specific program details, which will serve as the blueprint for the entire program.

The program objectives should be as specific as possible. For example, instead of stating "building loyalty with core retail customers," the objective should be to build a member base of 20,000 travel agents and create three levels to distinguish occasional, frequent, and top producers.

Second, targeted customer surveys should be conducted to gain prelaunch insight, which will be invaluable for the design of the program. The research should measure general market interest regarding the program and responses to the rewards and benefits offered, as well as overall customer attitudes, needs, and wants.

Finally, the review should include a detailed analysis of external challenges such as competing programs, as well as internal infrastructure challenges such as systems, staffing, communications, and administration capabilities, as well as budget requirements.

Based on this review, you will have sufficient information to develop a solid business plan for the program including goals and objectives, audience segmentation, a member recruitment plan, the communications strategy, the benefits and rewards structure, systems infrastructure, program measurements, the club organization (internal or outsourced), and the financials (program budget and point structure).

LOYALTY CHALLENGES

We have reviewed all the benefits of loyalty programs, but unfortunately, all is not rosy in loyalty land. There are some challenges to be faced.

Loyalty epidemic. The consumer marketplace is becoming saturated with loyalty programs, from frequent grocery shopper to frequent flier to frequent gasoline card to credit card loyalty programs to hotel and restaurant rewards to book clubs and movie watchers and frequent bagel eaters—and on and on. Almost every industry offers loyalty programs, and even though you are competing in the hospitality segment, your loyalty program is fighting for attention with all the programs in the market. There are two things to keep in mind. First, if you're going to do it, do it right; make your program count (with the right rewards, benefits, and communications). Running an undifferentiated, expected, copycat program will not a huge success story make. Second, you may need to narrow your focus. Try going after a specific segment or target travel agents instead of consumers; they are a much smaller crowd and may deliver a superior return on investment.

Benefits. It's easy to say that ownable and unique benefits will differentiate a loyalty program; it's not as easy to develop them. Meaningful benefits are not easy to define or may not be cheap enough to use. The solution lies in researching the market, collecting feedback from existing clients, surveying potential clients, and holding internal and external brainstorming sessions. Like a good brand strategy or campaign idea, great benefit ideas are out there; they just need to be uncovered. The second challenge is to avoid a disproportionately large emphasis on either soft or hard benefits. A good program needs both, in equilibrium. Focusing on hard benefits alone will create loyalty to points, not brands. Remember, hard benefits should build repeat patronage and soft benefits should develop brand relationships.

Cost. Loyalty programs are not cheap. They are a long-term investment and should eventually increase revenues and lower marketing costs, but be prepared to fight for them.

Partners. Most loyalty programs will have a variety of program partners, either as sponsoring companies, rewards partners, or redemption partners.

Just as with co-branding, the challenge is to choose the strategically correct partner brands for the program and keep the number of partners at a level that provides transparency for consumers.

Company buy-in. The loyalty program *must* be embraced and supported by the entire organization, starting at the top. It is a concept that will touch almost every department in any hospitality company and will be impossible to implement without a 100% consensus.

Misconceptions. The concept of loyalty is not very well understood and is surrounded with certain misconceptions. The most common misconception is that a loyalty program that rewards heavy users will make light users feel less important. The truth is that all customers should be treated equally, the only difference being that more frequent users will be rewarded more often or more lavishly. Another frequent misconception is the confusion of loyalty marketing with direct marketing. While direct marketing focuses on geographic or demographic segments and their responses to single offers, loyalty marketing rewards ongoing behavior and builds relationships on an individual basis.

Complacency. It is quite common for loyalty programs to become monotonous after the initial excitement wears off. A key challenge is to keep it continuously fresh and interesting with benefits, communications, updates, and news.

Privacy. This is an extremely sensitive issue, as loyalty programs collect plenty of data on their members. Customers are finding ways to protect their privacy, and good marketers are acknowledging that quest by using permission marketing. The principle of protecting a customer's privacy at all costs should be an integral part of any loyalty program.

FINAL EXIT

Even though you may plan to run your loyalty program perpetually, it should be launched and operated as a program with limited duration. This will give you an exit opportunity should market realities change, but it will not prevent you from extending its validity and duration indefinitely if everything goes according to plan. Not having an exit strategy will lead to many headaches and unnecessarily squandered dollars, not to mention brand repercussion, somewhere down the line. If you do have to terminate your program, don't try to sneak out of it; go out with a bang. Communicate vigorously, allow members sufficient time to redeem their points, and make them feel special and appreciated for having been members.

LOYALTY LINK

For excellent information on loyalty programs visit colloquy.com.

CHAPTER THIRTEEN

Marketing Operations

Efficiency is concerned with doing things right. Effectiveness is doing the right things.
—Peter F. Drucker

The previous chapters covered the key marketing functions. This chapter reviews several operational aspects of marketing.

HOW TO RUN A MARKETING DEPARTMENT

Being a marketing director (or any permutation of this position, from marketing manager to CMO) is hard work. It means devising market strategies and orchestrating marketing activities that will build brands and generate sales. The marketing department by its very nature is (or should be) related to all (or most) activities of the company, from research and product development to sales, operations, and finance.

As a marketing director, therefore, you will have to be part research analyst, sales manager, creative director, production coordinator, operations manager, accountant, media planner, photographer, retail store clerk, office manager, consumer (a male, a female, ages 15, 25, 34, 48, and 65 years), and many more. Thus an eclectic set of knowledge, skills, and experiences an outstanding marketing director makes.

But as the attempt to become thoroughly proficient in all these disciplines would certainly result in lunacy, the way to do it is to be a good manager of people, budgets, projects, and time. It also helps to keep educating yourself, learning where to look and what to look for, getting help from suppliers and professional consultants, and hiring people who are smarter than you.

Having been in charge of an international marketing department for several years, I've found that the following are some of the attributes of a strong marketing director:

- Have a sense of humor; marketing is fun.
- Work hard and work passionately.
- Develop the ability to perform and make decisions under pressure.
- Think visually.
- Have an insatiable interest in people, markets, and products.
- Be a browser with an inquisitive mind.
- Be willing to learn continuously and adjust your perspective.
- Learn to administer and control budgets (even though you hate it).
- Excel at cooperating with various departments.
- Believe in research.
- Be slow to engage in conflicts.
- Be resilient.
- Underpromise and overdeliver.
- Hire great people.
- Develop the ability to keep one eye on the details and the other on the big picture.

Nothing is as important in successfully managing a marketing department as follow-up. No amount of brilliant marketing is relevant if you miss deadlines, fail to finalize projects, or are unable to manage your employees' performance. I've seen good people fail repeatedly because they didn't have the discipline of proper follow-up. It is not easy to keep track of multiple projects, tasks, employees and offices, but there are many tools that can help. If you are computer dependent there's good organizational software, which, paired with some cool gadgets, will help you stay on top of things. I prefer the good old notebook. It forces me to review and rewrite all current project information on a daily basis.

It may be a cliché but it's true: building relationships is another key element in running a marketing department. People like to do business with people they like. So, the better your relationship is with clients, employees, co-workers, supervisors, suppliers, and professional consultants, the easier your work will be and the less work you will have to do yourself. You will be able to delegate to happy employees and service providers who will like doing the work for you. Thus, you will manage the process instead of the workload.

Honesty is another powerful management tool. Being honest with expectations, employees, co-workers, supervisors, clients, and suppliers will help you build a reputation for integrity. And it is hard to contradict integrity. A strong reputation for honesty will help you establish yourself as an authority.

Flexibility is often misconstrued as weakness, yet I see it as a sign of strength. If you are firm on every issue, you will become known not as strong but as difficult. Results are achieved by knowing when to be firm and when to be flexible; there is a huge difference between being reasonably flexible and not having a backbone. Or as David Ogilvy eloquently wrote: "A habit of graceful surrender on trivial issues will make you difficult to resist when you stand and fight on a major issue."

Complaining is a signal of weakness, so don't. The Japanese have a very strong stance on this. They believe that one shouldn't complain about one's company, job, or co-workers, as that will create a self-perpetuating negative momentum. Who can argue with that?

Finally, full ownership of responsibilities is what will make you a truly great marketing director. Accepting responsibility and credit in good times is easy. Accepting responsibility in times of trouble takes guts. And there will be times of trouble—mistakes made by you, your employees, your advertising agency, your printer—it really doesn't matter. You're in charge, so if you can never be held accountable and always try to dodge responsibility by blaming others, you are projecting weakness, not dependability.

MARKETING INFRASTRUCTURE

As all marketing activities must support both short-term (sales/bookings) and long-term (corporate/brand-building) objectives, the marketing infrastructure must be organized and integrated to facilitate long- and short-term projects with planning, development, and implementation while establishing and maintaining integration between marketing, sales, operations, and all other departments. To establish a fully integrated infrastructure requires strong leadership, with the objective of defining and directing an overall strategy and standardizing all marketing activities across all markets and market segments. Besides providing strategic direction, integration will help create a culture of mutual support and teamwork in which all team members and offices work together as one and support each other's efforts. Stronger involvement in the marketing process will help achieve better focus and a faster reaction to specific needs, rather than individual efforts that happen in a vacuum.

Often, marketing projects are reactionary, with marketing efforts and messages in the different markets being fragmented, with no unified strategic direction and many overlapping activities that do not necessarily meet the company's strategic objectives. The strategic marketing approach involves building an integrated system in which *each* marketing activity and *each* venue enhances and reinforces the whole. This means that you must coordinate communication and information for diverse projects, locations, offices, and activities to create a cohesive picture of the company and the brand. Creating a solid infrastructure will serve as the foundation for your marketing department.

ON BEING A LEADER

Sooner or later, you'll have employees reporting to you. This is a wonderful feeling. You have finally arrived; you are somebody's boss and can tell them what to do. Go ahead, indulge in your sense of power for 10 minutes and then do yourself a favor: become humble, more humble than you have ever been. Only humility in the face of power will make you a truly great leader. An old Italian proverb states that anybody can be polite to the king, but it takes a true gentlemen to be polite to the peasant. This is very true, so take it seriously. Everyone needs a sense of accomplishment, and bossing employees around will only result in mutual frustration. It has been my observation that truly great leaders are characterized by the following traits:

1. Truly great leaders do not take themselves too seriously. You're in charge, so be in charge with your actions and give the impression that you were born for this position. Boasting will make you look like an amateur. Filmmakers have a rule that perfectly applies here: show, don't tell.

2. Truly great leaders are tough in making decisions but gentle in executing them. Sometimes you have to make tough decisions or unpopular choices, such as laying off employees. If you manage to make difficult decisions but deliver them in a way that is compassionate and explains your reasoning, you will fortify your leadership role.

3. Truly great leaders are humble. I consider this the most important trait of all, and I can give two personal examples: (1) On the second day of my (very junior) job with Blue Diamond Growers in Sacramento, California, a man came to my desk with a coffee pot and served me a cup. I thanked him and introduced myself, only to learn that he was Walt Payne, the CEO. (2) I wrote a letter to the legendary advertising man David Ogilvy asking him to reveal a secret that he had alluded to in his book *Confessions of an Advertising Man;* he took the time to reply personally. (He said that a secret is a secret and he would be damned if he would reveal it. In a second letter, I asked him again. He replied again that he would not reveal the secret but also told me to contact his New York office for a job.)

4. Truly great leaders practice what they preach. There is nothing worse than a leader who doesn't apply her own rules to herself. You want respect? You have to give it first.

5. Truly great leaders don't complain. A leader who stands tall in the face of adversity will be admired and respected. Take advantage of tough situations to fortify your leadership.

6. Truly great leaders are honest in giving praise and criticism. If someone does a great job, tell them. If they do a bad job, teach them. Never criticize the person, though. Rather, focus on the task that went wrong.

7. Truly great leaders don't micro-manage. They coach. When I became senior director of marketing at Allegro, I asked my boss, the CEO, Benny Guevara, what his expectations were. He said: "Results is what I expect. I don't care if you come to work early, late, or at all. I don't want rule followers, I want decision makers. Don't just dream up ideas

and projects—land them." This empowerment made me start my day at 7 A.M. and finish at 10 P.M. Instead of imposing rules, he inspired me to create my own. He knew that I would impose stricter rules on myself than he could have ever expected.

8. Last, and perhaps most important, truly great leaders are not afraid of trying new things and making mistakes along the way. William Shakespeare put it more eloquently: "They say, best men are moulded out of faults, and, for the most, become much more the better for being a little bad."

Keep in mind, though, that you don't have to be the company president to be a leader. Even if you don't manage any employees, you can still apply these principles. It will be excellent training for when you become the CEO.

TRACKING RESULTS

Tracking the results of advertising and marketing activities is one surefire way of (1) running a knowledgeable marketing department and (2) becoming a marketing expert in your field. While others will skid around on the surface of guesswork, you will have hard data. Measurement is a purely operational marketing task; thus, it is important to plan it as an integral part of your marketing campaign. You can basically measure:

1. Calls to your call center (information and reservations)
2. Website traffic (visits and transactions)
3. Reservation conversion (from visits and calls)
4. Coupon redemption
5. Performance by account (regional, national, per brand, per location, total)
6. Branding (awareness, recall, appeals, benefits, features, etc.)

Measuring all calls is the basic form of tracking. It should be done by your telephone company if you are handling your reservation center in-house or by your reservation center if you're outsourcing. You can measure general call volumes from specific area codes. This information alone will give you a very good regional composite of your market. Overlaying this with demographic data will provide substantial insight into the background of your callers. One caution: make sure that the calls you measure are from prospective customers and not calls for complaints, from other divisions or something of that sort. Tracking calls to specific promotions requires more work on your behalf, but it pays off. Basically, you need to give your advertisements, mailers, or promotions a code unique to that particular activity and then have a mechanism in place so that at the point of contact, the prospect must identify the inquiry by mentioning that code. For example if you advertise in every issue of *Travel and Leisure*, you may code your March 2005 ad TL305. Then, every customer who calls is asked about the code by your phone staff.

Just as with calls, you may track general traffic to your website as well as measure the marketing impact of specific campaigns or promotions. Include a special code or link for each new promotion, and you will soon know which ad or promotion worked and which didn't.

Now, measuring call volume and website traffic is great if you are just giving information (as in a destination campaign), but if you have a reservation system at the other end, generating a lot of interest with no actual bookings is not as good. Thus, it is crucial to track calls and visits and then measure the conversion of those calls and visits into actual bookings. A reputable outsourced reservation center will be able to provide this type of information. If you're tracking calls in-house, set up a system or adjust your reservation software to facilitate this important activity.

A more traditional way of measuring promotion impact is coupon redemption. While common in consumer goods markets, coupon redemption never really took hold in hospitality and travel, partly due to the fact that travel distribution is not as structured as, say, distribution of food products. Nevertheless, coupons may be an excellent way of boosting production or interest and measuring their impact by monitoring redemption.

For many hospitality and tourism brands, allotments of inventory are pre-assigned to various larger accounts or clients, such as wholesalers, consortia, or incentive houses. Individual and group bookings in those allotments are handled by third parties and therefore are quite difficult to measure directly. In those cases, you must measure performance per account, per certain time period, and then calculate the return on the marketing investment for each account.

Finally, advertising campaigns have an impact on the market beyond the immediate call to action that they generate. They build positive associations and brand awareness, and they help position the brand in a specific way. So, measuring the impact of advertising and marketing campaigns on branding is crucial to gauge the effectiveness of specific campaigns and messages.

HOW HOSPITALITY MARKETING CAN AFFECT IMMEDIATE SALES

There are no magic formulas in marketing, and whoever claims otherwise is a phony. Often the complaint is raised that marketing is designed to be a long-term activity and that most marketing programs need many years to take effect. But who can afford to wait for years when the entire product inventory expires every 24 hours every day of the year? Yes, certain marketing programs will not produce immediate results; a rebranding project of an established brand may take many months and a significant budget. But there are marketing activities that can affect immediate sales.

Basically, marketing should be seen as an ongoing process that, if done properly, consistently, and continuously, will generate ongoing sales and produce desired results. Additionally, consistent marketing will provide ways to achieve immediate (short-term) results, such as reaching certain occupancy or sales levels during more difficult periods. For those times, there are several actions that will help produce immediate sales results for a hospitality company:

- **Special rates and packages.** Creating a special rate or package is often a good way to generate immediate sales hikes. This doesn't have to be a price discount offer. It may be a value-added offer or special package that makes the entire value proposition more attractive.
- **Sales blitz.** A series of targeted travel agent visits during a short period of time focused on promoting a single offer or destination can produce sales hikes.
- **Fax blast.** An intensive travel agent faxing campaign, pushing a certain offer, will help generate a spike in immediate sales through travel agents.
- **Newspaper advertising.** Direct advertising of a good offer in the travel section is always a good way to increase the call volume at the reservation center.
- **Direct mail and e-mail offers.** A targeted direct mail/e-mail offer promoting a special package or rate, with urgency of booking and limited availability, can increase interest, call volume, and reservations.
- **Internet offers.** People are constantly looking for great deals on the Internet. Post your hot deals on the sites of your Internet travel distributors. Most have a section for hot deals and special offers.
- **Website offers.** Create a hot deals section on your own website and post your hot deals for direct bookings or referrals to travel agents.
- **Internet travel auctions.** These auctions generate quick results. Also, since you are not advertising a discount, you are not ruining your image. The final price will be the winning bid and only if the necessary level has been met, so you can discount heavily on occasion without fear of repercussions.
- **GDS offers.** Distribute highly targeted special packages or offers to travel agents.
- **Booking bonuses and incentives.** For travel agents or consumers, special incentives may be that final push necessary to close the deal and increase sales. They should be kept short, sweet, and limited to create a sense of urgency.
- **Unused inventory.** Instead of a special push, use unused inventory to generate interest or barter for media space. Invite local journalists to stay for free. Organize farm trips. Give your inventory to charity.

While perhaps not effective immediately, these (and many similar) actions will eventually have an effect on the bottom line.

Nonetheless, if you have not done your marketing work diligently and continuously, no last-minute action, regardless of how radical, will yield the appropriate immediate results (if any at all). Actually, radical moves, more often than not, are desperation moves and are perceived as such by the marketplace. Always think of the implied message you are conveying to the marketplace before you embark on a special promotion.

TEMPUS FUGIT: MANAGE TIME OR IT WILL MANAGE YOU

Time is the end-all and be-all benchmark of performance. Budgets may be adjusted, results tweaked, and figures altered, but time is untouchable. Unlike the Rolling Stones' song, time is not on your side, so the active management of your time as a marketer should be a priority. The following six tips are helpful in managing time:

1. Maintain a daily list. Every day, list all actions that need to be completed that day and flag items for later follow-up. This will help you prioritize the daily, weekly, and monthly time invested in various tasks and projects.

2. Create project/production schedules. For each major project, a production schedule will be invaluable to keep things, people, and budgets on track.

3. Create three in-boxes: one for the day, one for the week, and one for review and filing. Empty them accordingly.

4. Handle small tasks at once. If it doesn't take more than 5 minutes, tackle small issues immediately and get them off your table.

5. Concentrate on the task at hand (also know as "taking a day at a time"). Don't procrastinate by thinking (or worrying) about three future projects instead of giving your full attention to the one at hand.

6. Communicate concisely and rapidly. Whether sending or receiving communications, manage the time you spend on the phone and on reading/writing e-mail, memoranda, letters, and proposals. If there is too much communication, request that written communications be no more than a few short paragraphs for memos and e-mails or include an executive summary for larger documents.

Following these six simple steps will greatly improve your efficiency and time consumption. There will still be days when hours seem to pass like minutes, but your overall performance will be vastly improved.

COMPETITIVE INFORMATION

You must keep abreast of what your competition is doing. An updated and comprehensive library with detailed information on competitors (pricing, brochures, advertisements, promotional materials, clippings, sales kits, media spending reports, annual plans, fact sheets) will serve as excellent reference when you are developing your marketing plans.

INTERNAL PR

Internal PR is not an area in which to be timid. A conscious effort to inform the entire organization about what your team and department have been doing and, more important, achieving is vital. Why? Because you have an internal audience. If you produce great results but operate as a hermit, you will be considered a good employee. If, however, you produce great results and inform your company about it, you will be on your way to achieving the status of expert (just don't forget to credit everyone who contributed to your success).

SIX GREAT SKILLS

Skill 1: Writing

In any working environment, chances are that a good portion (if not the majority) of your communication will be in writing—letters, memos, faxes, e-mails, reports, and presentations. Yet, it is amazing how bad written communication skills are in corporate offices.

In an excellent short book called *Writing That Works*, Kenneth Roman and Joel Raphaelson provide superb direction for the practical use of the written word. I highly recommend it, even if you only read the second chapter, which provides the following principles (parenthetical text mine): Don't mumble (say what you are trying to say). Make the organization of your writing clear (start with the topic and avoid unnecessary introductions). Use short paragraphs, short sentences, and short words. Make your writing vigorous, direct, and personal. Avoid vague modifiers (e.g., what is the "near future"?). Use specific, concrete language (don't beat around the bush). Choose the right word (are you inferring or implying? many words are often confused; learn their proper meaning). Make it perfect (know the proper spelling and avoid typos; you look sloppy if you don't). Come to the point. Write simply and naturally—the way you talk. Strike out words you don't need. Use current standard English. Don't write like a lawyer or bureaucrat. Keep in mind what your reader doesn't know. Punctuate carefully. Use facts and numbers with restraint. Write so that you cannot be misunderstood.

Another element that is crucially important in writing is to keep it short. Everyone is overloaded with print, broadcast, and online information. So, regardless of your eloquence, if you don't say what you want to say in a few short sentences or paragraphs, your communication will not be read.

Follow these principles and your writing will improve significantly. Another great little book on writing is William Strunk and E. B White's *Elements of Style*. Study both books, and your writing will improve dramatically.

Good writing skills pay off. Consider the following examples. A well-written letter to David Ogilvy, the legendary advertising man and founder of the Ogilvy and Mather advertising agency, resulted in a personal reply with a job offer at his agency's New York office. A concise 40-page report about the potential for entering the cruise industry presented to the top three company executives laid the groundwork for three significant job promotions in less than 2 years. A well-researched, well-written book proposal resulted in a publishing contract from one of the largest and most renowned publishers. You may have guessed it. I am writing about my own experiences.

You do not need a special gift for writing. You may not aspire to become the next Gabriel Garcia Marquez. You may even dislike writing. That's okay. Honing your writing skills will just help you communicate effectively and get your point across. And who doesn't want that?

Skill 2: Generating Ideas

While brainstorming may not be a skill per se, coming up with new ideas is. In today's world of commoditized products, bland marketing, and safe management, only new ideas can truly generate differentiation and value, both for the company and for the consumers. And brainstorming is one *funtastic* way of creating ideas. Cynics often mistakenly perceive it as a chaotic process of wasting time. I have come to believe that it is one of the best ways to generate ideas, involve employees with the company and product, and build camaraderie. Brainstorming is a technique that works for many different types of projects and areas of business. Besides advertising, it may be used for product development, customer service, promotions, public relations, human resources, operations, and even finance.

Choose a setting in which everyone feels relaxed and at ease. Then explain that this is not a formal meeting and there will be no presenters, but that everyone is encouraged to participate. Someone needs to conduct this event loosely, without being in charge. This person will provide general direction and summarize the findings. If you're the head of the department, it is probably best if you remain a participant and let someone else conduct the session. Stating its purpose and objective should start the session; just make sure that everyone understands that there are no right or wrong comments. Participants should not hold back, as brainstorming emphasizes quantity. All ideas and suggestions should be documented, and once the session is over you will likely have dozens of suggestions, most useless but a few good starts.

Skill 3: Implementing

Projects are how marketing work is organized and ideas get implemented. A lot has been said about project management, yet this remains quite a challenge for many marketing managers: too many deadlines, too many people, too little time, tight budgets, and the project is off schedule. This is why it is crucial that you first set up an integrated marketing infrastructure to aid you in the development of mechanisms that will help facilitate, manage, and control the implementation of all marketing and marketing-related projects.

The main steps in defining the marketing implementation process include:

- Defining the short-term needs (marketing in the markets, generate traffic/ sales, awareness)
- Defining the long-term needs (brand building, corporate communications, growth)
- Setting worldwide marketing/communications parameters (developing positioning identity)
- Defining the scope of involvement from each office and department (who does what and when)
- Developing project implementation teams

An integrated marketing decision-making process will also substantially improve the individual marketing budget control and in effect create economies of scale, achieving greater spending efficiency and thus stronger overall marketing effectiveness.

If managing projects is one of your weak spots and you're serious about getting help, there are courses you can take or you may try Project Challenge, interactive software that simulates the work environment and lets you play and learn how to manage projects.

Table 13.1 illustrates optimal project flow, with budget allocation, implementation teams, and result measurement.

Skill 4: Hiring and Firing

Do you think that hiring and firing people is not a skill? I have come to realize that this is one of the most important skills in managing a marketing department.

Hiring the right people will make or break your department, and while it is certainly more pleasant than giving someone the boot, it is a much more difficult task. Who should you hire? Talented people who are smarter than you and are hungry and willing to learn. They will be eager to work hard and will not succumb to the everyday routine. Watch out for the potential superstars, rare as they may be. They often come in unusual packages, without the "necessary" prerequisites of education or industry background, but they bring gusto for work, character, and plenty of gray matter. David Ogilvy used to say to his agency department heads: "If we hire people who are smaller than we are, we shall become a company of dwarfs. But if each of us hires people who are bigger than we are, we shall become a company of giants." How true.

Firing people is the most grueling task, yet it often needs to be done. Often managers refuse to fire questionable people on the grounds that they are doing an acceptable job. Their technical performance may be sound, but if they are otherwise detrimental to the performance of others or the entire office, they are doing more harm than good. I once had the task of turning around a

TABLE 13.1   Project Flow

Discovery phase	
Infrastructure	**Insight**
Marketing infrastructure	Audit and analysis
Revenue and profit objectives	Consumer research, perceptions, and attitudes
System capability	Customer segmentation
Resources	Behavior drives
Historical results	

Planning phase	
Project sections	**Strategy**
Priorities	Project strategy
Segmentation by market and profit potential	Market strategy
Objectives	Communication strategy
Project plan	Process strategy
	Budget strategy
	Deployment strategy

Implementation phase		
Implementation plan	**Development**	**Execution**
Budget allocation	Internal communications	Production schedule
Market projections	Sales support	Coordination with: support team, suppliers, vendors, distribution channels)
Media planning	Corporate support	
Creative plan	External communications	
Team allocation	Creative development (direct, advertising, collateral, point of sale, interactive, etc.)	Project controls
Training plan		Implementation

Feedback		
Consumer/market	**Financial**	**Project effectiveness**
Response	Cost per sale	Time to market
Brand appreciation	Return on investment	Budget control
Perceptions	Revenue/profit	Quality
Attitudes		Accuracy
Satisfaction		Team cooperation

marketing office that was troubled by inefficiency and squandered funds. After evaluating the employees' performance, I had to let everyone go and hired a very capable assistant. For 6 months I ran the department only with this in-credible person before all problems were resolved and the operation was back on track. We worked 12 hours every day, but it gave me a chance to set up everything properly and personally look into every functional aspect of the marketing operation. Then I was able to fill the necessary positions with sev-eral capable people and we had 2 stellar marketing years, after which I moved on (the added value to me was that my workload was radically reduced by having competent people pulling their weight). Who should you fire? Anyone who spreads gloom and brings down office morale; incurable office politi-cians, who waste too much of everyone's time; and prima donnas, who are too good to roll up their sleeves and actually work.

Skill 5: Presenting

Since you are in charge of the marketing function, chances are that you will have to make many presentations. These may be for customers, travel agents, reservations personnel, the board of directors, investors, media people, and others. Many people hate making presentations because they hate public speaking. They feel exposed and scrutinized. They are. Becoming good at mak-ing presentations involves knowing how to overcome your fears. While I've listed some of my own tips and techniques for presentations and training sem-inars in other parts of this book, here I'd like to confront 10 presentation myths that Ron Hoff describes as "fuddy duddy fundamentals" in his excellent book on making presentations *I Can See You Naked*:

1. "Don't be nervous." Telling presenters not to be nervous is like telling them to stop breathing. Everybody's nervous. Everybody. Which is good. A certain amount of nervousness gives your presentation an edge.

2. "Use a podium." Why? It restricts all movement and makes you look like a monster.

3. "State your objective." Hey, no offense, but we don't care what your objective is. What we care about (we, being your audience) is our objective. The "me generation" may be history, but people are still in-terested in what you can do for them, not what you can do for yourself.

4. "Speak slowly." Slow speakers can drive you nuts. It's like watching cement harden. News anchors speak between 165 and 195 words per minute (I've clocked them). Most presenters speak considerably slower than that- about 120 wpm.

5. "Tell a joke to get started." In most meetings, if you start with a joke just because you think it's funny, you're a candidate for immediate tune-out. A relevant, true story is so much better than a concocted joke that there is no comparison.

6. "Turn the lights low to show your slides." That's like saying, "Nighty, night."

7. "Cover all bases." "We try to cover everything and the audience remembers nothing." That may be the most prevalent self-criticism that I hear from presenters who have had bad luck in competitive presentations.

8. "Make it flow." Old-fashioned presentations flowed along like maple syrup—with smooth, immaculate bridges and transitions. TV has changed all that. Break it up. Jolt people. Surprise them.

9. "Summarize at the end." No—summarize all the way through. We call it "planting flags." Keep making it easy for people to remember.

10. "Keep control at all times." Don't try to be captain Queeg. You're likely to have a mutiny on your hands. Let an audience wrangle if it wants to. They'll feel better afterward, and you will come across as somebody who has enough confidence to give the audience some intellectual freedom.

Hoff finishes by saying, "The worst enemy of presentation is rigidity. The world has changed. Television is here. Holistics is here. Information delivery has gone through its biggest transformation in history. No wonder the old fundamentals of presentations are being debunked. Onward, friend, we've hardly started."

To all this I can only add: fail often to succeed sooner.

Skill 6: Training

"The desire of knowledge, like the thirst of riches, increases ever the acquisition of it," said Laurence Sterne. Knowledge and curiosity create a sort of self-fulfilling prophecy, and training is the easiest way to jump-start the knowledge-thirst momentum. Unfortunately, training is often neglected and postponed, as everyone is too busy doing their jobs. But coaching must be part of any marketing job. In the hustle and bustle of day-to-day work, it is quite difficult to set aside time for learning and training. The acquisition of knowledge at all levels, however, is the foundation on which an organization will thrive and grow strong. Coaching or training may take many forms, from product training for reservation centers to marketing discussions with operations personnel. In the hospitality industry, besides the physical structures, the product is defined by the people, and an ongoing training program must be at the core of the marketing strategy. Having observed many presenters, I can share with you what I have seen that works:

Involve the audience based on their self-interest Let's say that you are presenting information about your product portfolio to a room of reservation agents. You may say: (1) "This is our portfolio; besides standard rooms, we also have suites that have some extra features, as described in the manual" or (2) "For those of you who specialize in the family market, part of our product portfolio is optimal for families with children. Our reservation system allows you to presell the children's activities packages, so you can make a commission on the entire sale. The standard rooms are nice and suitable for two adults with two extra beds for children. The extra beds are subject to a fee, which can be handled on property or presold by you; this again allows you to make an extra commission. Finally, the suites have accommodations for four and certain added values included, such as the children's activities package and the parents' romantic moments package. There are no supplements to presell; but the suites have a higher rate and an extra booking bonus; thus, you will make an even larger commission selling the suites. Then for the couples market specialists, we have . . .": you get the idea. While version (1) is a typical boring, matter-of-fact litany, approach (2) qualifies the different parts of the audience based on their specialty or interest and provides them with factual information about maximizing their commissions.

Make it genuinely interesting   Use different materials—slides, video, handouts, quizzes, puzzles, games, toys, or any other aid that will make your training session interesting and entertaining. You can't bore people into paying attention.

Create a positive learning climate   Learning and training do not have to be confined to a classroom. Change the training venue to create a better learning climate. Hold your training in a park, on the beach, at a restaurant. Again, the idea is to break away from the boring and expected and facilitate the collective thinking process.

Reward participation   Even if you make the reward as dull as handing out dollar bills for every correct answer, create some reward system. It will make participants pay attention and may even trigger a little competitiveness.

Keep it as short and simple as possible (but not shorter or simpler than that)   Too many presenters ramble on and do not know when to stop. If you overcomplicate issues, you may feel compelled to overexplain. But you are not teaching thermodynamics. Just isolate the core elements of your topic, explain each of the elements with vigor, and stop.

CHAPTER FOURTEEN

Behind the Budget

Money is like a sixth sense without which you cannot make a complete use of the other five.
—W. Somerset Maugham

You may have a superb product, a great staff, and the smartest marketing plan, but if your company overexpands, or if your overhead, operational, or marketing costs prevent you from operating profitably and delivering on the bottom line, none of the above matters. The Internet boom-bust of 1999–2000 showed this perfectly. Therefore, this chapter is devoted to issues of figures and the bottom line. It discusses sources of business, marketing budgets, and cost-savings methods.

WHY IT PAYS NOT TO BE A BOTTOM-LINE PERSON

While seemingly contradicting this chapter's first sentence, there is a huge difference between delivering on the bottom line and being a bottom-line manager. The latter focuses solely on the bottom line and seem to lose track of other important issues.

Let's say that your company expanded its product portfolio and you need to increase market share on the West Coast dramatically, as most of your new destinations are not serviced from many other markets. You have several options: you could drop overall prices to attract visitors from all markets. You could drop prices just in certain markets. Or you could maintain prices and invest in the markets in which you need to grow.

Suppose you decide to do the last. Based on a careful review of the West Coast markets you realize that, considering the new location, there are three wholesalers who could triple or quadruple their current production in 3 years. Therefore, you decide to allocate disproportionately large marketing budgets to these wholesalers for 3 years. Additionally, you decide to support those distribution channel actions with your own brand marketing activities. The first year your wholesale marketing support, calculated as a percentage of the wholesalers' production, would be very high: 12–15%. (For example, if Operator A had annual production of $3 million, you provided marketing support of approximately $400,000, or slightly over 13%.) In the second year, each wholesaler's production grew to a level that reduced your marketing support to a more palatable 7–8%. (Thus, if Operator A's production grew to $5 million, the $400,000 marketing participation was reduced to 8%.) Finally, in the third year, the wholesalers' production grew so much that most of your support was a very acceptable 3–4%. (Production grew to approximately $12 million, and the $400,000 marketing support was 3.4%.) By that time, however, the wholesalers would have stopped looking at percentages and considered you a staple in their product portfolio, as well as a key player who invests significant budgets. The result would be that you not only delivered on the bottom line, but also grew profits, developed strategic relationships with key wholesalers, and in the process boosted brand recognition to enviable levels.

Conversely, a bottom-line person would have made the following calculation: Operator A has annual sales of $3 million; thus, your marketing support would have been $90,000 based on the standard 3%. If Operator A wants to increase your marketing support to $400,000, their production must grow to over $13 million. Guess what? Operator A doesn't care about your calculation, so your production remains where it has traditionally been. You, however, can proudly claim that you protected the bottom line, which in this case was the 3% rule.

But, amazingly, so did the first scenario.

MARKET STRATEGY: WHY YOU NEED THE SOB

All sales are good, right? Not really. Creating volume is one thing, maximizing revenue is another. The only way to know where your profits will come from is by having a source of business (SOB). The core sales objective for hotels, motels, resorts, cruise lines, and restaurants is to fill rooms, cabins, and tables to capacity. For destinations the core objective is to attract quality visitors, for airlines to fill the seats, and for car rental companies to rent all cars—all of this consistently and at the highest possible rate. The source of business will be your guiding light when it comes to reaching your sales, revenue, and profit objectives. Moreover, a realistic SOB will help you establish (or request) a realistic marketing budget. The SOB should define your production by geographical and regional markets, market segments, and distribution channels.

The data you will need to develop a solid and realistic SOB is your historic production data (occupancy, rates, revenues, sales data, seasonality patterns, geographic origin, market mix), competitive pricing, sales and marketing data, market trends, and economic forecasts. Once you have all this information, it's just a matter of compiling the data into a format that will allow you to create next year's projections. These projections will provide you with (1) high, normal, and low production levels, (2) expectations, (3) rates,

(4) revenues, (5) occupancy levels, and (6) trends. Once you have your SOB, you will also have a good indication of what marketing budget you will need to achieve that objective.

HOW MUCH IS ENOUGH?

This is the ____ million dollar question (you insert the figure). Management needs guidelines to be comfortable with the budget recommendations and approvals so that they can look good in front of the board of directors, investors, or owners. So, every year at budgeting time, as the question of how much money should be allocated to marketing lingers in everyone's mind, the need for an easy answer grows. Is it 3% of revenues or 5%? The 3% would be easily approved. It's a nice low percentage. But what if your competitors spend 13%? Well, they must know something we don't. Or they are simply crazy, splurging that way.

Welcome to the Twilight Zone. There is no simple formula for this task. Before you start to debate the total amount versus the percentage, it is important to define what the company shoves under the line item "Marketing Budget." Different companies define marketing differently, so this can include anything from the salaries of marketing personnel, office costs, and travel expenses to media dollars to all of the above. Thus, there's no point in fighting over a percentage before you know what needs to be covered by it. A 3% budget for marketing activities exclusively (advertising, direct mail, PR, Internet, and promotions) may be much better than a 6% budget that encompasses all sales- and marketing-related expenses as well as office and personnel costs.

Another point to keep in mind is to use the percentage to set an amount, not to operate on a sliding-scale budget. You are budgeting for future spending, so it is very difficult to work with percentages instead of a final amount. If management agrees to a marketing budget of 10% of revenues, you need to establish the final amount. Let's say that your revenue projection is $5 million, so your marketing budget will be $500,000. But what happens if you don't reach those revenue goals? What if you reach only $4.5 million? On a strict percentage basis your 10% budget will automatically drop to $450,000. Now let's say that this drop was due to the cancellation of some business in the last fiscal month of the year and that your entire $500,000 budget was already spent. Who is responsible for this $50,000 discrepancy? Conversely, what if you surpass revenue projections by $500,000? On a sliding scale, you should have an extra $50,000 in the budget. While it is virtually impossible to plan and operate on a sliding scale, there is room for flexibility. Marketing plans and expenditures should be rechecked and, if necessary, revised throughout the year. Budget commitments such as media buys should be made with a certain flexibility in mind. Just make sure that all of this is defined before the beginning of the next fiscal year.

Budgeting must not be a cookie-cutter process. You will need to budget differently for a period of new product and brand launches than for a period of maintenance (maintenance does not mean cutting back—launching new products means investing more!) or if you are the only player in the destination than if you have many competitors. Marketers may never get the marketing budgets they desire, but insufficient budgets mean paralysis. Charles Dickens said, "Annual income twenty pounds, annual expenditure nineteen nineteen and six, result happiness. Annual income twenty pounds, annual expenditure twenty pounds ought and six, result misery."

THREE FAULTY WAYS AND ONE CORRECT WAY TO SET YOUR MARKETING BUDGET

Let's say that you operate a luxurious 200-room resort in a popular destination. In a calendar year you'll have a total of 73,000 room nights to sell (365 × 200). Through the process of developing an SOB, you determined that your annual revenue goal is $8 million and your net profit goal is $1 million. Your SOB tells you that to achieve this revenue goal, you must have average year-round occupancy of 77% at an average daily rate of $142.3 (73,000 × 77% = 56,210 room nights × $142.3 = $8 million). Based on experience, knowledge, market trends, and professional advice, you determined that you need a marketing budget of $1.5 million to achieve those goals. Therefore, you are left with a total operational and administrative budget of $5.5 million.

Unfortunately, the marketing budget is seldom set as in this example. A variety of factors, among which is the lack of marketing accountability, have reduced the perception of marketing budgets to that of an expense. Thus the three most common formulas for setting marketing budgets are:

1. Last year's budgets with or without an inflation adjustment. This formula is erroneous because it bases the marketing budget on the assumption that last year's budget was done correctly.
2. Fixed percentage of sales. This formula is erroneous because it presents marketing as a direct function of sales instead of the reverse.
3. Same as that of the competition. This formula is erroneous because you are assuming that your competitors know what they are doing.

These formulas are faulty because they all approach marketing as a cost of sales rather than its driver. Furthermore, this type of budgeting (lack of a cause–effect relationship) places marketing on top of the list when costs need to be cut.

The optimal way of setting a marketing budget consists of defining your sales, revenue, and profit objectives (SOB), determining what marketing activities will generate the desired results, and then allocating the funds you will need to implement these activities so that you can achieve your objective. This is results-based budgeting. The problem lies in the lack of marketing accountability, as many companies do not measure marketing return on investment.

This is a pity, because if you don't know what drives your sales/revenues/profits, you cannot justify requests for budget increases, nor can you defend against budget cuts. There is no magic formula, though. The only way to know which marketing actions generate sales is by learning to gauge the returns by continuous testing, measuring, and research. Once you have developed mechanisms to track your marketing return on investment, you will be able to defend your marketing plan and your marketing budget will be treated as an investment rather than an expense.

MARKETING RETURN ON INVESTMENT

> Never ask of money spent
>
> Where the spender thinks it went.
>
> Nobody was ever meant
>
> To remember or invent
>
> What he did with every cent.

I once tried to use this limerick by Robert Frost (from "The Hardship of Accounting") when I was asked to justify budget allocations. I got a nice laugh, but still had to present the return on investment.

Measuring the results of marketing campaigns is not easy. It takes dedication, discipline, and commitment. The bottom line of marketing must be closely observed and controlled. Marketing is about ideas and results, and the ideas that are implemented must deliver measurable results. Accordingly, it should be handled as a business unit, which requires accountability (i.e., being able to measure marketing return on investment). Before you embark on any marketing activity, make sure that you have a mechanism in place to measure results. For more details on this topic read "Tracking Results" in Chapter 13.

MULTITASKING MARKETING ACTIVITIES

Whenever possible, have your marketing actions pull double duty. A by-product of integrating your marketing activities, this is an excellent way of maximizing your marketing budget. Extracting extra benefits may be achieved by arranging for a single effort to yield more than one benefit. This is not easy, but the most cost-effective marketing strategy combines two or three functions in a single advertising or promotional effort to achieve multiple objectives.

A great example of multiple benefits is a promotional campaign run by British Airways immediately following the Gulf War. Consumer confidence was at a low level, as the fear of terrorist attacks reduced load factors to only 30%. British Airways took full-page ads and double-page spreads in newspapers in over 60 countries and announced a sweepstakes promotion called "Everybody

Flies Free on April 23." The winners were to be chosen in a drawing. The multiple benefits included:

- Promotional benefit: the sweepstakes drawing attracted millions of entries.
- Brand strategy benefit: the campaign reinforced the airline's image as "the World's Favorite Airline."
- Market intelligence benefit: the sweepstakes entry forms created an exceptionally useful database with in-depth travel information.
- Publicity benefit: the airline received millions of dollars' worth of free media coverage.
- Sales benefit: the campaign helped British Airways return to pre–Gulf War levels in a few short months (talk about benefiting from marketing during a recession!).

A single campaign producing five major marketing benefits is quite an achievement. But even if you can't get such dramatic multiple results, smart marketing will help you occasionally score two goals with one throw. Watch out for such opportunities and use them to achieve their maximum potential.

CRITICAL MASS

There are thousands of ways to allocate funds from your budget. How to split it will largely depend on your product, the life cycle of your brand, the markets you are after, and so on. When you are on a limited budget, one of the most common mistakes is to spread yourself too thin. This happens when you try to be too many things to too many people.

With any budget, but especially a limited one, a very simple allocation guideline can be established by following the principle of Maslow's hierarchy of needs, which states that (1) some needs are more basic or critical than others; (2) the more basic needs must be satisfied at a minimum level before other needs are activated; and (3) as the basic needs become satisfied, more advanced ones come into play.

Following this principle, you'll develop a hierarchy of marketing activities with specific objectives and budgets, and you'll move to the next level only after achieving your marketing objectives in the current level. For example:

1. Start with the critical marketing activities that will affect immediate sales, such as creating a collateral piece, the fulfillment of this piece, coop marketing with wholesalers, GDS marketing, directory listings, group sales promotions, trade show participation, an ongoing fax campaign, familiarization trips for travel agents, and training and educational seminars for travel agents.

2. After you have covered these activities, move to the next level, which may include the design of a website, consumer promotions, direct marketing, booking incentives, and a public relations campaign.

3. Once you have allocated funds for those activities, you can place your own ads in the travel trade publications, hire sales reps in key markets, and organize publicity events.

4. Having covered the trade, you can then move into direct consumer advertising such as newspaper, magazine, and radio advertising and the development of a loyalty program.

5. Finally, if there's still money left in your budget, you can move into TV advertising and other marketing opportunities such as sponsorships.

Granted, it is difficult to know up front just which activity will yield the best results. But you must keep trying different approaches, testing the responses, and measuring your marketing return on investment. After a while you will know which activity delivered the best results, and you'll be able to optimize your budget allocations. Remember, whatever action you decide to take, to have an impact your brand must have critical mass, and however small your budget, it is always better to reach a small audience repeatedly than a large audience once.

BUDGET CONTROL

One of the most hated and most important administrative functions of any marketing job is the control of the marketing budget. And no, you cannot leave it to accounting. Tight budget control will help you optimize budget allocations and maximize brand exposure.

1. **Plan your spending.** This goes without saying. A well-planned budget allocation will allow you to keep tight control on how your money is spent.

2. **Create a marketing ledger.** This seems like tedious work but it is well worth doing. Create a spreadsheet with the total marketing budget and deduct every invoice or charge that you receive. This takes only a few minutes a week and will provide you with an accurate picture of your spending levels. It also serves as a double control to be reconciled with the accounting department at the end of the year.

3. **Create procedures.** The marketing department covers many functions, and a good proportion of the activities are repetitive. Take advantage of this and create solid procedures for processing these activities in an optimal way; otherwise, you will lose track of the money already spent.

4. **Become friends with your controller.** Marketing folk tend to see accountants as bean counters who don't understand the fine art of

splurging on marketing. In reality, though, aside from the occasional control freak, controllers can be turned into partners if you take the time to develop a solid relationship. Being partners doesn't mean splitting kickbacks, but rather making them understand the function of your job and making them see marketing as an investment rather than an expense. It will help if you can back up all spending by sales results you have achieved. Don't expect miracles, however; they did become accountants because of the left side of their brain.

5. **Leave a cushion.** *Always* leave a cushion of 10–20% of the total marketing budget. The cushion will help you cover unplanned expenses in case some new and interesting projects come up during the year or if you overspend on some projects.

6. **Budget approvals.** If you're responsible for controlling the budget, make sure that you're the only one allowed to approve spending. This is one of the few areas where being a control freak is actually okay.

7. **Benchmarking.** Always get at least three bids to benchmark the cost of any project you are initiating. This will keep everyone honest and will always keep you informed about the price range for project costs. Even if you have a dedicated printer or other supplier, it will not hurt to get an occasional bid just to confirm that you're still getting a good deal.

8. **Complimentaries.** You will, without a doubt, be bombarded with requests for complimentaries or freebies. These may include requests for charity donations, VIPs, employee family members, client staff, media visitors, travel agents, industry personnel, and many more. In hospitality, complimentaries are considered an easy giveaway because they "don't cost anything." But they do cost, and there is a fine line between being chivalrous and being taken for a ride. You don't want to be perceived as cheap, but you also cannot forget that your job is to sell the product, not give it away. My recommendation is to (a) create a budget for complimentaries and have them as a line item in the marketing budget; (b) minimize the number of people who are allowed to approve them; and (c) have a procedure in place for booking them.

PAY-FOR-PERFORMANCE

Just as you pay travel agents a commission, in certain situations you may want to try to negotiate performance-based compensation. This means that instead of a flat fee, you compensate the service provider based on the performance of a specific project. For example, when developing an e-commerce website, you could offer the web development company a package that includes a basic fee and commission on every transaction during the first 12 months. You may propose to pay a media outlet (magazine, website, etc.) based on the number of inquiries they generate. Granted, these are unorthodox methods, but in specific circumstances they may help preserve the budget.

BEWARE OF UNSOLICITED MARKETING PROPOSALS

As soon as you become the marketing decision maker, you'll be inundated with unsolicited proposals from various companies offering you anything from advertising space and sponsorships to professional services or asking for donations for charities, auctions, or research contributions. Except for a few sloppy ones, most proposals will contain some type of independent research study that will show that the publication has the highest readership or best demographic, the service will generate the best results, or the sponsorship of the event will yield the highest exposure.

You should evaluate each proposal carefully because among the majority of irrelevant ones you'll occasionally run into a great opportunity. Some companies will offer you participation in exchange for product (barter). But regardless of how low the cost of participation is, participate only if this promotion fits your strategy. Never participate just to be nice or because it's cheap. It is your company's budget, and you must allocate it to achieve maximum results.

If you think a proposal presents a good opportunity but you don't have any more money in the budget, offer to compensate based on performance. After all, the proposal was unsolicited, so if the offer is good, the company may agree.

MAXIMIZING YOUR BUDGET THROUGH BARTER

Especially in the travel and hospitality industry, barter may be an excellent way to maximize your marketing budget by using unused inventory. As marketing costs rise, bartering is becoming a popular way of funding various marketing-related expenses. Hospitality products represent some of the best barter material, and barter (or product exchange) companies are always interested in good hospitality inventory. In theory you can barter your product (rooms, cabins, tickets, meals) for anything under the sun, but the most common exchanges are for media, printing, and promotional items. The true value of bartering is in using excess inventory for goods and services instead of cash. Especially in hospitality, however, the additional benefits of bartering are the exposure of your product to an audience that would otherwise not be at your property and the ancillary non-rate income that will be generated by that new audience.

In the past, bartering had a dubious image due to shady deals. Nowadays, however, there are highly reputable companies that specialize in product exchange, and you can profit by working with them. Nevertheless, always check for references and recommendations before signing a contract.

When you are ready to negotiate a barter contract, consider the following:

- **Ratio.** Barter companies work with ratios, which means that they will require a larger amount of your barter credit for the cash value of the bartered item (e.g., media). Thus, for a straight cash media buy of $750,000, you may end up paying $1,125,000 in barter credits, which would represent a ratio of 1:1.5. If your product is in very high demand, you should try to avoid ratios.

- **Cash/barter blend.** Another way of making a barter agreement is by paying part in cash and part in barter. If the cash blend portion is significant, you should be able to avoid a ratio altogether. Especially for larger media buys, a cash/barter blend may be required, so try to find out how much your barter company will be paying for the media (large barter companies have highly negotiated media rates) to make sure that you get the best possible rates.

- **Cost benchmarking.** Benchmark the cost of the items you are acquiring through barter; that is, find out how much you would pay in cash. Otherwise, you may get hit with a high acquisition cost on top of a high ratio. Before you buy media through barter, check with your agency or media buying service to determine the media rates they are getting. In some cases, the media rates your agency gets due to volume buying may be so low that it will be cheaper to pay cash than barter. When you're bartering for merchandise such as promotional items or hard goods (anything from T-shirts to TV sets), these will commonly command a higher exchange value than your hospitality product. You must keep in mind that a TV set has a much longer shelf life than a hotel room, which expires every 24 hours; thus, it is valued in terms of hard dollars in comparison to your soft-dollar product.

- **Barter rates.** Carefully negotiate on what rates (room, cabin, ticket, etc.) you will base the agreement with your barter company. In bartering for media, it is fair to match the discount in rate to the media cost discount.

- **Resale restrictions.** Define exactly how the barter company is allowed to resell your inventory. This could include restricting sales to the public through travel agents, and so on. You don't want the market to be flooded by large amounts of your product at dumping prices.

- **Expiration date.** Always put an expiration date on your inventory; most agreements specify somewhere between 12 and 36 months.

- **Usage.** Specify and limit the volume of usage per agreed-upon time period. You don't want the barter company to use $1 million of non-paying inventory in the first month. In the case of a media buy, a fair approach is to allow the inventory to be used at a rate similar to the one at which you are being advertised. Another option is to prorate the inventory for the duration of the contract. Yet another option is to treat the inventory as an account and allocate a certain number of units per time period.

- **Blackout dates.** The barter agreement should include all blackout dates, such as major holidays, that will be excluded from the barter use.
- **Commissions.** Some barter companies try to charge a commission or negotiation fee for brokering the barter deal. This is a questionable practice; after all, they are in the barter business and should make their money on the exchange of goods.
- **Limitations.** Specify any limitations you need to include to protect your brand, budget, and company interests.
- **Control.** Define the mechanism for control of usage of your inventory and, especially in media buys, the verification of media placement. A reputable barter company will provide independent media verification (affidavits) and tearsheets as part of the agreement.
- **Reservations.** Develop a smooth reservation procedure for the bartered inventory. It benefits no one to hold large inventories without being able to liquidate them. The easiest way to do this is by treating the barter agent as an account and creating a special booking code.
- **Accounting.** Last but not least, accounting for bartered inventory is crucial. Involve your accounting department and establish proper procedures.

For additional information, contact the International Reciprocal Trade Association at irta.net or the National Association of Trade Exchanges at nate.org.

APPENDIX

The Marketing Plan

It is a bad plan that admits of no modification.
—Publilius Syrus, Maxims

THE MARKETING PLAN

A key responsibility of yours will be to create a detailed annual marketing plan. The purpose of this plan is to have a document that will summarize the objectives, strategies, actions, and budgets for each year. It is an excellent exercise for reviewing the marketing organization and process. The plan must be created and used as a tool; it does no good to produce an extensive document, and then put it on the shelf and forget about it.

Regardless of the company's size, the marketing plan should contain the following sections (in larger organizations, various sections may be developed by different departments, such as corporate strategic planning, sales, etc.):

Executive Summary

The executive summary should be no longer than one or two pages and should contain all key elements and conclusions from the marketing plan. This section is necessary to provide an instant overview to anyone who is interested in the company's planned market activities and expectations but doesn't have time to review the entire plan. In brief, it should specify:

- Next year's goals (revenue, occupancy, rate)
- Economic forecast and expectations
- Trends (market, distribution, consumer, travel, product)
- Current year-to-date results

- Recent year-over-year results
- Key current-year company developments
- Key information on competitors

Situation Overview

This section should review the current economic situation and forecast, and what effects the economic expectations will have on consumer and business behavior. It should also discuss the development of various trends in the industry and its segments relevant to the company.

Competitive Analysis

The competitive analysis should provide a detailed review of:

- Competitive products
- Competitive pricing comparison
- Competitive market and product developments
- Competitive marketing activities and budgets

SWOT Analysis

The SWOT (strengths, weaknesses, opportunities, threats) analysis should provide a detailed overview of where your product, company, locations, and brands stand within the business environment.

Distribution and Market Segment Analysis

The distribution analysis section should provide a detailed overview of the market mix. It should include a historical overview, year-to-date figures, and trends, expectations, percentages, potential, and objectives by market segment:

- End user (business, leisure, direct bookings, packages, loyal consumers)
- Retail (travel agents, consortia)
- Wholesale (wholesalers, tour operators)
- Corporate (corporate accounts, groups, meetings and incentives)
- Other (associations, private events, etc.)
- Regional (market origin)

Goals

The goals section should define all of the company's primary market goals, such as revenue, occupancy, and rate goals. Other strategic goals, such as increasing brand recognition and awareness, brand (re)positioning, gaining market share, entering new markets, and developing niche markets, should also be stated here.

Source of Business

The SOB will likely be developed in cooperation with various departments of the organization. It provides a detailed breakdown of the production forecast, sales quotas, and overall objectives. The SOB also serves as the guideline for formulating strategies and actions, as well as establishing the necessary marketing budget and staffing guide.

Strategies and Actions

This section lays out all the details of the entire plan:

1. Define marketing strategies and actions by market segment: consumer, travel agent, wholesale, corporate accounts, groups
2. Define overall marketing strategies and actions by action segment: public relations advertising, promotions, Internet marketing, events, retail travel trade marketing, wholesale coop marketing, and so on
3. Define strategies and actions by brand (pricing, product, distribution, promotion)
4. Define strategies and actions by product unit or location (pricing, product, distribution, promotion)

Marketing Budget

The final marketing budget should be included, and interrelationships should be established between key budget parameters and the various sections of the plan.

Marketing Staffing Guide

Based on the SOB, the marketing staffing guide should provide the organizational structure of the marketing department.

Intercompany Links

The intercompany links section should provide any additional company information related to or in support of the plan, such as sales strategies and action plans, corporate development plans, and so on.

Support Information

The support section may contain any facts and figures used to support the information presented in the plan. These may include flight schedules and capacities, destination trends, third-party destination campaign details, and similar related information.

Marketing plans should be used as working documents—as benchmarks for production, guides for budget allocation, and blueprints for strategy. Plenty of time needs to be devoted to the development of a solid plan. But regardless of how well conceived your plan is, you must always remember: plans don't fail, executions fail.

Epilogue

Seest thou a man diligent in his work. He shall stand before kings.
—The Bible, Proverbs 22:29

GNOTHY SEAUTON, A K A KNOW THYSELF

Diligence and dedication combined with passion and affinity will be the key to success in any marketing job. So, if you choose hospitality marketing as your profession, choose it for the right reasons. Don't choose it just because it sounds less boring than accounting. Choosing a career is a process; get to know yourself so that you know why you are making this career choice.

At 17 I needed to choose a college major and thus make my career choice. Since I loved sailing and windsurfing, I decided that it would be a great idea to study naval architecture. Combining my passion with my profession—designing boats and then sailing them—sounded wonderfully romantic. Then reality hit. Naval architecture was extremely technical and definitely the wrong choice. I had confused the passion of usage with the profession of engineering and wound up miserable. Even though I disliked the program from the first day and performed poorly in a variety of classes, it took me five semesters to decide to change majors. I was burdened by the perception that giving up something would make me a quitter. Only later in life did I realize that sticking with the wrong choice is the wrong choice and that change is actually good if done wisely. This became an important lesson. Learn from my experience: before you jump into a hospitality marketing career, find out if it is right for you.

WHAT IS YOUR JOB?

"That's not my job" or "This was not in my job description," employees often grumble. Well, if you want to do only what's written in your job description, don't complain that you're not getting ahead in professional life. Forget about the job description for a moment and focus on the job, which is to create immense value, to generate unfair advantages in the marketplace, to build enviable brands, to direct marketing campaigns that will make your competition squirm, to inspire your employees, and to wow your guests. Once you learn how to build brands, generate revenues, and grow profits, you'll be writing your own job description.

THE BRAND CALLED YOU

A few years ago, Tom Peters, the management guru, wrote an exceptional article in *Fast Company* titled "The Brand Called You." The basic premise, as the title indicates, is that since the old approach to career management (being a blindly loyal employee for 40 years) is no more, the new approach should be active management of you, not as an employee but as a brand.

Peters starts with the brand audit: "What is it that my product or service does that makes it different?" Define your strengths, your identifying characteristics, the attributes that make you stand apart from your colleagues, co-workers, supervisors, and others. Define what it is that you can deliver better/faster/cheaper/smarter than any of your "competitors." Then you can use those attributes to define the potential benefits you bring to your organization, or your projects, or your team; those attributes can facilitate. Just like a strong brand, you must stand for something in the minds of those in your environment.

Once you have defined your differentiating attributes and benefits, Peters states that you must actively promote or, in his words, "market the bejesus out of" your brand—to customers, colleagues, and your virtual network of associates, for visibility is key if you are to build that You-brand. How? Become an expert on your attributes. Write articles, speak, join projects outside of your immediate job description, teach a class, become a go-to person on that differentiating attribute. It's a self-fulfilling prophecy: BMW claims to have the ultimate driving machine. They develop technology and perfect their engines that make their cars the ultimate driving machines. Then those cars are accepted as the ultimate driving machines. Then they develop even better technology and engines that make their cars drive even better; thus, they support even more firmly the claim to have the ultimate driving machines. You get the idea.

Do not think about work or a job or even a career in the traditional linear sense, but as an investment in you. Perhaps not every job change is a promotion; perhaps not every promotion is a job change. The question to ask is whether a new job or promotion will add to your set of skills. Will it give you a chance to deepen your knowledge? Will it open up new worlds where you can learn a different approach, language, or technique? Will it give you a chance to work with some remarkable people and perhaps even pick up a mentor along the way?

You should read Peters' entire article at fastcompany.com, and I'll end this section with one of his remarks: "Forget about your resume. You don't have a resume. You've got a marketing brochure for the brand called You."

MARKETING CHALLENGES

As a hospitality marketing professional, you'll have to face several large challenges directly related to your job. They can be quite frustrating, and the likelihood that you'll have to deal with one or all of them is quite high, so it helps to be prepared.

1. **The intangibility challenge** Any marketing professional has to face this challenge: the fact that the profession is quite intangible. While operations, accounting, or human resources are very much structured and defined by a variety of rules such as operations manuals, accounting principles, and personnel guidelines, marketing is to a large degree empirical. There's no rule on exactly what outcome will be achieved by a certain advertisement or if a publicity event will produce a specific result in the third quarter. There are guidelines, which you have to study and learn. But there is no "marketing law" or "formula" that you can blindly follow, so you must become comfortable making decisions without a strict set of rules. The sooner you accept this fact and become comfortable with it, the sooner you will move past the fear of intangibility and start establishing your own set of guidelines and measures for progress and success.

2. **The consensus challenge** Whether you work for a hospitality or tourism company with one location and office or manage marketing for multiple destinations, products, brands, or offices, you'll have to work hard at building a consensus. Coordinating marketing projects and gaining acceptance by multiple internal audiences is no walk in the park. General managers, property sales managers, and regional managers sometimes have a lot of leverage when it comes to managing marketing activities pertaining to their product. It is wise to befriend them and create a group of allies long before you actually need to have them participate in your project.

3. **The product challenge** A big challenge of your job will be your product. The hospitality product is probably the most transparent and honest of all because the product equals the service and the service is visible throughout the consumption period. Unlike other service industries, where the service is performed behind closed doors, the hospitality product is completely transparent since the consumption happens within the product, not of the product. It must be re-created every day and is only as good as the worst mood of your most unhappy employee. This is not an easy proposition.

   On the other hand, this daily re-creation of the hospitality product can and should be used to the marketer's advantage. What other product category offers the ability to change the product completely from one day to another? A lousy can of soup will be lousy today, tomorrow, and the day after. The hospitality product can be radically changed in a rather short time.

Despite this fact, there is a strange tendency toward inertia among service companies throughout the world. That is, after the initial product launch excitement is gone, and following a certain level of growth, the product falls into an area of service complacency. There it lingers alongside many of the other hospitality and travel products competing in a sea of parity. No wonder customers treat them as commodities. Use this tendency to your advantage. Combat complacency. Make your product the hero of your market segment. It will pay off.

Once you've developed a product that is differentiated by its service quality and other features, you have to test it. Try it for yourself. Pay full price and experience it as an actual user. Pay for your friends to try it and give you an honest report. Keep doing this on a regular basis. It is the only way to know how the market is experiencing your product and the only way to maintain consistency. Oh, but that's not your job or responsibility; that's quality control's job and operations management's responsibility. Well then, welcome to oblivion and enjoy replying to all the complaint letters.

4. **The discounting challenge** Another big challenge is price discounting, also referred to as price promotions or specials. Unfortunately, discounting is a necessary evil and pricing adjustments are here to stay. The difference lies in the way discounting or price promotions are structured and executed. Thus, your company's pricing policy and structure should be developed with this fact in mind. What I mean is that price reductions should never be done as an afterthought. They should be worked into the original price structure at the time of seasonal or annual price development. The basic discount rate levels should be developed from the beginning and stowed away for later usage (if necessary). If you never have to use them, it means that you are having a fantastic season. If you do have to use them, you will know exactly which level of discount to apply.

5. **The budget challenge** Regardless of the size of your company, you will never have enough money in the marketing budget. There will always be an extra project for which you just won't have enough resources. Then there will be budget cuts. The easiest way to cut cost is by reducing the marketing budget, because it is intangible. The budget challenge is a serious one. Learn to defend your budget by providing full accountability and results tracked to specific actions. Knowing what actions (and corresponding budgets) will generate results will make budget requests easier and cuts more difficult.

6. **The recession marketing challenge** Studies show that companies that continue marketing during recession periods experience considerable subsequent market gains. This is due to the fact that while everyone's natural reaction is to constrict their marketing, your marketing expansion—or just maintenance of current levels—will have

double impact due to reduced market clutter and fewer players. This having been said, be prepared for an uphill battle. It is quite a challenge to convince a suspicious board of directors or cost-cutting-frenzied top management to continue investing in the market when returns are not going to be immediate. However, since this type of thinking is prevalent, that is exactly why you should be zagging when everyone else is zigging.

FINAL WORD

Many people wonder about the secret of marketing success. But the secret is: there isn't one. Just do your homework. Develop a strategy. Follow it. Insist on quality. Underpromise and overdeliver. Come up with ideas and then implement them. Produce results. Compete with yourself for your own excellence. Learn. Experiment. Push the envelope. Be honest. Scratch below the surface. Excel at what you do, but don't take yourself too seriously. Have fun. Smile. It's not about working hard. It's about working smart.

Index

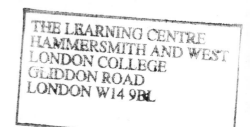